SPURGEON COMMENTARY

1 JOHN

SPURGEON COMMENTARY

1 JOHN

Charles H. Spurgeon

Elliot Ritzema

Editor

LEXHAM PRESS

Spurgeon Commentary: 1 John

Lexham Press, 1313 Bay St., Bellingham, WA 98225
LexhamPress.com

Print ISBN 9781683599333
Digital ISBN 9781683599340
Library of Congress Control Number 2025945652

First edition published 2014 as digital Logos edition. Second edition published 2026 as digital Logos edition and print volume.

Lexham Editorial: Elliot Ritzema, Jessi Strong, Lynnea Fraser, Kelsey Matthews, Carrie Sinclair Wolcott, Mandi Newell, Samuel Leon
Cover Design: Joshua Hunt
Typesetting Design: ProjectLuz.com

25 26 27 28 29 30 31 / US / 12 11 10 9 8 7 6 5 4 3 2 1

Contents

Foreword

Charles Haddon Spurgeon (1834–1892) was known in his day as the Prince of Preachers, and his preaching remains legendary among evangelicals today. But how was Spurgeon as an expositor of Scripture? Modern readers have sometimes wondered. Perhaps in reading one of his devotional works or in examining his "road to Christ" in a sermon, some have found Spurgeon too loose in his handling of Scripture. For these careful exegetes, their conclusion might be that he should be admired more as a homiletician than a Bible teacher. Can Spurgeon be a faithful guide for us as an expositor of Scripture?

Indeed, every preacher should be open to critique, and Spurgeon is no different. We should not be surprised to find areas of improvement for any one of his sermons. At the same time, my contention is that Spurgeon had an unwavering commitment to the faithful exposition of Scripture. This can be seen in three commitments he held: a commitment to study, accurate exposition, and preaching Christ.

1: A COMMITMENT TO STUDY

Spurgeon was adamant about the importance of study in the ministry. Speaking to his students, he warned them against those who relied on oratory skills to the exclusion of study. Some denominations, like the Quakers or Plymouth Brethren, would take pride in their pastors not preparing sermons and receiving a word directly from the Spirit. But Spurgeon believed that "churches are not to be held together except by an instructive ministry; a mere filling up of time with oratory will not suffice."[1] The only alternative, then, was for the preacher to be committed to the work of study. Spurgeon's ministry was steeped in his study of God's word, works of theology, biblical commentaries, devotional writings, edifying sermons, religious poetry and hymns, and much more.[2]

To be sure, this commitment to study will look different for every pastor. Spurgeon would have said that his sermon preparation was constant. Everywhere he went, he was always thinking about his sermons, meditating on Scripture, reading books, looking for sermon illustrations, and mulling over sermon outlines ("skeletons," he called them). But more specifically, Spurgeon's sermon preparation formally began on Saturday evenings, probably around 6 p.m., and it could run late into the night. During this time, he would select a sermon text (after much prayer) and devote most of his time to personal, intense study of each text. Only after that personal study would he consult other sources. He would lay out commentaries and sermon volumes from his favorite preachers and move among his books, gathering insights like a bee among flowers. All this prayer and study would culminate in a half-sheet outline he would bring into the pulpit. Spurgeon's notes were sparse, but they represented a life devoted to study. As he would say to his students, "All sermons ought to be well considered and prepared by the preacher; and, as much as possible, every minister should, with much prayer for heavenly guidance, enter fully into his subject, exert all his mental faculties in original thinking, and gather together all the information within his reach."[3]

More evidence for Spurgeon's laborious study can be found in his writings. In *The Treasury of David*, a seven-volume commentary on the Psalms, Spurgeon not only provides a robust commentary on all 150 psalms, but he shares his collection of all the best quotes that he could find from what others have written about the Psalms.

---

1. C. H. Spurgeon, *Lectures to My Students: A Selection from Addresses Delivered to the Students of the Pastors' College, Metropolitan Tabernacle*. First Series. (London: Passmore & Alabaster, 1875), 151.
2. This commitment can be seen in his pastoral library, which remains today at The Spurgeon Library on the campus of Midwestern Baptist Theological Seminary in Kansas City, MO.
3. Spurgeon, *Lectures*, 152.

These quotes show Spurgeon's reading to range far and wide from every theological tradition across the centuries of church history. It truly is remarkable. The other work highlighting Spurgeon's commitment to study is *Commenting and Commentaries*. In it, Spurgeon provides brief, personal comments on the value and usefulness of 1,437 commentaries for every book of the Bible. Many scholars and preachers, both Victorian and modern, have remarked on how accurate and insightful Spurgeon was in his comments. He was a preacher committed to the diligent study of God's word.

2: A COMMITMENT TO ACCURATE EXPOSITION

Additionally, Spurgeon believed in the importance of faithful exposition. As creative and original a preacher as he was, Spurgeon taught his students to be constrained by the text in their preaching. He warned against the dangers of over-spiritualizing the biblical text. "Do not violently strain a text by illegitimate spiritualizing. ... How dreadfully the word of God has been mauled and mangled by a certain band of preachers who have laid texts on the rack to make them reveal what they never would have otherwise spoken."[4] Such preaching would either harm the hearers as they lost confidence in their ability to understand the word of God or discredit the preacher's ministry as their pride and vanity were exposed. When it came to parables, metaphors, prophecies, and other illustrative texts, Spurgeon urged his students to be discreet and exercise good judgment in their interpretation. Some allegorizing or spiritualizing may be appropriate, but never while ignoring the text in its original context.

The importance of reading Scripture in its context is why Spurgeon was also committed to Scripture reading in every church gathering. Spurgeon's sermons were often based on a single verse of Scripture. But he always included a Scripture reading in every service to complement the sermon text. This would usually be a reading of the surrounding context of the sermon text. Or there could be multiple readings, with the other reading being from a related text in the opposite testament.

In these Scripture readings, Spurgeon did not merely read the text but commented on them. He provided brief "expositions,"

4. Spurgeon, *Lectures*, 103.

going verse-by-verse, explaining what each verse meant, and even making brief applications. The reason for all this was to equip his people to read their Bibles for themselves.

> We cannot expect to deliver much of the teaching of Holy Scripture by picking out verse by verse, and holding these up at random. The process resembles that of showing a house by exhibiting separate bricks. It would be an astounding absurdity if our friends used our private letters in this fashion, and interpreted them by short sentences disconnected and taken away from the context.[5]

In other words, a proper understanding of individual verses can only happen in the context of each chapter, which is to be understood in the context of the entire book and ultimately in the context of the whole Bible. Of course, to do this well, Spurgeon once again emphasized the importance of study to his students. In his own experience, he found himself preparing for these expositions as much, if not more, than for his sermons. "For the exposition, you must keep to the text, you must face the difficult points, and must search into the mind of the Spirit rather than your own. You will soon reveal your ignorance as an expositor if you do not study; therefore diligent reading will be forced upon you."[6]

Spurgeon found the discipline of expositing Scripture personally helpful in binding him to the word of God and not allowing him to rest on his rhetorical abilities. Having set up the sermon with a reading of the biblical context, it would have been wrong for him to preach the text in a totally unrelated direction. Instead, he always sought to have the sermon flow from the text in a way that was obvious to the listener. "The discourse should spring out of the text as a rule, and the more evidently it does so the better; but at all times, to say the least, it should have a very close relationship thereto."[7]

---

5. C. H. Spurgeon, *Commenting & Commentaries: Two Lectures Addressed to the Students of the Pastors' College, Metropolitan Tabernacle, Together with a Catalogue of Biblical Commentaries and Expositions* (London: Passmore & Alabaster, 1876), 22.
6. Spurgeon, *Commenting*, 24.
7. Spurgeon, *Lectures*, 74.

Spurgeon allowed some latitude in spiritualizing, "but liberty must not degenerate into license, and there must always be a connection, and something more than a remote connection—a real relationship between the sermon and its text."[8] As a preacher, Spurgeon was committed to disciplined and faithful exposition.

3: A COMMITMENT TO PREACHING CHRIST

Finally, Spurgeon was committed to preaching Christ in every sermon. As he famously declared in his first sermon in the newly built Metropolitan Tabernacle, "I would propose that the subject of the ministry of this house, as long as this platform shall stand, and as long as this house shall be frequented by worshipers, shall be the person of Jesus Christ."[9] Notice that Spurgeon's commitment was not so much to a message or a set of ideas. Instead, the good news of Christianity is found in the person of Christ. The gospel was intensely personal for Spurgeon, revealing a *Savior*. This commitment flowed from Spurgeon's understanding of Scripture.

The Bible culminates with the revelation of Jesus Christ, the Son of God. Therefore, when read in its proper, biblical-theological context, every text of Scripture points to Jesus. This was the tradition of English Puritanism in which Spurgeon was discipled. The Old Testament, in its narratives, poetry, laws, and prophecies, pointed forward to the coming Messiah. And the New Testament, in the Gospels and Epistles, revealed Jesus as the Messiah, the fulfillment of God's promises. Therefore, quoting a Welsh preacher, Spurgeon could say to his hearers,

> Don't you know young man that from every town, and every village, and every little hamlet in England, wherever it may be, there is a road to London?... And so from every text in Scripture, there is a road to the metropolis of the Scriptures, that is Christ. And my dear brother, your business is when you get to a text, to say, "Now what is the road to Christ?" and then preach a sermon, running along the road towards

---

8. Spurgeon, *Lectures*, 74.
9. C. H. Spurgeon, "The First Sermon in the Tabernacle," in *The Metropolitan Tabernacle Pulpit Sermons*, vol. 7 (London: Passmore & Alabaster, 1861), 169.

> the great metropolis—Christ. … I have never yet found a text that had not got a road to Christ in it, and if I ever do find one that has not a road to Christ in it, I will make one. I will go over hedge and ditch but I would get at my Master, for the sermon cannot do any good unless there is a savour of Christ in it.[10]

Spurgeon's commitment to preaching Christ was not homiletical but theological. Christ is the central meaning of the Scriptures. Therefore, in one way or another, the preacher should either find a road to Christ or make one. There may very well be worse and better roads to Christ in a text. But if the Scriptures exist to reveal Christ, this commitment to preaching Christ in every sermon is exactly right. This commitment makes Spurgeon a more trustworthy expositor of Scripture, not less.

CONCLUSION

Spurgeon's legacy is not of an entertainer or rhetorical performer. Rather, it is of a preacher committed to the accurate exposition of Scripture. Over forty years of ministry, he preached, taught, and wrote on virtually every book of the Bible, and he sought to do so faithfully. It is this teaching that continues to bear fruit. The Spurgeon Commentary series, then, seeks to compile the best of Spurgeon's biblical insights as a resource for Bible teachers today. Given his love of God's word and training preachers, he would have been pleased to see these books in the hands of pastors and church leaders. Being dead, Spurgeon still speaks, and I'm grateful for this series that gives voice to the Prince of Preachers in our day.

Geoff Chang

Kansas City, Missouri

January 30, 2024

10. C. H. Spurgeon, "Christ Precious to Believers," in *The New Park Street Pulpit Sermons*, vol. 5 (London: Passmore & Alabaster, 1859), 140.

Introduction

The great nineteenth-century Baptist preacher Charles Spurgeon crammed a remarkable amount of writing and speaking into his fifty-seven years. His words fill more than a hundred volumes. Although his sermons and writings touch on every book of the Bible at some point, he wrote commentaries only on Psalms (the multi-volume *Treasury of David*) and Matthew (*The Gospel of the Kingdom*). It can be difficult to find his teachings on other biblical books within his massive body of work.

That's why we created the Spurgeon Commentary series. The idea behind this series is simple: Take material from Spurgeon's sermons and writings and organize it into commentary format. This format includes several features I believe will be particularly helpful for both the devotional reader and the preacher preparing for a sermon.

Each section of the commentary includes three kinds of comments from Spurgeon: exposition, illustration, and application. The exposition sections do not simply deal with a block of biblical text as a whole; they are organized by *verse* as well as the *words within that verse*. This means that you can easily find what Spurgeon says about a particular verse or phrase. The individual phrases Spurgeon comments on within a verse are set in bold text. Some verses have long paragraphs of exposition, while others have a little or none at all. This reflects how much Spurgeon wrote on each verse. We have tried to include as much content as possible in places where Spurgeon wrote a lot, but unfortunately we have had to be selective at times.

When preachers are studying a text in preparation for a sermon, they often watch for good illustrations they can use to drive their point into the hearts of their listeners. To aid in this task, whenever

Spurgeon used a story or a comparison to illustrate a truth found in a verse, we have set that illustration apart for easy reference. Some sections of the commentary will have more illustrations than others, depending on how many Spurgeon used.

The application content at the end of each section contains Spurgeon's exhortations to his hearers to act on the truths he was drawing out from the text. We've often drawn the application content from a few different sermons on a passage. Each section of the commentary includes between one and four applications, depending on how much Spurgeon wrote and preached on that passage.

How much of this commentary is truly Spurgeon, and how much is from the editors? Hopefully, there is as much Spurgeon as possible, and the editors fade into the background. Section titles, including those for illustrations and applications, come from the editors. All other words are Spurgeon's, although we have updated his language in some places for greater readability. For example, we have changed "thee" and "thou" to "you." Additionally, we have supplied modern equivalents to archaic words that may be unfamiliar to today's reader. However, Bible quotations are taken from the King James Version (KJV), which Spurgeon used. It is often the case that when a word or phrase in the KJV is unfamiliar or misleading to us, it was to Spurgeon's audience as well, and he took the time to explain it.

In an effort to highlight Spurgeon's relevance to a present-day audience, we have left out discussions that were only applicable to the issues and controversies Spurgeon was speaking to in his own day. Instead, we've focused on the content that a present-day audience can relate to. Thankfully, much of what Spurgeon said and wrote is truly timeless. Although we have often gathered content from multiple sources in the same paragraph, we have not used ellipses, which would be more of a distraction than a help. Instead, we have included sources in a list at the end of each section of the commentary.

It is my hope that this commentary series will make Spurgeon's writings more accessible to today's readers, and perhaps even introduce him to people who have not had the pleasure of reading him before now. Through this series may it be, as it is written on the last page of his *Autobiography*, that Spurgeon "continues to preach the gospel he loved to proclaim while here—the gospel of salvation by grace, through faith in the precious blood of Jesus."[1]

Elliot Ritzema

Easter, 2024

1. C. H. Spurgeon, *C. H. Spurgeon's Autobiography, Compiled from His Diary, Letters, and Records, by His Wife and His Private Secretary: Volume 4, 1878–1892* (Chicago; New York; Toronto: Fleming H. Revell Company, 1900), 378.

John had an eagle's wing with which to soar aloft, and an eagle's eye with which to penetrate into great mysteries. And yet of all the writers of the Old or New Testament he is one of the simplest. He never endeavors to show you the greatness of his mind or the grandeur of his rhetoric; on the contrary, he speaks as a child to those who are children in the school of love. I would that all of us who try to teach others would remember this.

—Charles Spurgeon, "Helps to Full Assurance"

This epistle is specially perfumed with love. As you read it, you cannot help realizing that it was written by a very tender, gentle hand. And yet, when this loving writer is giving his last words in this epistle, the admonition with which he closes is this: "Little children, keep yourselves from idols." As love thus speaks in its fullness, let us be ready to give earnest attention to the message that it utters. John has, in this epistle, written much concerning the love of Jesus, as well he might, for he knew more about that love than any other man knew. And yet, when he had written concerning love to Jesus, he was moved to an intense jealousy lest, by any means, the hearts of those to whom he wrote should be turned aside from that dear Lover of their souls who deserved their entire affection. Therefore, not only love to them, but also love to Jesus, made him wind up his letter with these significant words: "Little children, keep yourselves from idols."

—Charles Spurgeon, "Idolatry Condemned"

1 JOHN 1

1 JOHN
1:1–4

1 That which was from the beginning, which we have heard,
which we have seen with our eyes, which we have looked upon,
and our hands have handled, of the Word of life; 2 (For the life
was manifested, and we have seen *it*, and bear witness, and shew
unto you that eternal life, which was with the Father, and was
manifested unto us;) 3 That which we have seen and heard declare
we unto you, that ye also may have fellowship with us: and truly our fellowship *is* with the Father, and with his Son Jesus Christ.
4 And these things write we unto you, that your joy may be full.

EXPOSITION

1 **That which was from the beginning** You remember how John begins his Gospel: "In the beginning was the Word" (John 1:1), and how a little later he says, "In him was life" (John 1:4). The Holy Spirit seems to have recalled those expressions to his mind, for he moves him to use them again.

which we have heard, which we have seen with our eyes The fact that Christ was really in the flesh, that he was no phantom, no shadow mocking the eyes that looked upon him, is exceedingly important. Hence John (whose style, by the way, in this epistle is precisely like the style that he uses in his Gospel) begins by declaring that Jesus Christ, the Son of God, who in his eternity was from the beginning, was really a substantial man, for he says, "We have heard" (hearing is good evidence); "We have seen with our eyes" (eyesight is good, clear evidence, certainly); "We have looked at" (this is better still, for this imports a deliberate, careful, circumspect gaze); but better still, "Our hands have touched," for John had leaned his head on Jesus Christ's bosom, and his hands had often met the real flesh and blood of the living Savior. We need have no doubt about the reality of Christ's incarnation when we have these open eyes and hands to give us evidence.

The facts of Christ's history on earth are recorded by eyewitnesses who could not be deceived concerning them. They exercised their various senses with regard to Christ—hearing, seeing, and touching him again and again. They were veracious witnesses, and they died in testimony of their faith in what they asserted. And when anything has been heard, seen, inspected, and even touched and handled, by a company of reliable witnesses, the testimony of such witnesses concerning it must be accepted as true.

of the Word of life There is something that every believer can do for his Lord. He must be able to tell of what he has tasted and handled of the Word of Life, and if he has not tasted and handled it, then he is not a child of God at all. The best teaching in the world is experimental. Nothing wins upon men like personal witnessing—not merely teaching the doctrine as we find it in the Book, but as we have felt it in its living power upon our own hearts. When we begin to tell of its effect upon ourselves, it is wonderful what power there is upon others in that testimony.

ILLUSTRATION

Telling Others What You Have Experienced

A person talks to me about a certain medicine, how it is compounded, what it looks like, how many drops must be taken at a dose, and so on. Well, I do not care to hear all that, and I soon forget it. But he tells me that for many months he was bedridden, he was in sore distress and in great pain, and like to die. Looking at him as he stands before me in perfect health, I am delighted with the change, and he says that it was that medicine which restored him. If I am a sick man in the same state as he was, I say to him, "Give me the name and address, for I must try that medicine for myself."

I believe that the simple witness of converted boys and girls, converted fathers and mothers and beloved friends, the witness that comes from the gray head that is backed up by years of godly living, has a wonderful power for the spread of the gospel, and we cannot expect that God will give us any very large blessing until the whole of us shall be at work for our Lord.

---

2 **For the life was manifested** That same eternal Being who is very God of very God, and is worthy to be called essentially Life, was made flesh and dwelt among us, and the apostles could say, "We beheld his glory" (John 1:14).

that eternal life, which was with the Father, and was manifested unto us The twelve apostles were favored with the most intimate intercourse with our blessed Lord, but I can hardly say that they entered into fellowship with him during his life on earth. Each of them might have been asked the question that our Savior put to one of them: "Have I been so long time with you, and yet hast thou not known me, Philip?" (John 14:9). But after Christ had ascended to heaven, and the Spirit of God had rested upon his disciples, and in proportion as the Spirit did rest upon them, all that they had seen, and heard, and handled of their Lord became a means of communion between himself and them. They were then able to realize what a very near, and dear, and deep, and familiar communion had been possible to them through having spent some three years or so with him in public and in private, and having actually seen him, and heard his voice, and felt the touch of his hand.

3 **That which we have seen and heard declare we unto you** What the apostles learned, they learned in order that they might tell it to others. All that John saw he was prepared to speak of

according to his ability, that others might have fellowship with him. Remember that, if you ever learn anything of Christ—if you have any enjoyment of his presence at any time—it is not for yourself alone, but for others also to share with you.

that ye also may have fellowship with us When fellowship is the sweetest, your desire is the strongest that others may have fellowship with you; and when, truly, your fellowship is with the Father, and with his Son Jesus Christ, you earnestly wish that the whole Christian brotherhood may share the blessing with you.

truly our fellowship is with the Father Fellowship with God was one of the richest privileges of unfallen man. The Lord God walked in the garden, and talked with Adam as a man talks with his friend. So long as he was willing and obedient, Adam ate the fat of the land, and among the rich dainties and "wines on the lees" (Isa 25:6) of which his soul was a partaker, we must number first and foremost unbroken communion with God, his Father and his Friend.

Sin, as it banished man from Eden, banished man from God, and from that time *our* face has been turned from the Most High, and *his* face has been turned from us—we have hated God, and God has been angry with us every day. Christ came into the world to restore to us our lost patrimony. It was the great object of his wondrous sacrifice to put us into a position that should be equal and even superior to that which we occupied in Adam before the fall. And as he has already restored to us many things that we lost, so among the rest—fellowship with God. Those who have by his grace believed, and have been washed by the precious blood, have peace with God through Jesus Christ our Lord; they are "no more strangers and foreigners, but fellow-citizens with the saints, and of the household of God" (Eph 2:19), and they have access with boldness into this grace wherein we stand.

and with his Son Jesus Christ John had been Christ's chosen companion, elect out of the elect to a choice and peculiar privilege. During the incarnation, he was one of the favored three who had enjoyed the closest intimacy with the Redeemer. He had seen Christ in his transfiguration, had witnessed the raising of the dead woman, had been with the Lord in the garden, and he had lingered with him even when the thrust was given after death and the blood and water flowed from his pierced heart. John had the nearest, the dearest, the closest fellowship with Christ in the flesh. As he had laid his head upon Christ's bosom, so had he laid all his thoughts and all the emotions of his mind upon the heart's love and divine affection of his Lord and Master.

But Christ was gone; it was no more possible to hear his voice, to see him with eyes, or to handle him with hands. Yet John had not lost his fellowship, though he knew him no more after the flesh, yet he knew him after a nobler sort. Nor was his fellowship less real, less close, less sweet, or less divine, than it had been when he had walked and talked with him, and had been privileged to eat and drink with him at that last sacred feast. John says, "Indeed our fellowship *is*"—not *was*—"*is* with the Father and with his Son Jesus Christ."

4 **And these things write we unto you** John seems to put the whole of the apostolic band, with himself, into the verse when he says, "These things write *we* unto you, that your joy may be full," as if joy would not be full unless inspired apostles should be commissioned of God to write in order to promote it. The Christian's joy needs looking after.

that your joy may be full Very closely does the apostle John resemble his Lord in the motive that prompted him to write this epistle! Remember how Christ said, in his last discourse to his disciples on the eve of his passion, "These things have I spoken unto you ... *that* your joy might be full" (John 15:11); and how he counseled them, "Ask, and ye shall receive, that your joy may be full" (John 16:24); and how he prayed to the Father for them, "that they may have my joy fulfilled in themselves" (John 17:13). Here, then, the beloved disciple, moved by the Spirit of God, reflects and follows out the same gracious purpose: "These things write we unto you, in order that your joy may be full."

What an evidence of our Savior's deep attachment to his people that he is not content with having made their ultimate salvation sure, but he is anxious concerning their present state of mind! He delights that his people should not only be safe, but happy; not merely saved, but rejoicing in his salvation. Hear this, people of God! The object of the revelation of Jesus Christ is that you may have joy—indeed, that you may have a heart full of joy, and that you may know what full joy means. Here below, we get but drops and dashes of joy unless we are brought into fellowship with God through Jesus Christ; then, we have the very joy of God in our souls. Oh, the delight of it! Oh, that you could all know it to the full!

APPLICATION

Fellowship with the Son

From the manger to the cross, and from the cross to the millennium, there should be in the Christian's experience a blessed fellowship. We ought to know Christ in his obscurity and littleness—the babe Christ being in our hearts. We ought to know him in his wilderness temptations—ourselves being tempted in all points. We ought to know him in his blasphemies and slanders—ourselves being accounted by man to be as Beelzebub; and as the offscouring of all things, we must know him in his passion, in his agony, and in his death, and then, "Thanks *be* to God, which giveth us the victory through our Lord Jesus Christ" (1 Cor 15:57), we may know him in his triumphs, in his ascension up on high, in his session at the right hand of God, and in his coming to judge the quick and the dead, for we, too, shall judge angels through Jesus Christ our Lord. We have, I hope, in some humble measure in these respects, fellowship with the Son Jesus Christ.

Fellowship around the Communion Table

How can we have fellowship with God in showing forth the death of Christ by means of the Lord's Supper? I think we can do so, first, *by coming to the conclusion that the sacrifice of Christ was an absolute necessity*. We are fully persuaded that God the Father would never have given up his only-begotten Son to die for human guilt if there had been any other way of saving lost sinners, and also that Jesus Christ would never have taken upon himself the awful burden of human guilt, and agreed to be bruised of the Father, if it had not been absolutely essential that he should die, or that man should, or that justice should; it must have been one of the three.

Next, while you are sitting around the communion table, endeavor so to think of the sufferings of Christ, that you will, in your measure, enter into the moods of his mind while he was suffering for you. As he felt a great horror of sin, ask the Lord to make you feel intense horror of it, and let the very thought of it wound you as it wounded him. He felt the shame of sin; then ask the Holy Spirit to teach you how shameful it is. In your mind and heart, crown sin with a crown of thorns like that with which it crowned your Lord. Spit at sin, and scoff at sin, even as sin scoffed and spat at your Lord. Yet further, our Lord Jesus felt that justice must be honored; so feel in your soul, as you come to communion, that the justice of God must be honored, and magnified, and glorified. Have fellowship with Christ in feeling that, cost what it may, God must never be unjust.

Then, again, I pray the Holy Spirit *to help you, and to help me, to glorify God concerning the death of Christ while we are at his table*. As you eat the bread, and drink the wine, think of what Christ suffered, and of the mysterious way in which his sufferings have brought glory to the Father's name. I do truly believe that, when Christ bore the sins of his people up to the tree, and away from the tree, the justice of God was more honored than it would have been if all the elect had been sent to hell forever. If our sins had been punished upon ourselves, with the utmost rigor of the divine law, that law would not have been so honored, throughout the entire universe of intelligent beings, as it now must be when they hear that God himself would sooner pay the penalty of sin than allow his law to be broken with impunity.

Next, you can enter into fellowship, at the communion table *by loving Christ, your Mediator, as well as by glorifying God the Father*. You know that God loves Jesus Christ; I mean, the man Christ Jesus,

God and man in one person. He loves him, not only in his essential Godhead, as he ever must love him, but he also loves him for his work's sake. With what delight do the Father's eyes ever rest on his Son! How sweetly does he say to him, "Well done!" How does he delight to honor and glorify him! Do you not also feel something of the same sort of love to Christ as you gather around his table? Ask the Spirit of God to cause you to be enamored of Christ, and to make him to be "altogether lovely" (Song 5:16) in your eyes.

Joy to the Full

If you have lost the joy of the Lord, I pray you do not think that your loss is a small one. I have heard of a minister who once said that a Christian lost nothing by his sin, and then he added—except his joy. Well, what else would you have him lose? Is that not quite enough? To lose the light of my Father's countenance, to lose my full assurance of my interest in Christ, is to lose my best and purest delight; is this not a loss quite great enough?

Let us walk prayerfully, let us walk carefully, that we may possess unbroken peace and joy to the full. Let none of us sit down in misery and be content to be there. There is such a thing as becoming habituated to melancholy. My own tendency is sometimes to get into that state of mind, but, by the grace of God, I shake it off, for I know it will not do. If we once begin to give way to this foolishness, we shall soon forge chains for ourselves that we cannot easily break. Take down your harp from the willow, believer. Do not let your fingers neglect the well-known strings. Come, let us be happy and joyful! If we have looked sad for a while, let us now be brightened by thoughts of Christ. At any rate, let us not be satisfied until we have shaken off this lethargy and misery, and have once again come into the proper and healthy state in which a child of God should be ever found—namely, a state of spiritual joy.

1 JOHN 1:5–10

5 This then is the message which we have heard of him, and declare unto you, that God is light, and in him is no darkness at all. 6
If we say that we have fellowship with him, and walk in darkness,
we lie, and do not the truth: 7 But if we walk in the light, as he is
in the light, we have fellowship one with another, and the blood
of Jesus Christ his Son cleanseth us from all sin. 8 If we say that
we have no sin, we deceive ourselves, and the truth is not in us.
9 If we confess our sins, he is faithful and just to forgive us our
sins, and to cleanse us from all unrighteousness. 10 If we say that
we have not sinned, we make him a liar, and his word is not in us.

EXPOSITION

5 **God is light** Not *a* light, nor *the* light, though he is both, but that he *is* light. Scripture uses the term *light* for knowledge, for purity, for prosperity, for happiness, and for truth. God is light—and then in his usual style John, who not only tells you a truth but always guards it, adds, "and there is no darkness in him at all."

and in him is no darkness at all There is no darkness of sin, or ignorance, or error about God.

6 **If we say that we have fellowship with him** The apostle warns us against *saying* more than we have made our own by experience. He hints at the solemn difference between empty profession and gracious reality. To have fellowship with God is a great matter, but merely to *say* that we have fellowship with him is a totally different thing. John warns us that if we *say* that which our characters do not support, we lie. He leaves

it just so, without a word of softening or excuse. Between saying and being, between saying and doing, there may be all the difference in the world.

and walk in darkness This does not mean walking in the darkness of sorrow, for there are many of God's people who walk in the darkness of doubts and fears, and yet they have fellowship with God. Indeed, they sometimes have fellowship with Christ all the better for the darkness of the path along which they walk. The darkness meant here is the darkness of sin, the darkness of untruthfulness. If I walk in a lie, or walk in sin, and then profess to have fellowship with God, I have lied and do not practice the truth.

we lie, and do not the truth There were certain people in John's day who said, "We have fellowship with God." They did not explain how they had come by it; perhaps they claimed to have reached it by philosophical speculation, by exact reasoning, or by long-continued meditation. Whatever the road, they said that they had reached the city of God and were in communion with the Great Being. John saw that they walked in darkness, rejecting the light of divine revelation from above and the pure light of the Holy Spirit within. He also saw that they themselves were not true, and that their lives were not pure, and therefore he warned them that they were speaking and acting a lie. Their life was a lie, for they were not walking in the truth. Their profession that they had fellowship with God was another lie, for God can have no fellowship with falsehood. "God is light, and in him is no darkness at all"; therefore, he cannot hold any communion with darkness.

John draws the lines very tightly and judges with unflinching fidelity. The disciple whom Jesus loved spoke like the son of thunder that he was when he had to deal with shams. It is the part of true love to be honest and to expose that which would be injurious to those it loves. The one who will gloss over a falsehood loves in word only. Learn, then, that if men boast of fellowship with God and do not receive the revelation of his word, they lie and do not know the truth.

7 **But if we walk** The Christian life is described as walking, which implies *activity*. Christian life feeds upon contemplation, but it displays itself in action. Fellowship with God necessitates action, since to be with God we must "walk with God." The living God is not inactive, motionless, aimless. "My Father," says Jesus, "worketh hitherto, and I work" (John 5:17). We must maintain fellowship with God chiefly in the character of active workers or in that of willing sufferers. Walking implies activity, but it must be *of a continuous kind*. Neither this step, nor that, nor the next, can make a walk. We must be moving onward and onward, and remain in that exercise, or we cease from walking. Holy walking includes perseverance in obedience and continuance in service. It is not he that begins, but he that continues who is the true Christian.

It is of no use to pretend to have light in the brain so as to comprehend all knowledge, so as to be sound and orthodox in one's doctrinal opinions—this will be of no vital service so far as the great point of salvation is concerned. A man may think he has much light, but if it is only notional and doctrinal, and is not the light that enlightens his nature and develops itself in his practical walk, he lies when he talks of being in the light, for he is in darkness altogether. Nor is it truthful to pretend or profess that we have light within in the form of experience if we do not walk in it. For where the light is true, it is quite certain to show itself. If there is a candle within the lantern, its light will stream forth into the surrounding darkness, and those who have eyes will be able to see it. I have no right to say I have light unless I walk in it.

The Christian, then, is in the light, and he is *practically* in it; his walk and conversation are regulated by truth, by holiness, and by the divine knowledge that God has been pleased to bestow upon him. He walks in the light of faith, in another path than that which is trodden by men who have nothing but the light of sense. He sees him who is invisible, and the sight of the invisible God operates upon his soul. He looks into eternity, he observes the dread reward of sin and the blessed gift of God to those who trust in Jesus, and eternal realities have an effect upon his whole manner and conversation. Hence he is a man in the light, walking in that light.

in the light What is this light in which the Christian walks? *It is the light of grace.* In our natural state we are in darkness, and under the dominion of the Prince of Darkness. The apostle says of us Gentiles, "Having the understanding darkened, being alienated from the life of God through the ignorance that is in them, because of the blindness of their heart" (Eph 4:18). When the grace of God comes, the dayspring from on high visits us. The Holy Spirit brings us out from under the dominion of the old nature by creating within us a new life, and he brings us out from under the tyranny of the Prince of Darkness by opening our eyes to see and our minds to understand celestial truth. The opening of our blind eyes and the pouring in of the light of truth are from the Lord. This is a work in which he is as fully seen in the glory of his Godhead as when in the natural creation he said, "Let there be light: and there was light" (Gen 1:3). The entrance of God's word into the mind by the power of the Holy Spirit gives us light as to ourselves, our sin, and our danger. With this comes light as to the way of salvation through Jesus Christ, and light as to the mind of God concerning our sanctification. True knowledge takes the place of ignorance, and a desire for purity becomes supreme over the love of sin. Paul says, "For ye were sometimes darkness, but now are ye light in the Lord" (Eph 5:8).

ILLUSTRATION

Do You Pay a Doctor to Lie to You?

Do you not know that plain dealing is more precious than rubies? Would you not say to your physician, "Put me under the severest examination, and let me know the truth"? Would you pay him a fee so that he might deceive you?

As to your soul, do you not desire to know the very worst of your case? If you would rather be comfortable than be safe, then you and I are not of one mind. I want to walk in the light, free from deception, knowing truly and thoroughly my own place before the heart-searching God. I would rather not cry, "Peace, peace," where there is no peace. I do not desire the comfort that grows out of delusion. We must build on truth, and nothing else but truth.

---

as he is in the light Can we ever attain to this? Shall poor flesh and blood ever be able to walk as clearly in the light as he is whom we call "Our Father," of whom it is written, "God is light, and in him is no darkness at all" (1 John 1:5)? Certainly this is the model that is set before us, for the Savior himself said, "Be ye therefore perfect, even as your Father which is in heaven is perfect" (Matt 5:48). If we take anything short of absolute perfection as our model of life, we shall certainly, even if we should attain to our ideal, fall short of the glory of God.

But what does it mean that the Christian is to walk in light as God is in the light? I think it indicates likeness, but not degree. We are as truly in the light, we are as heartily in the light, we are as sincerely in the light, as honestly in the light, though we cannot be there in the same degree. I cannot dwell in the sun; it is too bright a place for my residence. But I can *walk* in the light of the sun though I cannot dwell in it. And so God is the light; he is himself the sun, and I can walk in the light as he is in the light, though I cannot attain to the same degree of perfection, and excellence, and purity, and truth, in which the Lord himself resides.

ILLUSTRATION

Striving for the Noble Ideal

The youthful artist, as he grasps his early pencil, can hardly hope to equal Raphael or Michelangelo, but still, if he did not have a noble ideal before his mind, he would only attain to something very mean and ordinary.

Heavenly fingers point us to the Lord Jesus as the great exemplar of his people, and the Holy Spirit works in us a likeness to him.

---

we have fellowship one with another As you read this verse, it looks very much as if all that was meant was fellowship with your brother Christians; but this, according to able critics, would not convey the sense of the original. "We have mutual fellowship; there is communion between God and our souls"—this is the sense of the passage.

God in the light and man in the light have much in common. They are now abiding in one element, for they are dwelling in one light. They are now both concerned about the same thing, and their aims are undivided: God loves truth, and so do those who are renewed in heart. It has come to pass that the great Lord and his enlightened ones see things in the same light. God with his great vision beholds more than we can, yet he does not see more than the truth; we with our narrow perceptions see the truth, and cannot tolerate falsehood. Now we can speak with God, since we speak truth; he can converse with us, since we are ready to hear the truth. In prayer and praise we are no longer false, and therefore the Lord can hear us. His word falls also upon an honest mind, and so its meaning is perceived. Now we can also act together: the great God and his poor feeble children are striving together for truth and righteousness.

and the blood of Jesus Christ his Son Blood is precious at all times, but this is no blood of a mere man: it is the blood of an innocent man—better still, it is the blood of man in union with Deity—"his Son!" God's Son! Angels cast their crowns before him! All the choral symphonies of heaven surround his glorious throne "over all, God blessed for ever. Amen" (Rom 9:5). And yet he yields his blood, takes upon himself the form of a servant, and then is scourged and pierced, bruised and torn, and at last slain; for nothing but the blood of Deity could make atonement for human sin.

Observe that here *nothing is said about rites and ceremonies.* It does not say, "and the waters of baptism, together with the blood of Jesus his Son, cleanses us." Not a word—whether it shall be the sprinkling in infancy, or immersion of believers—nothing is said about it. It is the blood, the blood only, without a drop of baptismal water. *Nothing is here said about sacraments*—what some call "the blessed Eucharist" is not dragged in here—nothing about eating bread and drinking wine. It is the blood, nothing but the blood: "the blood of Jesus Christ his Son."

Perceive, too, that *nothing is said about Christian experience as a means of cleansing*. The text does not say that our walking in the light cleanses us from sin. It does not say that our having fellowship with God cleanses us from sin—these go with cleansing, but they have no connection as cause and result—it is the blood, and the blood alone that purges us from sin.

Observe, yet again, that in the verse *there is no hint given of any emotions, feelings, or attainments cooperating with the blood to take away sin.* Christ took the sins of his people and was punished for those sins as if he had been himself a sinner, and so sin is taken away from us. In no sense, degree, shape, or form is sin removed by attainments, emotions, feelings, or experiences. The blood is the one atonement; the blood, without any mixture of anything besides, completes and finishes the work, for "ye are complete in him" (Col 2:10).

cleanseth us "Cleanseth," says the text—not "*shall* cleanse." There are multitudes who think that as a dying hope they may look forward to pardon, and perhaps within a few hours of their dissolution they may be able to say, "My sins are pardoned." Such people can never have read God's Word—or, if they have read it, they have read it with unbelieving eyes. The moment a sinner trusts Jesus, that sinner is as fully forgiven as he will be when the light of the glory of God shall shine upon his resurrection countenance. Forgiveness of sin is a present thing—a privilege for this day, a joy for this very hour. Whoever walks in the light as God is in the light has fellowship with God, and has at this moment the perfect pardon of sin.

In the very highest state to which we can attain in this world—namely, walking in the light as God is in the light and having fellowship with him—even then we shall sin, and shall still need the blood of Christ to cleanse us from its stain. So those err exceedingly who say that the Christian man can or does live utterly free from sin. Either they have lowered the standard by which they judge the actions of men, or they excuse themselves on some antinomian principle, or else they must be altogether ignorant of the truth about the matter, for "if we walk in the light, as God is in the light," and have fellowship with him, still, "the blood of Jesus Christ his Son cleanseth us from all sin." Therefore, there is sin needing to be cleansed, for Christ does no superfluous work.

ILLUSTRATION

Head Learning vs. Heart Learning

I have heard of a naturalist who thought himself exceedingly wise with regard to the natural history of birds. Yet he had learned all he knew in his study, and had never so much as seen a bird either flying through the air or sitting upon its perch. He was a fool, although he thought himself exceedingly wise.

And there are some men who, like him, think themselves great theologians. They might even pretend to take a doctor's degree in divinity, and yet, if we came to the root of the matter and asked them whether they ever saw or felt any of these things of which they talked, they would have to say, "No; I know these things in the letter, but not in the spirit. I understand them as a matter of theory, but not as things of my own consciousness and experience."

Be assured that as the naturalist who was merely the student of other men's observations knew nothing, so the man who pretends to religion but has never entered into the depths and power of its doctrines, or felt the influence of them upon his heart, knows nothing whatsoever. All the knowledge he pretends to is but varnished ignorance. There are some sciences that may be learned by the head, but the science of Christ crucified can only be learned by the heart.

---

from all sin Dwell on the word "all" for a moment. Our sins are great—every sin is great, but there are some that in our apprehension seem to be greater than others. It is amazing how the ingenuity of man seems to have exhausted itself in inventing fresh crimes. Surely it is not possible to invent a new sin. But if it is, man will invent it before long, for man seems exceedingly cunning and full of wisdom in the discovery of means of destroying himself and the endeavor to injure his Maker. But there are some sins that show a diabolical extent of degraded ingenuity—some sins of which it would be a shame to speak, of which it would be disgraceful to think. But note here: "The blood of Jesus cleanseth us from *all* sin." There may be some sins of which a man cannot speak, but there is no sin that the blood of Christ cannot wash away.

Just take the word "all" in another sense, not only as taking in all sorts of sin, but as comprehending the great aggregate mass of sin. Let only the blood be applied to our consciences, and all our guilt is removed and cast away forever. All—none left, not one solitary stain remaining—all gone, like Israel's enemies, all drowned in the Red Sea, so that there was not one of them left, all swept away, not so much as the remembrance of them remaining.

8 **If we say that we have no sin** Our deceitful heart suggests to us that we should deny our present sinfulness, and so claim fellowship with God on the ground that we are holy, and so

may draw near to the holy God. It is suggested to our hearts that we should say that "we have no sin," and are neither guilty by act nor defiled in nature. This is a bold assertion, and he who makes it has no truth in him, but at different times it has been made and stoutly maintained by very different persons.

Some have arrived at it by denying altogether the doctrine of original sin. They will not allow that there is a fault and natural corruption in the nature of every man whereby man is very far gone from original righteousness and is of his own nature inclined to evil. If you should venture to plead that you have no sin on the ground that your nature is not evil, I ask you to rid your heart of that lie, for a lie it is through and through. I do not care how honest your parentage or how noble your ancestry is—there is a bias in you toward evil. Your animal passions and even your mental faculties are unhinged and out of order, and unless some power beyond your own shall keep your desires in check, you will soon prove the depravity of your nature by overt acts of transgression.

It is not uncommon for others to arrive at the same conclusion by another road. They say that they have no sin by various feelings and beliefs that they, as a rule, ascribe to the Holy Spirit. Now, if any man says that all tendency to sin is gone from him, that his heart is at all times perfect, and his desires always pure, so that he has no sin in him whatsoever, he may have traveled a very different road from the character we just now warned, but he has reached the same conclusion, and we have but one word for both boasters. It is the word of our text: "If we say that we do not have sin, we deceive ourselves and the truth is not in us."

Some, however, have reached this position by another route. They plead that though they may have sin, yet they are not bad at heart. They look upon *sin* as a technical term, and though they admit in words that they have sin, yet they practically deny it by saying, "I have a good heart at bottom; I always was well intentioned from the very first. True, what I have done does not appear to be right according to the very severe judgment of the law of God, but I cannot help that. I only followed my nature, and cannot be blamed, for I never meant to do anything wrong either to God or man. I have always been kind to the poor and have done the right thing all around. I know I have—of course we all have—erred here and there, but you cannot expect a fellow to be perfect. I can't say I see anything to find fault with." Thus they in effect say they have no sin. In so saying or feeling they prove that the truth is not in them. They are either deplorably ignorant as to what holiness is, or else they are willfully uttering a falsehood; in either case, the truth is not in them.

we deceive ourselves To deceive another requires a measure of cunning, but to deceive yourself requires far more. Our deceitful heart reveals an almost satanic shrewdness in self-deception. It readily enough makes the worse appear the better reason, and it states a lie so that it wears the fashion of truth. If you say you have no sin, you have achieved a fearful success: you have put out your own eyes and perverted your own reason! You have fed on falsehood until it has entered into your very being and rendered you incapable of truth. I know you claim to be very sincere in your belief of your own rightness, and it would be very hard to persuade you out of your fond notions. But this is all the worse, for you have completely deceived yourself so much the more. Now that you call darkness light and boast that your blindness is true sight, we mourn over you as all but hopeless, and we fear that the Lord should leave you to perish because you cling so tightly to a lie.

ILLUSTRATION

Deceiving Yourself Like the Ostrich

The ostrich is reported to bury her head in the sand and then suppose herself safe, but she is captured all the more speedily. We may shut our eyes and say, "I do not have sin," but in so doing, instead of securing eternal salvation, we shall as practically give ourselves up to the destroyer as the bird of the desert is fabled to do.

---

and the truth is not in us Let a man say, "I do not have sin," and he has condemned himself out of his own mouth. The text says of such a man the truth is not in him, and he who does not have truth in him is not saved. The absence of confession of present sin means the absence of the light of truth and sincerity. God saves all sorts of people, however black their sins. But the man with a false spirit, the pharisaic washer of the outside of the cup while the inside is foul, is the last person who is likely to be saved. A main point in conversion consists in being honest, for it is the honest and good ground that receives the seed.

9 **If we confess our sins** Observe that John does not say, "If we confess our *sin*." He had been speaking of that in the eighth verse, but here he uses the plural to include both sin in its essence and in its actual development in our life. We are to confess both the inward sin and the outward fruit of it.

That is the point; he who says that he has no sins will not confess them. He who believes himself to be perfect cannot enjoy the blessing described in this verse. To deny that we have any sin is to walk in darkness and to show we are without the light that would reveal our sin to us. If we are walking in darkness, we cannot be in fellowship with God. But to see sin in ourselves from day to day, humbly to confess it, and mourn over it, is to walk in the light. And, walking in the light, we shall have fellowship with God, who is light.

ILLUSTRATION

Do Not Be Satisfied until the Disease Is Gone

Suppose you go to a surgeon because you have some deadly cancer growing upon you. You want to have it removed, and you know there are a great many physicians who will profess to cure such things, but in reality only give temporary ease. You keep clear from all these. You are well aware that if only a little root of the growth should be left, it will grow again. So you say outright to the surgeon,

"There is my disease; I will tell you all the symptoms of it. I only ask to have a thorough cure, cost what it may in money or pain. I make no reserve, just do whatever you feel is best in the case, but make clean work of it. If you have the knife in your hand, do not spare it out of pity for my pain, but be just with me. Cut out the disease, roots and all, so that it may be a complete cure."

Even in the same manner, go to the Lord and say, "Lord, there is my sin. I confess it all; do not allow me to have any peace unless it is true peace; do not let me have any comfort unless I get it from Christ. And if there must be more conviction of sin and more alarm of conscience, if there must be deeper gashes and sterner cuts into my soul, Lord, do not spare me; purge me from the secret depravity of my nature, and make me pure. Your holiness is what I crave, and I cannot be satisfied until you make me holy, even as you are holy."

---

he is faithful The text means just this: treat God truthfully, and he will treat you truthfully. Make no pretensions before God, but lay bare your soul. Let him see it as it is, and then he will be faithful and just to forgive you your sins and to cleanse you from all unrighteousness. Note the beauty of that expression; God will deal with you in *faithfulness*. His nature is mercy, and you naturally expect that if you confess your sin to a merciful God, he will deal mercifully with you and be faithful to his nature—and he will be so. But he has also given a promise that if the wicked forsake his way and the unrighteous man his thoughts and turn unto the Lord, he will have mercy upon him. Depend upon it, he will be faithful to his promise. The blood of Jesus Christ has made a full atonement, and God will be faithful to that atonement. He will deal with you on the grounds of the covenant of grace, of which the sacrifice of Jesus is the seal, and therein also he will be true to you.

and just to forgive us our sins If I understand this text, it means this: that it is an act of justice on God's part to forgive the sinner who makes a confession of his sin to God. It is not that the sinner deserves forgiveness; that can never be. Sin can never merit anything but punishment, and repentance is no atonement for sin. Not that God is bound from any necessity of his nature to forgive everyone that repents, because repentance does not have in itself sufficient efficacy and power to merit forgiveness at the hand of God. Yet, nevertheless, it is a truth that, because God is just, he must forgive every sinner who confesses his sin.

God's justice demands that the sinner should be forgiven if he seeks mercy, for this reason: Christ died on purpose to secure pardon for every seeking soul. Now, I hold it to be an axiom, a self-evident truth, that whatever Christ died for he will have. I cannot believe that when he paid to his Father the price of blood, and groans and tears, he bought something that the Father will not give him. Now, Christ died to purchase the pardon of sin for all those who believe in him, and do you suppose that the Father will rob him of that which he has bought so dearly? No, God would be untrue to his own Son—he would break his oath to his well-beloved and only begotten Son—if he were not to give pardon, peace, and purity to every soul that comes to God through Jesus Christ our Lord.

and to cleanse us from all unrighteousness This must include the vilest sin that ever stained human nature, the blackest crime that ever came from the black heart of man. And now John is very careful, when he strikes a blow, to hit completely. He has already smitten those who say they have no sin, and now he smites those who say they did not at one time have any.

10 **If we say that we have not sinned** Some get to this point by saying that what they did was not really sin to any extent; or, at any rate, if it would have been sin in other people, it was no sin in them. Considering their strong passions, they wonder they were not worse, and considering the circumstances of

their case, they do not see how they could have done otherwise: in a word, they have not sinned at all. There is another class who say, "All these [commandments] have I kept from my youth up: what lack I yet?" (Matt 19:20). This self-justification clearly makes God a liar. For what does the cross of Calvary mean, what do those streams of blood mean, what do those agonies to the death mean? God has acted out a gigantic lie if we have no sin, for he has provided a propitiation for a thing that does not exist.

we make him a liar, and his word is not in us We conceive of things as they appear, but God sees them as they exist. "For man looketh on the outward appearance, but the LORD looketh on the heart" (1 Sam 16:7). The dress of things impresses *us*, but all things are naked and open before *him*. The Lord never misrepresents, nor has fellowship with misrepresentation. We are forever hurrying about with our paint and varnish and tinsel, laboring to make the meaner thing appear equal to the more precious, and spending our skill in making the sham seem as brilliant as the reality. But all this is contrary to the way of the Lord. Everything is true in God, and everything is seen in its reality by his all-discerning eye. Because he is light, he deals with things in the light, treating them as they are.

APPLICATION

Walking in the Light of God's Word

The truth of God is spiritual, and the natural man is carnal, and therefore the natural man will not receive the teaching that comes from God. By this test will you know whether the true light is shining upon you: Do you believe what God has revealed in his Word? or are you your own teacher—maker of your own faith? He cannot be a disciple who does not learn, but invents. Do you hear the teaching of the Lord Jesus, and believe it? I repeat it; you must not only *say* that you believe it, but you must indeed and truly believe the things that God has revealed. You will know by this whether you are a child of light or a child of darkness. Are the doctrines of grace essential verities with you? Whatever God has said about sin, righteousness, judgment to come, are you ready to accept it at once? Whatever he has revealed concerning himself, his Son, his Holy Spirit, the cross, life, death, hell, and the eternal future, do you believe it unfeignedly? This is to walk in the light. All other teaching is darkness.

Look Only to the Blood

Whereas there are some who urge you to look to your doctrinal intelligence as a ground of comfort, I ask you to look only to the blood. Whereas there are others who would set up a standard of Christian experience and urge that this is to be the channel of your consolation, I pray you, while you prize both doctrine and experience, rest your soul's weight nowhere but in the precious blood. Some would lead you to high degrees of fellowship. Follow them, but not when they would lead you away from the simple position of a sinner resting upon the blood. There are those who could teach you mysticism, and would have you rejoice in the light within; follow them as far as they have the warrant of God's Word, but never take your foot from that Rock of Ages, where the only safe standing can be found. Some of my brothers are very fond of preaching Christ in his second advent—I rejoice wherein they preach the truth concerning Christ glorified, but I conjure you do not build your hope on Christ glorified, nor on Christ to come, but on "Christ crucified" (1 Cor 1:23).

Remember that in the matter of taking away sin, the first thing is not the throne, but the cross; not the reigning Savior, but the bleeding Savior; not the King in his glory, but the Redeemer in his shame. Do not care to be studying dates of prophecies if burdened with sin, but seek your chief, your best comfort in the blood of Jesus Christ, which cleanses us from all sin. Here is the polestar of your salvation; sail by it and you shall reach the port of peace.

Come to God as You Are

Our only safe course—and may the Spirit of God grant us grace to follow it—is to come to God as we actually are, and ask him to deal with us, in Christ Jesus, according to our actual condition. If we are to walk with God at all it must be in the light, and if we once walk in the light with him our condition will tally with the description of verse seven;

we shall see sin in ourselves and daily feel the blood of Jesus Christ cleansing us from it. Only on the footing of daily confessed and pardoned sin can there be any fellowship between us and the eternal God this side of heaven, for that footing is the only one consistent with the facts of the case. Let us daily ask the Lord to keep us in a truthful spirit, admitting the truth, both concerning ourselves and our Lord, feeling its power, and desiring to be taught still more of it. Let us pray him to deal with us not according to our suppositions but according to the fact, and let us entreat him never to allow us to rejoice in fancied blessings, such as might satisfy our proud, half-stupefied conscience, but to give to us the real blessings of genuine forgiveness and effectual cleansing from all unrighteousness.

What Confessing Sins Looks Like

To confess sin does not mean merely on one occasion to repeat a catalog of sins before God in private, nor at certain set seasons to rehearse a list of our faults, but it means a lifelong acknowledgment of our sin. We must take our places as men who have sinned, and never attempt to occupy the position of innocent beings. We are to look toward God as a man ought to look who has transgressed. When a man prayerfully begs that he may feel the power of the blood of Jesus, he is confessing sin, for is not the blood of Jesus needed because of our sin? The daily exercise of faith in Jesus Christ is a confession of sin, for nobody would need to believe in a Savior unless he had sin.

Baptism is a confession of sin; who needs to be buried with Christ if he is alive by a righteousness of his own? To come to the communion table and remember there the atoning sacrifice is a confession of sin; for we would need no remembrance of our blessed Substitute if we were not sinners. Confession of sin is best carried out when we deal with God as those who have offended him, not as those who feel that they are innocent. We are to act before the Lord as those who know that sin is in them. We ought to watch as those who feel that the battle is not fought, and therefore we cannot lay down our armor and our sword. We should so live as those who know that the race is not run, and therefore they press forward. We ought to be prayerfully dependent upon God, as those who know that if they were left by divine grace they would go back unto perdition.

1 JOHN 2

1 JOHN 2:1–11

1 My little children, these things write I unto you, that ye sin
not. And if any man sin, we have an advocate with the Father,
Jesus Christ the righteous: 2 And he is the propitiation for our
sins: and not for ours only, but also for the sins of the whole
world. 3 And hereby we do know that we know him, if we keep
his commandments. 4 He that saith, I know him, and keepeth
not his commandments, is a liar, and the truth is not in him.
5 But whoso keepeth his word, in him verily is the love of
God perfected: hereby know we that we are in him. 6 He that
saith he abideth in him ought himself also so to walk, even as
he walked. 7 Brethren, I write no new commandment unto you,
but an old commandment which ye had from the beginning.
The old commandment is the word which ye have heard from
the beginning. 8 Again, a new commandment I write unto you,
which thing is true in him and in you: because the darkness is
past, and the true light now shineth. 9 He that saith he is in the
light, and hateth his brother, is in darkness even until now. 10 He
that loveth his brother abideth in the light, and there is none occasion of stumbling in him. 11 But he that hateth his brother is in
darkness, and walketh in darkness, and knoweth not whither
he goeth, because that darkness hath blinded his eyes.

EXPOSITION

1 **My little children** The apostle John presents us with a very clear and emphatic testimony to the doctrine of full and free forgiveness of sin. He declares that the blood of Jesus Christ, God's dear Son, cleanses us from all sin (1:7), and that if any man sin, we have an Advocate. It is most evident that he is not afraid of doing mischief by stating this truth

too broadly; on the contrary, he makes this statement with the view of promoting the sanctity of his "little children."

ILLUSTRATION

Children Are Prone to Get Dirty

Children are very apt to get into the mire. Most mothers will tell you, I think, that if there is a pool of mud anywhere within a mile, her firstborn joy and comfort will find it and get into it if he possibly can. No matter how often a child is washed he seems always to need washing again: if there is a method by which he can foul his hands and his face, your pretty cherub is most ingenious to find it out.

I am afraid this is too much the case with the children of God. There is so much of carnality about us, so much of the old Adam, that the question is not into which sin we fall, but into which sin we do not fall.

---

that ye sin not The object of this bold declaration of the love of the Father to his sinning children is "in order that you may not sin." This is a triumphant answer to the grossly untruthful objection that is so often urged by the adversaries of the gospel against the doctrines of free grace—that they lead men to licentiousness. It does not appear that the apostle John thought so, for in order that these "little children" should not sin, he actually declares to them the very doctrine that our opponents call licentious.

Those men who think that God's grace, when fully, fairly, and plainly preached, will lead men into sin, do not know what they say. It is neither according to nature nor to grace for men to find an argument for sin in the goodness of God. Human nature is bad enough, but even a natural conscience revolts at the baseness of sinning because grace abounds. Shall I hate God because he is kind to me? Shall I curse him because he blesses me? I venture to affirm that very few men reason this way. Man has found out many inventions, but such arguments are so transparently abominable that few consciences are so dead as to tolerate them.

Bad as human nature is, it seldom turns the goodness of God into an argument for rebelling against him. As for souls renewed by grace, they can never be guilty of such infamy. The believer in Jesus reasons in quite another fashion. Is God so good? Then I will not grieve him. Is he so ready to forgive my transgressions? Then I will love him and offend no more. Gratitude has bands that are stronger than iron, although softer than silk. Do not think that the Christian needs to be flogged to virtue by the whip of the law! Do not dream that we hate sin merely because of the hell that follows it! If there were no heaven for the righteous, the sons of God would follow after goodness because their regenerated spirit pants for it. And if there were no hell for the wicked, from the necessity of his newborn nature the true Christian would strive to escape from all iniquity. Loved by God, we feel we must love him in return.

ILLUSTRATION

Preach the Gospel, Even If Some Distort the Gospel

Shall we keep back the children's bread lest the dogs should steal the crumbs? Shall we destroy health-restoring drugs because fools may poison themselves with them? Shall all the trees be cut down for fear the owls should build their nest in them? Shall the sea be dried up because sharks swim in it?

Shall the pure virgin truth be condemned because gross villains have forged her name and abused her character? God forbid. Let us never blush to preach the whole gospel, and to preach its full forgiveness of sin in the boldest and baldest manner.

---

if any man sin Although the gentle hand of the beloved disciple uses such mild and tender terms, putting it as a supposition, as if it were an astonishing thing after so much love, mercy, kindness, that we should sin, yet John very well knew that all the saints do sin, for he has himself declared that if any man says that he does not sin he is a liar, and the truth is not in him (1:8). Saints are, without exception, still sinners.

But far be it from me to deny that divine grace has wrought a wondrous change; it would be no grace at all if it had not. It will be well to note this change. The Christian no longer loves sin: it is the object of his sternest horror; he no longer regards it as a mere trifle, plays with it, or talks of it with unconcern. He looks upon it as a deadly serpent, whose very shadow is to be avoided. He would no more venture voluntarily to put its cup to his lip than a man would drink poison who had once almost lost his life through it. Sin is dejected in the Christian's heart, though it is not ejected. Sin may enter the heart, and fight for dominion, but it cannot sit upon the throne.

ILLUSTRATION

Christians May Sin, but Sin Is Not Their Element

The swallow dips his wing into the brook, and then he is up again into the skies, soaring toward the sun. The duck can swim in the pool or dive under the water—it is in its element. So the Christian just sometimes touches with his wing the streams of earth, but then he is up again where he should be. It is only the sinner that can swim in sin and delight in it.

You may drive the swine and the sheep together side by side. They come to some mire, and they both fall into it, and both stain themselves. But you soon detect the difference in nature between them: for while the swine lies and wallows with intense gusto, the sheep is up again, escaping as soon as possible from the filth. So with the Christian: he falls, God knows how many times, but he rises up again. It is not his nature to lie in sin. He abhors himself that he should ever fall to the ground at all, while the ungodly goes on in his wicked way until sin becomes a habit, and habit like an iron net has entangled him in its meshes.

---

we have an advocate It does not say, "If anyone sins he has forfeited his advocate," but "we have an advocate," sinners though we are. All the sin that a believer ever did or can be allowed to commit cannot destroy his interest in the Lord Jesus Christ. Indeed, in some sense Jesus is only mine when I can claim the name of sinner. I cannot have an advocate unless I do sin; I do not want one. Who wants an advocate to plead his cause in a court of law if there is no suit against him? Sin is a charge against me. I am a sinner; I have an advocate.

All the sin that a believer can commit cannot mar his interest in Christ, though it may mar his enjoyment of that interest for the present. This doctrine, instead of driving men to sin, will draw them to love that gracious and immutable God who, notwithstanding all our sin and care and woe, will never allow us to perish.

with the Father If I am a sinner then there is a court, and there is one who sits as Judge—the Father. There is a charge against me; otherwise I would not need an advocate to meet it. This implies that I have sinned. There is an adversary to press his suit against me, and he would hardly venture to do this if there were no sin. There must be a right of reply on my part; I must have the right to put in a disclaimer in court, and to stand up and plead before the bar of justice. He who has a right to plead in court is the man who is accused, and the man who has some offense. If I were neither accused nor had been a sinner, then I would have no right to occupy the time of the court. But, being a sinner, and being brought up on that charge, and having one who presses the charge against me, I have a right to reply, and that reply, through God's good grace, I have a right to make through my advocate.

Jesus Let us say, concerning our advocate, that he is ordained with a special view to sinners. All his names and attributes prove him to be a suitable advocate. You and I, who though saved are still sinners, may safely put our case into his hands, for see who he is: Jesus is the name of one who became man for my sake. He knows what sore temptations mean. He understands what trials mean, what afflictions mean. I am glad I have one who will be interested in my welfare, and will plead for me as a friend for a friend, and as a brother for a brother. I thank God that, though I sin, I still have Jesus who is my "brother … born for adversity" (Prov 17:17), the friend of sinners, and will therefore plead the sinner's part.

Christ Notice, next, it is "Jesus *Christ*"—*Christos*—the anointed. This shows *his authority* to plead. Jesus Christ has a right to plead, for he is the Father's own appointed, the Father's own anointed. He is Christ, and therefore authorized. But I add, he is Christ, and therefore *qualified*, for the anointing has also qualified him for his work. He can plead better than Judah pleaded when he spoke for Benjamin (Gen 43:9). He can plead so as to move the heart of God and prevail. What words of tenderness, what sentences of persuasion will he use when he stands up to plead for me! But more, he is Christ, that is, he is God's Messiah. Therefore, God would not send him unless he *guaranteed him*. If God should send into this world a Savior who could not save, then God would have no mercy. God's appointing and sending Christ is a guarantee of Christ's success.

the righteous Notice next, it is "Jesus Christ *the righteous*." This is not only his character, but it is his plea. It is his character, and if my advocate is righteous then I am sure he would not take up a bad cause. But how can he do this? He meets the charge of unrighteousness against me by this plea on his part: that *he* is righteous. He seems to say to the great Father on the day when the sinner stands arraigned: "Yes, my Father, that sinner was unrighteous, but remember that I was accepted as his substitute. I stood to keep the law for him, and gave my active obedience. I went up to the cross and bled, and so gave my passive obedience;

I have covered him from head to foot with my doing and my dying. I have so arrayed him that not even the angels are adorned as he is, for though they may be clothed with the perfect righteousness of a creature, I have given him the righteousness of God himself." What more can be asked for the sinner than this? Jesus Christ the righteous stands up to plead for me, and pleads his righteousness. And he does this not if I do not sin, but if I do sin.

2 **he is the propitiation for our sins** That God should deal with us as to our virtues, if we had any; that he should deal with us as to our love, if we had any, might not seem so difficult; but that he should send his Son to dwell with us as sinners—ay, and to come into contact with our sins, and thus to take the sword, not only by its hilt, but by its blade, and plunge it into his own heart, and die because of it, this is a miracle of miracles. O friends, Christ never gave himself for our righteousness, but he laid down his life for our sins. He viewed us as sinners when he came to save us.

and not for ours only, but also for the sins of the whole world By which is meant, not only that Jesus Christ died for Gentiles as well as Jews, and for some of all nations, but that there is that in the atonement of Christ which might be sufficient for every creature under heaven if God had so chosen every creature. The limitation lies, not in the value of the atonement itself, but in the design and intention of the Eternal God. God sent his Son to lay down his life for his sheep. We know that Christ redeemed us from among men, so that the redemption is particularly and specially for the elect; yet at the same time the price offered was so precious, the blood was so infinite in value, that if every man that ever lived had to be redeemed Christ could have done it. It is this that makes us bold to preach the gospel to every creature, since we know there is no limit in the value of the atonement, though still we know that the design of it is for the chosen people of God alone.

3 **hereby we do know that we know him** What, then, is it to know Christ? Of course, we have never seen him. Many years ago he left this world and ascended to his Father. Still we can know him. It is possible. There have been thousands, and even

millions, who have had a personal acquaintance with him whom, though they have not seen, they loved, and in whom they have rejoiced with joy unspeakable and full of glory.

To "know" is a word used in Scripture in several senses. Sometimes it means *to acknowledge*, as when we read of a certain Pharaoh "which knew not Joseph" (Exod 1:8); that is, he did not acknowledge any obligation of the state or kingdom to Joseph. He did not remember what had been done by that great man. So too, Christ says that his sheep "know" his voice. They acknowledge his voice as being the voice of their Shepherd, and cheerfully follow where their Shepherd leads. Now, it is a matter of the first necessity to acknowledge Christ, that he is God, that he is the Son of the Father, that he is the Savior of his people, and the rightful Monarch of the world—to acknowledge more, that you accept him as your Savior, as your King, as your Prophet, as your Priest. This is, in a certain sense, to know Christ; that is, to own and confess in your heart that he is God, in the glory of God the Father; that he is your Redeemer; that his blood has washed you, and his righteousness covers you; that he is your salvation, your only hope, and your fondest desire.

The word "know" means, in the next place, *to believe*—as in that passage, "By his knowledge shall my righteous servant justify many" (Isa 53:11), where it is evidently meant that by the knowledge of him, that is to say, by faith in Christ Jesus, he would justify many. To "know" and to "believe" are sometimes used in Scripture as convertible terms. Now, in this sense we must know Christ: we must believe him; we must trust him; we must accept the reports of the prophets and apostles respecting him. We must subscribe to them, practically, with all our heart, and soul, and strength, and lean the whole burden of our everlasting destiny upon his finished work. To know him, then, is to acknowledge him and to believe in him.

This is not all. The word "know" often means *experience*. It is said of our Lord that he "knew no sin" (2 Cor 5:21)—that is to say, he never experienced sin; he never became a sinner. To know Christ, then, we must feel and prove his power, his pardoning power, his power of love over the heart, his reigning power in subduing our passions, his comforting power, his enlightening power, his elevating power, and all those other blessed influences that through the Holy Spirit proceed from Christ. This is to experience him.

And once more, to "know" in Scripture often means *to commune*. Every believer needs to know Christ by having an acquaintance with him, by speaking with him in prayer and praise, by laying bare one's heart to his heart, receiving from him the divine secret and imparting to him the full confession of all our sins and griefs. In a word, to know Christ is very much the same as to know any other person.

ILLUSTRATION

Knowing Christ Is Like Knowing Any Other

When you know a man, if he is your intimate friend, you trust him, you love him, you esteem him, you are on speaking terms with him. You not only bow to him in the street, but you go to his house, you sit down with him at his table. At other times, you hold counsel with him, or you ask his assistance. He comes to your house and you hold familiar association with one another.

The soul must be on such terms with Christ. He must not be merely a historic personage of whom we read in the page of Scripture, but a real person with whom we can speak in spirit, commune in heart, and be united in the bonds of love. We must know him, his very person, so as to love and to trust him as a real Lord to us. Judge, then, whether you really and indeed in this sense "know" Christ.

---

if we keep his commandments It should be the object of every Christian to find out what Christ's command is, and this done, never to ask another question, but receive it with meekness, meditate on its holy sanction, and venerate it as the law of the Lord's house. If Christ has said it I dare not cavil, argue, or question, much less rebel. It is mine to keep his commandments in my heart as a sacred trust, as precious treasures more to be desired than gold, and with a yet increasing relish, as luxuries to the taste, sweeter than honey or the honeycomb. But to keep them *in our hearts, we must earnestly desire to fulfill them*. By reason of the fall we cannot perfectly keep the commands of Christ, but the heart keeps them as the standard of purity, and it would be perfect if it could. The Christian's only desire is to be exactly like Christ. It pains him that he falls short of his image; it gives him great joy if he can feel that the Holy Spirit is working in him anything like conformity to the divine will. His heart is right toward God, sincerely so.

Not that this is enough, unless there is a constant, persevering aim *to fulfill his commandments in our lives*. Depend on it that the lack of practical obedience to Christ is the root of 999 out of every 1,000 of our doubts and fears. The roots of our fears are in our sins. Search there, and you shall find the cause of soul-trouble. I believe many a child of God walks in darkness because he does not obey the word of the Lord. Take for your motto the sentence that the mother of Jesus addressed to the servants at the marriage in Cana of Galilee—"Whatsoever he saith unto you, do it" (John 2:5). Do you often hear the precept with never a thought of heeding it? Then beware lest you "suddenly be destroyed, and that without remedy" (Prov 29:1).

ILLUSTRATION

Knowing Through Obedience

When our Lord met the disciples at Emmaus and talked with them, they did not know him while he talked with them. But when do you think they knew that they knew him? It was not until they performed an act of obedience by offering hospitality to a stranger. Then he was known to them in the breaking of bread.

Yes, there is a blessed eye-clearing to many a child of God when he gives of his bread to the poor and needy, and when he comes to the table of the Lord in remembrance of his death. He shall then know that he knows him. We are told that the cherubim have wings, but they also have hands under their wings. True children of God have knowledge, but they have practice under their knowledge. You have no good proof that you are a child of God because you have the wings of knowledge unless you also have the hands of practice.

---

4 **He that saith, I know him, and keepeth not his commandments** The man that says, "I know Christ" and does not keep his commandments is making his own damnation sure. He signs, seals, and stamps it every day. By his profession of being a follower of Christ he confesses that he knows what he ought to be; yet by his actions he proves that he is not what he ought to be, and so he is bearing witness against himself, judging himself, condemning his own soul, and challenging the dread sentence of everlasting perdition. God save us from such a lie as this.

is a liar Not only in this case, but all through his epistles, John continues to unravel the tangled web of hypocrisy. Ah, that deceit should steal such gentle shapes and seem like truth! It was his constant aim to show the diverging point between facts and sayings, between realities and professions, between those who have and those who only say that they have.

ILLUSTRATION

Lying Without Speaking

People can tell lies when they hold their tongues. There was a little girl at school who always held her hand up when the boys and girls were asked to show that they knew the answer to any question that had been put to them. One afternoon she held her hand up when she did not know the answer, and a classmate said to her, "Jane, you did not know that." And she said, "No; but I thought teacher would think better of me if she thought I knew it." "But," said the other, "that is telling a lie with your hand."

Yes, and you may equally act a lie. A man who professes to be a Christian when he is not hangs out false colors on Sunday, and all through the week he plays the liar's part. If his profession were true, surely his conduct would be consistent with it!

---

and the truth is not in him The man who begins by lying about his relation to God soon becomes inured to lying in the community of his fellow men. Some of the greatest rogueries and robberies ever committed have been perpetrated by professing Christian men. How often when we have heard of a gigantic fraud has there been some canting hypocrite or other connected with it! This is very natural, and it is scarcely surprising. When the man had come to deceive himself, to dissemble in sacred things, and to lie to God, he was such a practiced hand that the devil could not find a fitter vassal to lie to men. You may flatter yourself with the vain conceit that you will never cheat anybody. I am not so sure. If a man would rob God, he would rob his mother. If he once gives the lie to God by making a false profession, I do not know where he may stay his hand. Who would have sold Christ for twenty pieces of silver? Who but Judas, the one who professed to be his follower, his disciple, his private secretary, and his treasurer, though all the while his heart was false to his Lord? It is a traitorous profession that breeds gigantic sins.

5 **whoso keepeth his word** When we try to be, in every respect, what God's Word tells us we ought to be, then we may know that we are in God. But if we walk carelessly, if we take no

account of our actions, but do, after a random fashion, whatever comes into our foolish hearts, then have we no evidence at all that we are in God.

know that we are in him When every word of his is precious to us, and when we strive to live according to his precepts, then we know that "we are in him." This is even more than knowing that we know him, for it is the assurance that we are united to him by a living connection that can never be broken.

6 **He that saith he abideth in him** That is exactly what every Christian does say. He cannot be a Christian unless this is true of him, and he cannot fully enjoy his religion unless he assuredly knows that he is in Christ, and can boldly say as much. We must be in Christ, and abidingly in Christ, or else we are not saved in the Lord. It is our union with Christ that makes us Christians. By union with him as our life we truly live—live in the favor of God. We are in Christ as the manslayer was in the city of refuge: we abide in him as our sanctuary and shelter. We have fled for refuge to him who is the hope set before us in the gospel; even as David and his men sheltered themselves in the caves of En-gedi, so we hide ourselves in Christ.

ought himself also so to walk, even as he walked The first thing about a Christian is initiation, initiation into Christ; the next thing is imitation, the imitation of Christ. We cannot be Christians unless we are in Christ, and we are not truly in Christ unless in him we live and move and have our being, and the life of Christ is lived over again by us according to our measure. "Be ye therefore followers of God, as dear children" (Eph 5:1). It is the nature of children to imitate their parents. Be imitators of Christ as good soldiers who cannot have a better model for their soldierly life than their Captain and Lord. Should we not be very grateful to Christ that he deigns to be our example? If he were not perfectly able to meet all our other wants, if he were an expiation and nothing else, we should glory in him as our atoning sacrifice, for we always put that to the front, and magnify the virtue of his precious blood beyond everything. But at the same time we need an example, and it is delightful to find it where we find our pardon and justification. Those who are saved from the death of sin need to be guided in the life of holiness, and it is infinitely condescending on the part of Christ that he becomes an example to such poor creatures as we are.

ILLUSTRATION

Great Leaders Lead by Example

It is said to have been the distinguishing mark of Caesar as a soldier that he never said to his followers, "Go!" but he always said, "Come!" Of Alexander, also, it was noted that in weary marches he was sure to be on foot with his warriors, and in fierce attacks he always was in the vanguard. The most persuasive sermon is the example that leads the way.

This certainly is one trait in the Good Shepherd's character: "And when he putteth forth his own sheep, he goeth before them" (John 10:4). If Jesus bids us do anything, he first does it himself.

---

7 **Brethren, I write no new commandment unto you** The love of our brother is in one sense an old command, for it is the substance of the second table of the law. But the gospel sets it in a new light beneath the cross, and binds us to keep it by new and powerful obligations.

8 **a new commandment I write unto you** That which is new in the gospel, in one sense, is not new in another; for, though John was about to write what he called a new commandment, yet at the same time he was writing something that was not novel, something that was not grafted upon the gospel, but that grows naturally out of it, namely, the law of love.

the darkness is past, and the true light now shineth Children of light may for a time walk in the darkness of sorrow; but from the darkness of untruthfulness, ignorance, sin, and unbelief they have been delivered. In these respects the darkness is passing away, and the true light is already shining. Moral darkness is contrary to their newborn nature: they cannot endure it.

9 **He that saith he is in the light, and hateth his brother** To *have* a thing, or to boast that you have it—to *be*, or to pretend to be, such-and-such a character—are as opposite as white and black, as light and darkness. Indeed, we scarcely need revelation to tell us this, for it is so in secular things, and it must be certainly applicable to religion. We meet in common life with persons who say that they are rich, but this does not make them so. They apply for credit and say that they are wealthy when they are worth nothing. Companies will ask for your money with which they may speculate, and they say that they are sound, but they are oftentimes found to be rotten; though some of them make a very fair show in the prospectus, the result appears very foul in the winding up of the association.

Rest assured, then, that if in these temporal matters to say is not the same thing as to be or to do, neither is it so in spiritual things. A minister may say that he is sent from God and yet be a wolf in sheep's clothing. A man may say that he unites himself to the church of God, but he may be no better than a hypocrite and an alien who has no part in her fellowship. We may say that we pray, and yet never a prayer may come from our hearts. We may say to our fellow men that we are Christians, and yet we may never have been born again—never have obtained the precious faith of God's elect—never have been washed in the blood of Jesus Christ. And as you would not be satisfied with merely saying that you are rich—as you lack the title deeds of the broad acres; as you want to hear the coins chink in your box; as you want the real thing, and not the mere saying of it—so do not be put off with the mere profession of religion. Do not be content with a bare assertion, or think that is enough; but seek to have your own profession verified by the witness of heaven, as well as by that of your own conscience.

ILLUSTRATION

Exposed by the Light

If any man dares to tell me that he lives for a single day without a sinful deed, I will dare to tell him that he never knew himself. Only look at your own room. If you disturb it, I see only a little dust floating about in it, but if a stray sunbeam shall enter through the window I see millions upon millions of little motes dancing up and down. I discover that the whole of what I supposed to be clear, pure air is filled with innumerable atoms of all sorts of things, and that I am breathing these even in the purest atmosphere.

So is it with our heart and life. When the Spirit shines into us we see that the atmosphere of life is as full of sin as it can hold, and a man may sooner count the hairs of his head, or the sands upon the sea shore, or the drops of the dew of the morning upon the grass, than count the sins of a single day.

---

10 **He that loveth his brother abideth in the light** A loving spirit, kind, generous, forgiving, unselfish, seeking the good of others—this is one of the best proofs that our natural darkness has gone and that true spiritual light is within us. Some persons think very much of the doctrine of Christ, but very little of the Spirit of Christ. Let such remember that it is written, "Now if any man have not the Spirit of Christ, he is none of his" (Rom 8:9). If we do not know what it is to love, then we do not in the scriptural sense know what it is to live; we are dead. Hatred is the cerement in which the dead soul is wound up, the grave clothes in which it is put away in the tomb; but love is the garment of life in which a truly quickened spirit arrays itself. The one who is full of hatred dwells in darkness, but he who loves abides in the light. Note how love and life and light are most blessedly linked to one another.

11 **he that hateth his brother is in darkness** Love is the true test of light, the light that leads us to love God, to love Christ, to love the truth, to love God's people—yes, and to love the whole world of men for their good. This is the love that attests the light we have to be the very light of God.

darkness hath blinded his eyes Hatred is darkness, love is light; the revengeful man is an heir of eternal midnight. Let us purge ourselves from all anger, malice, and envy, for these are evils of the darkest dye.

APPLICATION

Continually Come to Christ as a Sinner

Every day I find it most healthy to my own soul to try and walk as a saint, but in order to do so I must continually come to Christ as a sinner. I would seek to be perfect; I would strain after every virtue, and forsake every false way. But still, as to my standing before God, I find it happiest to sit where I sat when I first looked to Jesus, on the rock of his works, having nothing to do with my own righteousness, but only with his. Depend on it, the happiest way of living is to live as a poor sinner and as nothing at all, having Jesus Christ as all in all. You may have all your growth in sanctification, all your progress in grace, all the development of your virtues that you want, but still I earnestly ask you never to put any of these where Christ should be. If you have begun in Christ, then finish in Christ. If you have begun in the flesh and then go on in the flesh, we know what the sure result will be. But if you have begun with Jesus Christ as your Alpha, let him be your Omega. I ask you never to think you are rising when you get above this, for it is not rising but slipping downward to your ruin. Still a sinner, but still having an advocate with the Father, Jesus Christ the righteous—let this be the spirit of your everyday life.

In Doubt as to Knowing Christ?

Some Christians who do know Christ are in great doubt as to whether they know him. This ought not to be. It is too solemn a matter to be left to chance or conjecture. I believe there are saved ones who do not know for sure that they are saved. They are often raising the question that never ought to be a question. No man ought to be content to leave that unsettled, for if you are not a saved man, you are a condemned man. If you are not forgiven, your sins lie on you. You are now in danger of hell if you are not now secure of heaven, for there is no place between these two. You are either a child of God or not. Why do you say, "I hope I am a child of God, yet I do not know; I hope, yet not know that I am forgiven"? You ought not to be in such suspense. You are either one or the other—either a saint or a sinner, either saved or lost, either walking in the light or walking in the dark.

What Is Needed to Walk as Christ Walked

First, it is necessary to have a *nature like that of Christ*. You cannot give out sweet waters so long as the fountains are impure. "Ye must be born again" (John 3:7). There is no walking with Jesus in newness of life unless we have a new heart and a right spirit. See to it that your nature is renewed—that the Holy Ghost has wrought in you a resurrection from among the dead. For, if not, your walk and conversation will savor of death and corruption. A new creature is essential to likeness to Christ: it is not possible that the carnal mind should wear the image of Jesus.

That being done, the next thing that is necessary is *a constant anointing of the Holy Spirit*. Can any Christian do without the Holy Spirit? Then I am afraid that he is no Christian. But, as for us, we feel every day that we must cry for a fresh visitation of the Spirit, a renewed sense of indwelling, a fresh anointing from the Holy One of Israel, or else we cannot walk as Christ walked.

And then, again, there must be in us a *strong resolve* that we will walk as Christ walked; for our Lord himself did not lead that holy life without stern resolution. He set his face like a flint that he would do the right; and he did the right. Do not be led astray by thoughtlessly following your fellow men: it is a poor, sheepish business, that running in crowds. Dare to be singular; dare to stand alone. Stand to it firmly that you will follow Christ. A Christian man in a discussion attempted to defend the truth, but his opponent grew angry, and cried out vehemently again and again, "Hear me! Hear me!" At last the good man answered, "No, I shall not hear you, nor shall you hear me; but let us both sit down and hear the word of the Lord." And that is the thing to do: to be hearing Christ and following him; not I to learn of you, nor you of me, but both of Christ: so shall we end all controversy in a blessed agreement at his feet. God help us to get there.

And so, once again, I add that if we want to walk as Christ walked, we must have much *communion with him*. We cannot possibly get to be like Christ except by being with him. I wish that we could rise to be so much like the Savior that we should resemble a certain ancient saint who died a martyr's death, to whom the world said, "What are you?" He said, "I am a Christian." They asked, "What trade do you follow?" And he said, "I am a Christian." They inquired, "What language do you speak?" And he said, "I am a Christian." "But what treasures do you have?" said they; and he replied, "I am a Christian." They asked him what friends he had, and he said, "I am a Christian," for all he was, and all he had, and all he wished to be, and all he hoped to be, were all wrapped up in Christ. If you live with Christ you will be absorbed by him, and he will embrace the whole of your existence. In consequence, your walk will be like his.

Take care that you do not in all things copy any but Christ. If I set my watch by the watch of one of my friends, and he sets his watch by that of another friend, we may all be wrong together. If we shall, each one, take his time from the sun, we shall all be right. There is nothing like going to the fountainhead. Take your lessons in holiness, not from a poor erring disciple, but from the infallible Master. God help you to do so.

1 JOHN
2:12–29

12 I write unto you, little children, because your sins are forgiv-
en you for his name's sake. 13 I write unto you, fathers, because
ye have known him *that is* from the beginning. I write unto you,
young men, because ye have overcome the wicked one. I write
unto you, little children, because ye have known the Father.
14 I have written unto you, fathers, because ye have known him
that is from the beginning. I have written unto you, young men,
because ye are strong, and the word of God abideth in you, and
ye have overcome the wicked one. 15 Love not the world, neither
the things *that are* in the world. If any man love the world, the
love of the Father is not in him. 16 For all that *is* in the world, the
lust of the flesh, and the lust of the eyes, and the pride of life, is
not of the Father, but is of the world. 17 And the world passeth
away, and the lust thereof: but he that doeth the will of God abideth for ever. 18 Little children, it is the last time: and as ye have
heard that antichrist shall come, even now are there many antichrists; whereby we know that it is the last time. 19 They went
out from us, but they were not of us; for if they had been of us,
they would *no doubt* have continued with us: but *they went out*,
that they might be made manifest that they were not all of us.
20 But ye have an unction from the Holy One, and ye know all
things. 21 I have not written unto you because ye know not the
truth, but because ye know it, and that no lie is of the truth.
22 Who is a liar but he that denieth that Jesus is the Christ? He
is antichrist, that denieth the Father and the Son. 23 Whosoever
denieth the Son, the same hath not the Father: *(but) he that
acknowledgeth the Son hath the Father also.* 24 Let that therefore
abide in you, which ye have heard from the beginning. If that
which ye have heard from the beginning shall remain in you, ye
also shall continue in the Son, and in the Father. 25 And this is

the promise that he hath promised us, *even* eternal life. [26] These *things* have I written unto you concerning them that seduce you. [27] But the anointing which ye have received of him abideth in you, and ye need not that any man teach you: but as the same anointing teacheth you of all things, and is truth, and is no lie, and even as it hath taught you, ye shall abide in him. [28] And now, little children, abide in him; that, when he shall appear, we may have confidence, and not be ashamed before him at his coming. [29] If ye know that he is righteous, ye know that every one that doeth righteousness is born of him.

EXPOSITION

12 **I write unto you** Remember what order of man John was—that disciple whom Jesus loved, whose head had leaned on Jesus's bosom, whose eyes had seen the King in his beauty, and whose strengthened gaze had looked within the gates of pearl. This is he who at one time saw the pierced heart of the Well-beloved pouring forth blood and water (John 19:34), and at another beheld the Lion of the tribe of Judah take the book and loose its seven seals (Rev 5:5). It is the apostle of love who says to us, "I am writing to you." Let us carefully note what the Spirit says to us by his servant John.

little children It is thought by many wise interpreters that under this term John includes the whole church of God, and that afterwards he divides that church into two companies—the fathers and the young men: those who under one aspect are all "little children" are under another regarded as young men or fathers. There is very much to support this view in several instances in this epistle. John is evidently addressing all the saints when he speaks of them as "my little children," as, for instance, in 3:18, and also in the closing verse, "Little children, keep yourselves from idols" (5:21). Surely, all the saints are included in these exhortations. There is a sense in which every Christian is still a little child, a sense in which he ought to be so—ever dependent upon the great Father, ever ready to receive the word of the Father without questioning, ever teachable, ever restful in the Father's care, and full of love to him who is his all in all. We must necessarily always be children before God. Our finite capacity is so limited that we are mere babes in knowledge in the presence of infinite wisdom, and as very sucklings in understanding when contrasted with the great Father of spirits. We know enough to make us know that we know very little. The most advanced intellects in the church are but as infants compared with the Ancient of Days.

Still, I am inclined to think that in this case John really does divide the entire church into three classes: the babes in grace, or the children, those who have not long been born into the family. Then follow the young men: these are the second class, and they are a valued body of Christians, in the fullness of their vigor; strong in faith, giving glory to God; mighty in prayer; vehement in action, bold in testimony.

Then there is the third class: the fathers, the mature, the experienced. These do not quite so much delight in war as the young men do, but at home they diligently care for the household of faith, watching over the feeble, strengthening and comforting them. These are able by their experience to answer gainsayers, to edify the untaught, and to guide the ignorant. Their knowledge is deep, and they are, therefore, able to become teachers of others; they are men of spiritual force, and have come to the full stature of men in Christ Jesus; therefore they are the solid strength of the church. If the young men are the church's arm, these are the church's backbone. We need to have many such, though it is to be feared that our churches are much like the apostolic ones, of which Paul said, "Yet have ye not many fathers" (1 Cor 4:15).

because your sins are forgiven you This is a privilege extremely desired by the little children. They have only recently felt the burden of guilt; they still smart under the lashes of conscience; the Spirit of God has but newly convinced them of sin, of righteousness, and of judgment. Therefore, above everything, their prayer is, "Father, forgive me." To them the remission of sins stands out as the first and most desirable of all blessings. Truly they are right in their estimate; for what possession is there which can be called a blessing at all until sin be forgiven?

Here let me observe that the forgiveness of sins is *assuredly the possession of the new beginner* in the divine life. He is as certainly forgiven as he ever shall be. The forgiveness of sins is not a matter of degrees or of growth. It is done in an instant and done forever, never to be reversed. The child of God who was born only yesterday is not as completely sanctified as he will be; he is not as completely instructed as he will be; he is not as completely conformed to the image of Christ as he will be; but he is as completely pardoned as the full-grown saint.

ILLUSTRATION

Sins Cast into the Depths

The Egyptians at the Red Sea were not destroyed little by little; they were not swallowed up in the flood a regiment at a time; the eager depths that had by miracle been divided for a time leaped together, and Pharaoh and his hosts, all of them, were covered, to be seen no more forever. Sing unto the Lord, for he has triumphed gloriously; "the depths have covered them" (Exod 15:5). The Israelites had barely set their foot upon the other side of the Red Sea, and yet all their enemies were as completely drowned as when the people entered into the promised land.

It is even so with you who have newly believed in Christ: your sins are cast into the depths of the sea. Your iniquities are subdued by the Lord Jesus, who has come to save his people from their sins. Therefore, little children, praise your God, and sing unto his name with all your might, "who forgiveth all thine iniquities; who health all thy diseases" (Ps 103:3).

---

for his name's sake That is, for the sake of Jesus, for the sake of his glorious person, for the sake of his honorable offices, for the sake of his blood-shedding and atoning death, for the sake of his glorious resurrection, for the sake of his perpetual intercession before the throne of God. Your sins are not forgiven because of anything you are or hope to be, nor because of anything that you have done or have suffered. You are forgiven for Christ's name's sake, and all the saints of God can say the same. This is a sure ground of hope. There is no quicksand, but a solid rock is under our foot. If the pardon had been granted for our own work's sake, it might have been reversed upon our disobedience. But since sin is pardoned for Christ's sake, the pardon is irreversible, since there is no change in Christ.

13 **I write unto you, fathers** "Fathers" are *persons of maturity*, men who are not raw and green; not fresh recruits, unaccustomed to march or fight, but old legionaries who have used their swords on others, and are themselves scarred with wounds received in conflict. These men know what they know, for they have thought over the gospel, studied it, considered it, and having so considered it have embraced it with full intensity of conviction. Usually we mean by "fathers" men who have become developed in grace, mature in character, decided in conviction, clear in statement, and accurate in judgment. These can discern between things that differ, and are not deceived by the philosophies that allure the ignorant. They know the voice of the Shepherd, and they will not follow a stranger. The younger folk may be bewitched so that they do not obey the truth, but these are not fascinated by error. New converts in their difficulties resort to these fathers, for doubts that bewilder the beginner are simplicity itself to those who are taught by the Lord. These are the watchmen on the walls who detect where insidious doubt is creeping in, where deadly error under the guise of truth is slyly undermining the faith of the church. To that end, the Lord has instructed them and given them to have their senses exercised to discern between good and evil. Among them

are men who have understanding of the times to know what Israel ought to do (1 Chr 12:32).

But there is something more than this in Christian fatherhood. The fathers of the church are men of heart, who *naturally care for the souls of others*. It is a grand thing when Christian men and Christian women come to this, that they are not perpetually thinking of their own salvation and of their own souls being fed under the ministry, but they care most of all for those who are weak and feeble in the church. During a service their thoughts go out for those assembled. They are anxious as to how that stranger may be impressed by the sermon, how an anxious spirit may be comforted, how a backsliding brother may be restored, how one who is growing somewhat chill may be revived. This paternal care betokens a true father in the church.

ILLUSTRATION

Fathers in War

I have seen in the army a number of veterans marching in front, an ornament and an honor to the whole company. Your short-service men come and go, but these tried men stick to the colors and are the backbone of the regiment. If a tough bit of fighting has to be done, you must rely upon such as these. Like Napoleon's Old Guard, they cannot be shaken or driven back; the smell of powder does not alarm them, nor the whistling of the shot, nor the roar of the artillery. They have seen such things before. They can also bide their time and wait, which is a great thing in a soldier. When at last they are bidden to charge, they leap like lions on their prey, and the enemy is driven before them.

Such men we have in the church of God, and such we need: men that are not flattered by opposition or made to lose their heads by excitement. They believe in God, and if others doubt, they are not infected by their folly. They know; they are certain; they have put their feet down, and will not move from their persuasion. When the time comes for action, they are ready for it, and throw their whole weight so heartily into the war that every charge tells.

---

because ye have known him Observe here *the concentration of their knowledge.* Twice he says, "Ye have known him that is from the beginning." Now, a babe in grace knows twenty things; a young man in Christ knows ten things; but a father in Christ knows one thing, and that one thing he knows thoroughly. It is very natural for us at first to divide our little stream into many rivulets, but as we grow gray in grace we pour it all into one channel, and then it runs with a force efficient for our life's work. I trust I know many doctrines, many precepts and many teachings, but more and more my knowledge gathers about my Lord, even as the bees swarm around their queen. May it come to this with us all: "I determined not to know any thing among you, save Jesus Christ, and him crucified" (1 Cor 2:2).

that is from the beginning Note *the peculiarity of their knowledge as to its object:* they know "him that is from the beginning." Do the babes in Christ not know the Lord Jesus? Yes, they do, but they do not know him in his full character. They know him as having forgiven their sins, and that is much, but it is not all. In gracious maturity the Christian sees the blessed persons of the Divine Trinity entering into a compact for the salvation of men, and he sees the Son of God himself from the beginning acting as the representative of his elect, and taking upon himself to answer on their behalf to the Father. He sees the Eternal Son there and then becoming the sponsor and the surety for his chosen, engaging to pay their debt and make recompense to the injured justice of God on account of their sins. He sees that covenant even from of old ordered in all things and sure in the hand of him who was from the beginning.

I write unto you, young men In the Christian church there is an order of Christians who have grown so much that they can no longer be called "babes in grace," yet they are not so far matured that they can be exactly called "fathers." These, who form the middle class of the spiritual-minded, are styled "young men." Understand that the apostle is not writing here to any according to their bodily age; he is using human age as a metaphor and figure for representing growth in the spiritual life. Age, according to the flesh, often differs much from the condition of the spirit. Many old men are still no more than "babes," some children in years are even now "young men" in grace, while not a few young men are "fathers" in the church while young in years. God has endowed certain of his servants with great grace, and made them mature in their youth: such were Joseph, Samuel, David, Josiah, and Timothy.

These young men are not babes. They have been in Christ too long for that. They are no longer novices, to whom the Lord's house is strange. They have been born unto God probably now for years. The things they hoped for at first they have to a large extent realized; they know now what once they could not understand. They are not now confined to milk diet; they can eat meat and digest it well. They have discernment, having had their senses exercised by use, so that they are not so liable to be misled as they were in their infancy. And while they have been longer in the way, so also have they now grown stronger in the way. It is not a weak and timorous faith that they now possess; they believe firmly and stoutly and are able to do battle for the "faith which was once delivered unto the saints" (Jude 3), for they are strong in the Lord and in the power of his might. They are wiser now than they used to be. When they were children they knew enough to save them, for they knew the Father, and that was blessed knowledge; but now they know far more of the word of God that abides in them through their earnest, prayerful, believing reception of it. Now they have a clearer idea of the breadth and length and depth and height of the work of redemption, for they have been taught by God. They even venture to enjoy the deep things of God, and the covenant is by no means an unknown thing among them. They have been under the blessed teaching of the Spirit of God, and from him they have received an anointing so that they know all things (1 John 2:20). In knowledge they are no more children, but men in Christ Jesus. Thus they are distinguished from the babes in Christ.

They are not yet fathers because they are not yet so established, confirmed, and settled as the fathers are, who know what they believe, and know it with a certainty of full assurance that nothing can shake. They have not yet had the experience of fathers, and consequently have not all their prudence and foresight: they are richer in zeal than in judgment. They have not yet acquired the nursing faculty so precious in the church as the product of growth, experience, maturity, and affection; they are going on to that, and in a short time they will have reached it, but as yet they have other work to do more suitable to their vigor. Do not suppose that when we say they are not to be called "fathers" that they are not, therefore, very valuable to the community; for in some senses they are quite equal to the fathers, and in one or two respects they may even be superior to them. The fathers are for contemplation; they study deep and see far, and so they "have known him that is from the beginning"; but a measure of their energy for action may have gone through stress of years. These young men are born to fight; they are the militia of the church, they have to contend for her faith, and to extend the Redeemer's kingdom. They should do so, for they are strong. This is their lot, and the Lord help them to fulfill their calling. These must for years to come be our active spirits: they are our strength and our hope. The fathers must soon go off the stage; their maturity in grace shows that they are ready for glory, and it is not God's way to keep his shocks of corn in the field when once they are fully ripe for the garner—perfect men shall be gathered up with the perfect, and shall enter into their proper sphere. The fathers, therefore, must soon be gone; and when they are gone, to whom are we to look for a succession but to these young men? We hope to have them with us for many years, valiant for the truth, steadfast in the faith, ripening in spirit, and growingly made fit to take their seats among the glorified saints above.

Judge whether you are fairly to be ranked among the young men. Have no regard to the matter of sex, for there is neither male nor female in Christ Jesus. Judge whether you are fit to be ranked among those whose full-grown and vigorous life entitles them to stand among the effectives of the church, the vigorous manhood of the seed of Israel.

because ye have overcome the wicked one Why does Satan attack this class of men most? I reckon, first, because Satan is not always sure that the babes in grace are in grace, and therefore he does not always attack beginners. But when they are sufficiently developed to make him see who and what they are, then he arouses his wrath. Those who have clean escaped from him he will weary and worry to the utmost of his power.

A friend writes to me to inquire whether Satan knows our thoughts. Of course he does not, as God does. Satan pretty shrewdly guesses at them from our actions and our words, and perhaps even from manifestations on our countenances, but it is the Lord alone who knows the thoughts of men immediately and by themselves. Satan is an old hand at studying human nature: he has been near six thousand years watching and tempting men and women, and therefore he is full of cunning. But he is not omniscient, and therefore it may be that he thinks such and such a person is so little in grace that perhaps he is not in grace at all, so he lets him alone. But as soon as it is certain that the man is of the royal seed, then the devil is at him. I do not know whether our Lord was ever tempted at Nazareth while he was yet in his obscurity, but the moment he was baptized, and the Spirit of God came upon him, he was taken into the wilderness to be tempted by the devil.

14 **I have written** Probably you ask, "Why does John say first, 'I am writing' (2:12), and then, 'I have written'?" There is a beautiful touch of nature in this speedy change of tense.

John was an extremely old man, and therefore while he says, "I am writing," he adds, "I have written," as if he felt that it might be the last time that he should take his pen in hand. Very soon with him the present tense would change into the past, and he indicates the fact by changing his mode of speech. Perhaps he even felt that possibly before the letter reached the brothers to whom he addressed it he would be no more among the sons of men. Therefore he says, "I am writing," indicating that while he was still with them, with warm and loving heart he solemnly exhorted them; and then he adds, "I have written," as if he had recorded his dying testimony, and left it as his last legacy of love. To us, today, John's words run altogether in the past tense—"I have written"—but we need not therefore forget that they were the well-considered words of a venerated father in Christ, and that he wrote them as one so near to his departure that he regarded himself as already on the move, and therefore scarcely knew which tense to use.

"I write" and "I have written" also indicate the abiding need of men: they require the same teaching from time to time. I suppose that John alludes to his Gospel when he says, "I have written," and now, a little later, he writes his epistle and says "I write"—giving in each case the same teaching. Men's natures are still the same, men's spiritual conflicts and dangers are still the same, and hence the same truth is suitable, not only from day to day, but from century to century. There is but one food for soul hunger, and but one help in spiritual danger. The true teacher evermore comes to men with the same truth, because men continue to have the same dangers, necessities, sorrows, and hopes.

because ye have known him that is from the beginning The tiniest babe in the family of God knows the Father, for, as we have seen, *his sins are forgiven him*. By whom is that pardon given? Why, by the Father. Therefore, he who has had his sins forgiven necessarily knows the Father. When the poor prodigal felt the kisses of his father's love and saw the best robe adorning his person, then he knew the Father.

All the philosophers in the world do not know so much of the Father God as a forgiven sinner knows. I go a little further: if there are any who have never fallen into sin, but are like the ninety-nine just persons who need no repentance, or like the elder brother who had never at any time transgressed his father's commandment, I say that these do not know and cannot know the Father as the forgiven child does. The Father's heart comes out most fully and expressly when he says, "Bring forth the best robe, and put it on him; and put a ring on his hand, and shoes on his feet. ... For this my son was dead, and is alive again; he was lost, and is found" (Luke 15:22, 24). Then, as he looks up through his tears and sees the ineffable smile of the Father's affection, the forgiven child knows the Father. The very least child of grace, having received the forgiveness of sin, knows the Father in this most important sense.

ILLUSTRATION

Little Children Know Their Father

Think of your dear little one at home. He cannot yet read a letter in a book; he knows nothing of the things that his elder brother studies; but he knows his father. He may not know very much about his father; he could not certainly speak to others about his father's business or his father's wealth, but yet he knows him. The child cannot help his father, or understand what his father does; but he knows his father, and would choose him out from among a thousand. See how his eyes twinkle now that father has come home; see him stretch out his little hands; see how eager he is to get into these dear arms! He knows his father, and never forgets that knowledge.

Dear child of God, this is a piece of knowledge that you have also; and in this you will yield to none of all the sacred family.

I have written unto you, young men, because ye are strong This does not imply that any measure of spiritual strength was in them by nature, for the apostle Paul clearly puts it otherwise concerning our natural state, saying, "For when we were yet without strength ... Christ died for the ungodly" (Rom 5:6). By nature we are without strength to do anything that is good and right. We are strong as a wild bull to dash headlong into everything that is evil; strong as a lion to fight against all that is good and Godlike. But for all spiritual things and holy things, we are utterly infirm and incapable; indeed, we are as dead men until God the Holy Spirit deals with us.

Neither does the apostle here at all allude to the strength of the body in young men, for in a spiritual sense this is rather their weakness than their strength. The man who is strong in the flesh is too often for that very reason strongly tempted to sins of the flesh; hence the apostle bids his young friend to "flee also youthful lusts" (2 Tim 2:22). The time of life in which a young man is found is full of perils, and so is the spiritual condition of which it is the type. The young man cannot reckon on vigor of the flesh as contributing toward real strength; he has rather to ask for more strength from on high lest the animal vigor that is within him should drag down his spirit. He is glad to be in robust health that he may bear much toil in the Lord's cause, but he is not proud of it, for he remembers that the Lord "delighteth not in the strength of the horse: he taketh not pleasure in the legs of a man" (Ps 147:10).

These young men in grace are strong, first of all, *in faith*, according to that exhortation, "Be strong, fear not" (Isa 35:4). They have known the Lord now for some time, and they have enjoyed that perfect peace which comes of forgiven sin. They have noticed the work of the Spirit within themselves, and they know that it is no delusion, but a divine change. Now they not only believe in Christ, but they know that they believe in him. They know whom they have believed, and they are convinced that he is able to guard what they have committed to him (2 Tim 1:12).

This strength makes a man strong *to endure*. Blessed is that man who is so strong that he never complains of his trials, never whimpers and frets because he is made to share in the humiliations and griefs of his covenant head. He expected to bear the cross when he became a follower of the Crucified, and he is not now made weary and faint when it presses upon him. It is a fair sight to see young Isaac bearing the wood for the sacrifice, young Joseph bearing the fetters in prison with holy joy, young Samson carrying away the gates of Gaza, bars and all, and young David praising God with his harp though Saul is feeling for his javelin. Such are the exploits of the young men who count it all joy when they fall into manifold trials for Christ's sake.

This strength shows itself, next, in *laboring for Christ*. The young man in Christ is a great worker. He has so much strength that he cannot sit still; he would be ashamed to leave the burden and heat of the day to be borne by others. He is up and at it according to his calling and ability. He has asked his Lord as a favor to give him something to do. His prayer has been, "Show me what you would have me to do," and having received an answer he is found in the vineyard trenching the soil, removing the weeds, pruning the vines, and attending to such labors as the seasons demand. These are the men that work our reformations; these are the men who conduct our missions; these are the men who launch out into the deep for Christ. They make the vanguard of the host of God, and largely compose the main body of her forces.

So also are these young men strong *to resist attack*. They are assaulted, but they carry with them the shield of faith with which they "quench all the fiery darts of the wicked" (Eph 6:16). Wherever they go, if they meet with other tempted ones, they spring to the front to espouse their cause. They are ready in the day of battle to meet attacks upon the faith with the sword of the Spirit. They will yield no point of faith, but defend the truth at all hazards.

Furthermore, these young men are not only strong for resistance, but they are strong *for attack*. They carry the war into the enemy's territory. If there is anything to be done, they are like Jonathan and his armor-bearer, eager for the fray. They are very zealous for the Lord of hosts, and are prompt to undertake toil and travail for Jesus's sake. They smite down error, and set up truth; they believe great things, attempt great things, and expect great things, and the Lord is with them.

the word of God abideth in you Notice that John not only mentions "the word of God," but the word of God *in you*. The inspired word must be received into a willing mind. How? The Book that lies *there* is to be pleaded *here*, in the inmost heart, by the work of the Holy Ghost upon the mind. All of *this* letter has to be translated into spirit and life. "The word of God abideth in you"—that is, first to know it, then remember it and treasure it up in your heart. Following this, you must understand it and learn the analogy of faith by comparing spiritual things with spiritual until you have learned the system of divine truth and are able to set it forth and plead for it. It is, next, to have the word in your affections, to love it so that it is as honey or the droppings of the honeycomb to you. When this is the case, you must and shall overcome the wicked one. A man instructed in the Scriptures is like an armed knight who, when he goes among the throng, inflicts many wounds but suffers none, for he is locked up in steel.

But that is not all. It is not the word of God in you alone; "the word of God *abideth* in you." It is always there; it cannot be removed from you. If a man gets the Bible into him he is all right, because he is full and there is no room for evil. When you have filled a measure full of wheat, you have effectually shut the chaff out. Men go after novel and false doctrines because they do not really know the truth; if the truth had gotten into them and filled them, they would not have room for these daydreams.

ILLUSTRATION

Letting the Word of God Abide

Her Majesty was on the south side of the water today, but she does not abide there. All the pomp and sunshine of her presence have vanished, and Westminster Bridge and Stangate are as they were before.

The word of God sometimes comes with royal pomp into the minds of young men. They are affected by it for a time, and they rejoice in it, but that blessed word soon departs, and they are none the better for that which they have heard. Multitudes still are stony-ground hearers; they receive the word with joy, but they have no root, and by and by they all wither away. The model young man in the text (1 John 2:14) is not of this kind. The word of God abides in him.

ye have overcome the wicked one In what sense have these young men conquered the evil one?

First, in the fact that they have broken away from his power. They were once his slaves; they are not so now. They once slept beneath his roof in perfect peace, but conscience raised an uproar, and the Spirit of God troubled them, and they escaped his power. Once Satan never troubled them at all. Why should he? They were good friends. Now he tempts them and worries them and assaults them because they have left his service, engaged themselves to a new master, and become the enemies of him who was once their god. The strong man has been turned out by one stronger than he; Jesus has carried the fortress of the heart by storm and driven out the foe.

Moreover, these young men have overcome the evil one in the very fact of their opposition to him. When a man resists Satan, he is victorious over Satan in that very resistance. Satan's empire consists in the yielding of our will to his will. But when our will revolts against him, then we have already in a measure overcome him. A Christian man has both defensive and offensive weapons. He has a shield as well as a sword, but Satan has fiery darts and nothing else. I never read of his having any shield whatsoever, so that when we resist him he is bound to run away. He has no defense for himself, and the fact of our resistance is in itself a victory.

But besides that, some of us who are young men in Christ have won many a victory over Satan. We have been tempted, but the mighty grace of God has come to the rescue, and we have not yielded. Can you not look back, not with pharisaic boasting, but with gracious exultation, over many an evil habit that once had mastery over you, but that is master no longer? "But thanks be to God, which giveth us the victory through our Lord Jesus Christ" (1 Cor 15:57). Hear what the Spirit says to you when John writes to you. Because you have overcome the wicked one, he says, "Love not the world, neither the things that are in the world" (1 John 2:15).

Once more, in Christ Jesus we have entirely overcome the wicked one already. The enemy we have to contend with is a vanquished foe—our Lord and Master met him and destroyed him. Our Lord overthrew him who had the power of death, that is, the devil, and therefore Satan does not have the power of death any longer. The keys of death and of hell are at the girdle of Christ. Let us take courage and abide steadfast in the faith, for we have in our Lord Jesus overcome the wicked one. We are more than conquerors through him that has loved us.

15 **Love not the world, neither the things that are in the world** Your affections are meant for something better than these transient and defiled things, so do not let your heart's love flow out to things so soiled and base. "Set your affection on things above, not on things on the earth" (Col 3:2).

Now, one might soon misunderstand this position, and by degrees look down from a pharisaic elevation and say, "I do not belong to this world. I am superior to it and utterly despise it. I take no interest in its welfare; it is too lowly a thing for me to care about." I think I have seen something of this sort in certain brothers who promulgate the theory that a few are to be rescued from the wreck that is breaking up and going to pieces on the beach. Just a few may be brought to shore, but all hope that the vessel itself will ever float again is gone. We have nothing to do but to load the lifeboats with one here and there, and pull away from the wreck with all speed. I do not believe in this theory, and I hope I never shall. I feel a yearning toward the blinded sons of men; I cannot take complacency in them, but I feel a love of benevolence toward them. Every Christian who has realized the love of Christ must, I think, feel the same. I believe that the kingdoms of this world will yet become the kingdom of our Lord and of his Christ.

ILLUSTRATION

Loving the World as a Foster Child

Now we feel such love to the world as that which the nurse has toward her foster child. It may be a very tiresome child, but she is entrusted with it. Because its hunger cannot be appeased unless she feeds it, and its nakedness cannot be clothed unless she wraps it up, its needs and its weaknesses appeal to her pity and she cares for it until by degrees her heart warms into an intense affection toward it.

That is the sort of feeling which our Lord would have us cultivate toward mankind.

If any man love the world, the love of the Father is not in him These two things are such deadly opposites that they cannot live together. Where the love of the Father is, there cannot be the love of the world. There is no room in us for two loves. The love of the world is essentially idolatry, and God will not be worshiped side by side with idols. You cannot send your heart at the same time in two opposite ways—toward evil and toward good. You must make a choice between the two.

Does not this text draw a very sharp distinction between those who love the Lord, and those who do not love him?

Remember that this is the language of John, the apostle of love, but true love is honest, outspoken, heart-searching, heart-trying. Do not imagine that there is any love for your souls in the heart of the preacher who preaches smooth things, and who flatters you with his "Peace, peace," when there is no peace. No, the highest, deepest, most heaven-inspired love is that which searches and tries the heart lest there should be any deception there.

16 **the lust of the flesh, and the lust of the eyes, and the pride of life** That devil's trinity "is not from the Father, but is from the world." While you are not to love the world you must take care that you *do not fall victim to any of the lusts of this present evil world,* such as the lust of the flesh. We have to speak very solemnly and admit that the most advanced saint still needs to be warned against the lust of the flesh, the indulgence of appetites that so readily lead men to sin.

Then there is the lust of the eyes. David fell into that when he repined because of the prosperity of the wicked, and was obliged to confess, "So foolish was I, and ignorant" (Ps 73:22). He looked at the prosperous wicked till he began to fret himself about them. That lust of the eye, in desiring more for yourself and envying those that have more—never let it happen.

And the pride of life—that thirsting to be thought respectable, that emulation of others, that struggling after honor and such like—this must not be. You are men, and must "put childish things away" (1 Cor 13:11). Do not fall prey to vanities: these toys are for the children of the world, not for you who are so near to the glory of the Lord. You are grown ripe in grace, and will soon enter heaven: live accordingly. Let all earthly things lie like babies' baubles beneath your feet while you rise to the manhood of your soul.

17 **And the world passeth away** It is only a puff, a phantom, a bubble, a mirage that will melt away as you try to approach it; there is nothing substantial in it. It ought not, then, to be difficult to make a choice between these fleeting shadows and the everlasting substance.

but he that doeth the will of God abideth for ever Not, "the one who does some great thing to be seen by men"; not, "the one who builds a row of poorhouses, or leaves a great mass of money to charity when he dies, because he could not possibly carry it away with him"; not, "the one who sounds a trumpet before him to let everybody know what a good man he is"; not, "the one who needs to outdistance everybody else"; but, "the one who does the will of God remains forever." Obedience to the will of God is the pathway to perpetual honor and everlasting joy. Everything else is transient, fleeting, and soon passes away, but the one who does the will of God has entered into the eternal regions, and he has himself become one of those who remain forever. Do not be carried away, therefore, from your old firm foundation, and from your eternal union to Christ.

18 **it is the last time** You may read the passage, "It is the last hour," as if John wanted to show how late it was, and how soon Christ would come.

even now are there many antichrists And now, I think, even more than when John wrote, is this the case. Antichrists are multiplying on all sides, and there are even worse evils to come than we have seen as yet. It therefore behooves Christians to be on the watch, and to let this truth comfort them, that "it is the last hour." Only get through this dispensation, and the battle is ended. Even though the dispensation should be protracted beyond our hope and desire, yet, still, get through it and it is over. This is to be the last charge of our great adversary and all his hosts. Stand fast, therefore, you soldiers of the Cross; stand like rocks amid the onslaught of the waves, and the victory shall yet be yours.

19 **they went out from us** Many of the antichrists came out of the church; they sprang up from among the followers of Christ. The worst of men go out from among the best of men. The raw material for a devil was an angel. To make a Judas, you must make him out of an apostle. May God purify his professing church, since even in her own loins she breeds adversaries of the faith.

they were not all of us There is a separating process always going on in the professing church, and the most effectual winnowing fan of all is a faithful ministry. After a while, some of our hearers do not like what we say; it is too personal, too cutting, too searching. They want to listen to that kind of preaching that will allow them to go on comfortably in their sins, and to have the reputation of living even while they are dead. How constantly our Lord's teaching kept on sifting his disciples! After one of his utterances concerning human inability apart from divine grace, we read, "From that time many of his disciples went back, and walked no more with him" (John 6:66). As he continually brought out some of the deeper truths as his disciples were able to bear them, there were certain of the mixed multitude that had joined with his followers who went off this way and that way. It is always so, and so must it be, under the faithful preaching of the Word. You must not be astonished or grieved when it is so.

20 **ye have an unction from the Holy One** You are taught by God, so you know all that is needed for the attainment of true godliness and the accomplishment of the divine purposes.

and ye know all things You who know God—and even the little children, the babes in Christ, know the Father—know all things. You will not be led astray and deceived by these antichrists who have gone out into the world. The Spirit of God will teach you as you need to know. He will so instruct you that you shall know all that is for your soul's good, and for his own glory.

He does not mean that the saints know everything, but they judge, they discern, they know truth from error. When doctrine presents itself to you, you know whether it is of Christ or of antichrist, and act accordingly. You are able to judge, to discern, and to distinguish.

21 **no lie is of the truth** That which is of man's making is false, "But the word of the Lord endureth for ever. And this is the word which by the gospel is preached unto you" (1 Pet 1:25).

22 **he that denieth that Jesus is the Christ** Some pretend to honor the Father while they dishonor the Son, but this can never really be done. Jesus truly said, "I and my Father are one" (John 10:30), so that he who denies the Son denies the Father also.

23 **Whosoever denieth the Son, the same hath not the Father** Those who deny the deity of Christ practically deny the divine fatherhood of God. It is not possible for us to understand the rest of the truth if we do not believe in Christ, who is *the* Truth.

24 **that which ye have heard from the beginning shall remain in you** Little children are very fickle. The toys that they cry for one day they break the next; young minds change with the wind. So, little children, there are many evil ones who will endeavor to seduce you from the truth of God, and as you have a natural instability of mind as yet, for you are only newly converted, it is well to be on your guard against those who would mislead you. Until we are rooted and grounded in the truth, new things have great charms for us, especially if they have about them a great show of holiness and zeal for God. Listen, then, dear children newly born into the Savior's family: "What you have heard from the beginning must remain in you."

Your hope has come from a belief in Christ as God has borne witness to him. Abide in the truth that you received from the beginning, for in your earliest days it wrought salvation in you. The foundation of your faith is not a changeable doctrine; you rest on a sure word of testimony. Truth is, in its very nature, fixed and unalterable. You know more about it than you did; but the thing itself is still the same, and must be the same. Take care that you remain in it. You will find it difficult to do so, for there is an element of changeableness about yourself: you must overcome this by grace. You will find many elements of seduction in the outside world. There are men whose business it is to shake the faith of others, and thereby to gain a reputation for cleverness and depth of thought. Some seem to think it an ambition worthy of a Christian to be always questioning, or, as the apostle puts it, to be "ever learning, and never able to come to the knowledge of the truth" (2 Tim 3:7). To throw doubt into minds that, by a gracious certainty, have been made blessed, is their chosen life's work. Therefore, you will be often led to try your foundation, and at times you will tremble as you cling to it.

continue in the Son, and in the Father Since it was the truth that was revealed to them at first, there was no need of a later revelation to correct the mistakes of the first, as some foolishly and falsely teach nowadays.

25 **eternal life** Not transient life, but eternal life, is the great promise of the covenant of grace, and abiding in Christ we possess it.

26 **them that seduce you** They would lead you astray if they could, so beware of them. "Forewarned is forearmed."

27 **the anointing which ye have received of him abideth in you** The Holy Ghost brings the truth home to your heart with savor and unction, endearing it to your inmost soul. The truth has so saturated you through the anointing that you cannot give it up. Has not your Lord said, "The water that I shall give him shall be in him a well of water springing up into everlasting life" (John 4:14)?

28 **And now, little children** John lived to a great age; the tradition is that they used to carry him into the assembly, and, when he could do nothing else, he would lift his hand, and simply say, "Little children, love one another." Here, to show his tender concern for those to whom he wrote, he called them "little children." He could not wish them a greater blessing out of the depth of his heart's affection than that they should faithfully abide in Christ.

abide in him John says, "Little children, abide in him." How sweetly those words must have flowed from the lips and the pen of such a venerable saint! I think he is in this the echo of the Lord Jesus. In John 15 the Lord Jesus said, "Abide in me, and I in you. As the branch cannot bear fruit of itself, except it abide in the vine; no more can ye, except ye abide in me. ... If ye abide in me, and my words abide in you, ye shall ask what ye will, and it shall be done unto you" (John 15:4, 7). That word "abide" was a very favorite one with the Lord Jesus, and it became equally dear to that disciple whom Jesus loved.

ILLUSTRATION

Abiding in Christ Like Living in a Home

I was speaking yesterday to a friend who had bought a pleasant house, with a large garden. He said to me, "I now feel as if I had a home. I have lived in London for years, and I have changed from one house to another with as little regret as a man feels in changing a bus; but I have always longed for the home feeling that hung about my father's house in the country. There we loved the cozy rooms and the lookouts from the little windows, and the corner cupboards in the kitchen. As for the garden and the field, they yielded us constant delight, for there was that bush in the garden where the robin had built, and the tree with the blackbird's nest. We knew where the pike lay in the pool, and where the tortoise had buried itself for the winter, and where the first primroses would be found in the spring. There is a vast difference between a house and a home."

That is what John means with regard to Christ in 1 John 2:28: we are not merely to call on him, but to abide in him. Do not go to Jesus one day and to the world another day. Do not be a lodger with him, but abide in him. My friend spoke of changing from one bus to another, and I fear that some change from Christ to the world when the day changes from Sunday to Monday; but it should not be so. Say with Moses, "Lord, thou hast been our dwelling place in all generations" (Ps 90:1).

Why does the apostle urge us to remain in Christ? Is there any likelihood of our going away? Yes, for in this very chapter he mentions apostates, who from disciples had degenerated into antichrists, of whom he says, "They went out from us, but they were not of us; for if they had been of us, they would no doubt have continued with us" (1 John 2:19). "Remain in him," then, and do not turn aside to crooked ways, as many professing Christians have done. The Savior once said to his apostles, "Will ye also go away?" (John 6:67), and they answered him with that other question, "Lord, to whom shall we go?" (John 6:68). I hope your heart is so conscious that he has the words of eternal life that you could not dream of going elsewhere.

when he shall appear Notice how John puts it. He uses two words for the same thing: "when he shall appear," and "at his coming." The second advent may be viewed in two lights. First, as the appearing of one who is here already, but is hidden; and next, as the coming of one who is absent. In the first sense, we know that our Lord Jesus Christ abides in his church, according to his word, "Lo, I am with you alway, even unto the end of the world" (Matt 28:20). Yet though spiritually present, he is unseen. Our Lord will, all of a sudden, be "manifested," as the Revised Version has it. The spiritual and secret presence of Christ will become a visible and manifest presence in the day of his appearing.

As to our Lord's "revealing," John would have us abide in Christ, that we may have confidence when he appears. Confidence at his appearing is the high reward of constant abiding in Christ. The apostle keeps most prominent "the revealing" as an argument. A thousand things are to happen at our Lord's appearing, but John does not mention one of them. He does not hold it up as a thing to be desired that we may have confidence amid the wreck of matter and the crash of worlds, when the stars shall fall like autumn leaves, when the sun shall be turned into darkness and the moon into blood, when the graves shall be opened and the dead shall rise, or when the heavens, being on fire, shall be dissolved, and the elements shall melt with fervent heat, the earth also, and the works that are in it shall be burned up. Those will be direful times, days of terror and dismay. But it is not of these that he speaks particularly, for he regards all these events as swallowed up in the one great fact of the glorious appearing of our Lord and Savior Jesus Christ.

we may have confidence The apostle exhorts us *by a motive in which he takes his share*. Look at that little word: it runs, "that *we* may have confidence." The beloved John needed to have confidence at the appearing of the Lord, and confidence fetched from the same source as that to which he directed his little children. They must abide in Christ, that they might have confidence, and the dearest of the apostles must practice the same abiding. How wisely, and yet how sweetly, he puts himself on our level in this matter!

His desire is that we may have confidence if he appears all of a sudden. What does he mean by having confidence when he shall appear? Why, this: that if you abide in him when you do not see him, you will be very bold should he suddenly reveal himself. Before he appears, you have dwelt in him, and he has dwelt in you; what fear could his appearing cause you? The word translated "confidence" means freedom of speech. If our divine Lord were to appear in a moment, we should not lose our tongue through fear, but should welcome him with glad acclaim. Faith has so realized him that if suddenly he were to appear to the senses, it would be no surprise to you; and, assuredly, it would cause you joy rather than dismay. You would feel that you at last enjoyed what you had long expected, and saw somewhat more closely a friend with whom you had long been familiar. I trust that some of us live in such a style that if our Lord were to appear suddenly, it would cause no alarm to us. We have believed him to be present, though unseen, and it will not affect our conduct when he steps from behind the curtain and stands in the open light.

O Lord Jesus, if you were now to stand in our midst, we should remember that we had your presence before, and lived in it, and now we should only be the more assured of that which we before knew by faith. We shall behold our Lord with confidence, freedom, assurance, and delight, feeling perfectly at home with him. The believer who abides in his Lord would be only a little startled by his sudden appearing. He is serving his Lord now, and he would go on serving him. He loves him now, and he would go on loving him. Only as he would have a clearer view of him would he feel a more intense consecration to him.

at his coming The apostle also uses the term "at his coming," or "his presence." This is the same thing from another point of view. In a certain evident sense our Lord is absent: "He is not here, for he is risen" (Matt 28:6). He has gone his way unto the Father. In that respect he will come a second time, "unto them that look for him shall he appear the second time without sin unto salvation" (Heb 9:28). He who has gone from us will come in like manner as he was seen to go up into heaven. There is thus a difference of aspect between the second advent when it is described as "his revealing" and "his coming." John pleads the glorious manifestation of our Lord under both of these views as a reason for abiding in him.

29 **every one that doeth righteousness is born of him** What your Lord bids you, continue to do. Call no man Master, but in all things submit your thoughts, your words, and your acts to the rule of the Lord Jesus. Obey him by whose obedience you are justified. Be precise and prompt in your execution of his commands. If others regard you as morbidly conscientious, do not heed their opinion, but "remain in him." The rule of the Master is always binding on all his disciples, and they depart from him in heart when they err from his rule.

APPLICATION

Little Children, Remain in Him

The beloved John speaks unto us as unto little children, for none of us is much more. We are not such wonderfully knowing people as certain of our neighbors; we are not such learned scientists and acute critics as they are; neither do we have their marvelous moral consciousness, which is superior to inspiration itself. Therefore, we are bound by our very feebleness to venture less than they do. Let the men of the world choose what paths they want; we feel bound to abide in Christ because we know no other place of safety. They may push off into the sea of speculation; our smaller boats must hug the shore of certainty. To us, however, it is no small comfort that the Lord has revealed to babes the things that are hidden from the wise and prudent. Those who become as little children enter into the kingdom of heaven.

Cling to the Lord Jesus in your feebleness, in your fickleness, in your nothingness; and abidingly take him to be everything to you. "The conies are but a feeble folk, yet make they their houses in the rocks" (Prov 30:26); be like them. Abide in the rifts of the Rock of Ages, and let nothing tempt you to leave your stronghold. You are no lion, able to fight your foes and deliver yourself by main strength. You are only a little badger, and you will be wise to hide rather than fight. "Little children, abide in him" (1 John 2:28).

Young Men and the Word Within

If the young man inquires for tools and weapons with which to serve his Master, I refer him to this point in the text: "The word of God abideth in you" (1 John 2:14). If you desire to teach others, you do not have to ask what the lesson shall be, for it resides in you. Do you want a text that will impress the careless? What impressed you? You cannot have a better one. You desire to speak a word in season from the word of God that will be likely to comfort the disconsolate? What has comforted your own soul? You cannot have a better guide. You have in your own experience a tutor that cannot fail you, and you also have an encouragement that cannot be taken from you. The word of God within you will well up like a spring, and truth and grace will pour forth from you in rivers.

I have heard our Lord compared to a man carrying a water pot. As he carried it upon his shoulder, the water fell dropping, dropping, dropping, so that everyone could track the water bearer. So should all his people be, carrying such a fullness of grace that everyone should know where they have been by that which they have left behind. He who has lain in the beds of spices will perfume the air through which he walks. One who, like Asher, has "dipped his foot in oil" (Deut 33:24), will leave his footprints behind him. When the living and incorruptible seed remains within, the divine instincts of the new nature will guide you to the wisest methods of activity. You will do the right thing under the inward impulse rather than the written law, and your personal salvation will be your prime qualification for seeking out others of your Master's flock.

Fathers Should Be Loving

John has been saying to you, dear fathers, and indeed to all of us who are in Christ, that we should *love one another*. If you are truly fathers you cannot help loving all the family. The fatherly instinct is love, and fathers in Christ should be brimful of it. Little ones should be induced by our loving spirit to come around us, feeling that if nobody else loves them, we do; if nobody else cares for them, we do.

I have known a father in Christ to whom a convert would speak much more readily than he would to his own earthly father or mother. I suppose they see an invitation in the faces of these fathers. I do not quite know how they find it out, but somehow converts feel that such a person is a man whom they could address, or a woman whom they could talk with. These fathers and mothers are full of love, and their speech betrays the fact. I know some men who are like great harbors for ships: a soul tossed with tempest makes for them as for a harbor. May you and I be just such persons, and may the Holy Spirit use us for the good of others.

What Have You Been Doing in His Absence?

What have you been doing while he has been absent? This is a question for a servant to answer at his Lord's arrival. You are left in his house to take care of it while he is in the faraway country. If you have been beating his servants, and eating and drinking with the drunken, you will be greatly ashamed when he returns. His coming will be in itself a judgment. "But who may abide the day of his coming? And who shall stand when he appeareth?" (Mal 3:2). Blessed is that man who, with all his faults, has been so sanctified by grace that he will not be ashamed at his Lord's coming.

Who is that man? It is the man who has learned to abide in Christ. What is the way to prepare for Christ's coming? By the study of prophecies? Yes, if you are sufficiently instructed to be able to understand them. "To be prepared for the Lord's coming," some enthusiasts might say, "should I not spend a month in seclusion, and get out of this wicked world?" You may, if you like; and especially you will do so if you are lazy. But the one scriptural prescription for preparing for his coming is this: "Abide in him" (1 John 2:28). If you remain in the faith of him, holding his truth, following his example, and making him your dwelling place, your Lord may come at any hour, and you will welcome him. The cloud, the great white throne, the blast of trumpets, the angelic attendants of the last assize, the trembling of creation, and the rolling up of the universe as a worn-out garment, will have no alarms for you; for you will "not be ashamed before him at his coming" (1 John 2:28).

1 JOHN 3

1 JOHN
3:1–10

[1] Behold, what manner of love the Father hath bestowed upon us, that we should be called the sons of God: therefore the world knoweth us not, because it knew him not. [2] Beloved, now are we the sons of God, and it doth not yet appear what we shall be: but we know that, when he shall appear, we shall be like him; for we shall see him as he is. [3] And every man that hath this hope in him purifieth himself, even as he is pure. [4] Whosoever committeth sin transgresseth also the law: for sin is the transgression of the law. [5] And ye know that he was manifested to take away our sins; and in him is no sin. [6] Whosoever abideth in him sinneth not: whosoever sinneth hath not seen him, neither known him. [7] Little children, let no man deceive you: he that doeth righteousness is righteous, even as he is righteous. [8] He that committeth sin is of the devil; for the devil sinneth from the beginning. For this purpose the Son of God was manifested, that he might destroy the works of the devil. [9] Whosoever is born of God doth not commit sin; for his seed remaineth in him: and he cannot sin, because he is born of God. [10] In this the children of God are manifest, and the children of the devil: whosoever doeth not righteousness is not of God, neither he that loveth not his brother.

EXPOSITION

1 **Behold** This word "see" is a word of wonder. John had lived among wonders. John's life, from the time of his conversion, was a life of wonders, not only in what he saw with his natural eye, but in all the sights that the Lord gave him to see with his spiritual eye when he appeared to him in "the isle that is called Patmos" (Rev 1:9). His life was crowned with wonders in his memorable escape from martyrdom, when, according

to tradition, he was cast into a cauldron of boiling oil but came out unharmed, his Master having determined that he was not by martyrdom to glorify his name. If ever there was a seer among men to whom wonders became common things, it was John. Yet as he wrote this heavenly epistle, he could not help bursting out in exclamations of amazement such as do not generally come from writers so much as from speakers: "*See*," says he, "*See* what sort of love!"

But this "see" is also a note of instruction. It is as if the man of God said, "Stand still, and consider the extraordinary love of God." Do not speak of it, for some of these things slip glibly from the tongue. Sit down, and ponder, and weigh, mark, and behold. *See* what sort of love. Here, take your glass, and look at it microscopically. Study it. Wonder at it. Study it with every faculty concentrated on it; you shall find new excellences in it every time you look into it. "See what sort of love"—the very manner of it is exceedingly sublime and adorable. Do not merely glance and go your way. Stop and rest, and pry into this secret, comparing this love with all other loves, and the manner of it with the manner of men. Come here, and dig where there are nuggets of pure gold to reward every moment of your industry. Sink your shafts here, and go into the depths to bring up this priceless treasure. *See:* read, mark, learn, inwardly digest, and still *see* again. Look, and look, and look on; there will be no end to the discoveries you will make. When you have looked, remember that you have not been gazing upon a mere appearance, but have beheld an actual fact: "Behold, what manner of love the Father hath bestowed upon us, that we should be called the sons of God." When you have beheld this, then look again, and behold with equal admiration that it is no supposition, or fancy, or romance. The Lord calls us children, "*and we are.*"

what manner of love "Behold what manner of ______" What is the word? "What sort of *gift* the Father has given to us that we should be called the children of God"? It might have been so written, and have been quite correct; but it is not so written. "Behold what sort of *honor* the Father has given"? No, no!

"Behold what sort of *love* the Father has given to us." It is as much as to say that the adopting of a man to be a son of God is an act that involves so much of love that you are bidden especially to fix your eyes on the love of it and to notice its manner.

Now just think for a minute what *intense* love is manifested to that man who is favored to be called a child of God. It is love in the highest degree. What love you would have in your heart if you were to take a wanton and malicious enemy and say, "You shall be my son"! If one had wronged you, and despised you, and defied your authority, and you should say to him, "You shall be my child from this time forward," what a singular deed of love would this be! Yet it might not be very much for you to do, for you may be, after all, nothing very great. It would, however, be the utmost your love could devise. Only think of what it must be for God—even that infinite and eternal Spirit—to say, "You will be my child. I will take you, though you are an heir of wrath, and make you mine." In this, indeed, is love; love worth the beholding.

It is certainly an *undeserved* love, because no man can possibly deserve to be made into a child of God. Grace in this instance is the sole source of the stream of goodness. You might think it possible that you could deserve some ordinary gift, but you could not deserve such a benefit as to be made a son of God. If you had never sinned, I do not see that you could have had any right to sonship. The most faithful service does not make a servant into a son. If you had been perfect, what would you have given to God as purchase money for this high dignity? He is great and glorious without your service. To be promoted to be a prince of the royal blood of heaven—it is not possible for any man to deserve this. No works can climb to this lofty place; only faith can reach it by the power of grace. "But as many as received him, to them gave he power to become the sons of God" (John 1:12). This power, this privilege, this honor of sonship before God, is gained in no other way but that of faith.

There is *everlasting* love in it. If God makes you to be called a son of God, that is done, and done forever; it never can be undone. Here is the joy of it. The servant does not abide in the house forever, but a son abides always. The relationships that come of service begin and end. You know it is so among men. You can say to a hired servant, "Take your money and be gone," but you cannot say that to your son. Whatever you give him or do not give him, if he is your son, he *is* your son, and always must be so. This is especially true of the children of God—they are not only called the children of God, but it is added, "*and we are.*" Indeed we are, and ever shall be, his sons. We are made really to be what we are said to be. We are *called* the children of God, and *we are* the children of God, and this cannot be undone.

It is *infinite* love that knows no end. It is the love of the Father—that glorious person of the blessed Trinity in whom the fountain of all grace is seen. It is the Father who in boundless love has called us to be his sons. Jesus says, "the Father himself loveth you" (John 16:27). It is not the death of Jesus that moved the heart of the Father to love us, as some fondly dream. The truth is that the Father's love is the reason why Jesus was given. How it unveils the heart of the Father when we see that he who gave his Son for us has also bestowed upon us this manner of love, that we should be called his sons! Let us adore and love the great Father of our spirits, whose love is the first cause of all our blessedness.

the Father hath bestowed upon us It is bestowed upon us men and women. We are poor creatures when we make the best of ourselves, and yet he calls us sons of God. "For unto which of the angels said he at any time, 'Thou art my Son?'" (Heb 1:5). This dignity is reserved for us, whom he has made a little lower than the angels. Think of what his Only-begotten Son is like—that glorious Son of God of whom he says, "Let all the angels of God worship him" (Heb 1:6). See how in splendor of beneficence he deigns to call us also his sons, and so to put us side by side with the Only-begotten—not on an equality as far as his Godhead is concerned, for that cannot be, but bestowing on us that same love with which he loves his Son. He loves us in Christ even as he loves Christ himself. See what sort of love it is, that *we* should be adopted and regenerated by the living God.

that we should be called the sons of God *Who calls us so?* That is the wonder. Men take upon themselves great names without any right to them. There are degrees among men that are degrees of shame because the persons who wear them were never justly entitled to them. It is one thing for us to call ourselves children of God, and another thing for the Father to bestow his love so that we are truly called the sons of God. From where comes this princely title of "children of God"? Who calls the saints the children of God?

The Father himself does so. He speaks to them as unto children. He deals with them as with sons. He is pleased in infinite love to bid them say, "Our Father," and he answers to them by calling them children and heirs. He acknowledges their sonship, and pities them as a father pities his children. He has called them sons, saying, "'And will be a Father unto you, and ye shall be my sons and daughters,' saith the Lord Almighty" (2 Cor 6:18). Oh, what a blessing it is to have God calling you his child; the great Almighty and Infinite One looking upon you with a Father's love, and saying, "You are my son"! He speaks the truth, and we may believe it, and be sure. He knows his own children, and gives the name of sons to none whom he will in the end disown. He calls us his children, *and we are*.

Who has called us the sons of God? *Jesus himself*, the firstborn among many brothers, has called us so. Did he not speak of "my Father and your Father" (John 20:17)? What did he mean when he was not ashamed to call us brothers (Heb 2:11)? Everywhere our dear Lord and Master speaks of us as belonging to the one family of which he is the Head. By sweetly taking us into union with himself Jesus practically calls us sons of God, *and we are*.

The Holy Spirit also dwells in all the heirs of heaven, and thereby calls them sons of God. He bears witness with our spirit that we are the sons of God, and it is he who is given to us to be "the Spirit of adoption, whereby we cry, Abba, Father" (Rom 8:15). That "Abba, Father," of ours is prompted by the Spirit of grace, who would never prompt a stranger and an alien to claim kinship with the Lord. The witness of the Holy

Spirit is the witness of truth. A filial spirit implanted by the Spirit of God cannot deceive us. Thus Father, Son, and Holy Ghost call us the children of God, *and we are.*

ILLUSTRATION

Ashamed to Call Him Father

I have heard of a fine gentleman in London, dressed in all his best, walking out in the park. He had a poor old father who lived in the country, and who came up dressed in his rustic clothes to see his son. As the son was not at home when the father reached the house, he went into the park to find him. Now the fine gentleman did not absolutely disown his father, but he went out of the park at a pretty sharp trot, for fear anybody should say, "Who is that country fellow you were talking with?" He did not like to acknowledge his father, because he was a laborer.

That is mean as the mud in the kennel, is it not? We could not thus wonder if the glorious Lord refused to own us. There is such a come-down from the loftiness of his holiness to the depth of our faultiness. But yet he has such love, such a manner of love, that he bestows upon us this honor that we should be openly called the sons of God.

---

and we are When the apostle had said, "We should be called children of God," he then adds that we are not only to be called so, but *we are* so. The glory of it is that we now have this thing. We have it in possession: "*and we are.*" This little interjected assertion brings most forcibly before my own mind the truth of our present sonship toward God.

Adoption gives us the name of God's children, the new birth gives us the nature of God's children, and so in both senses *we are*. Adoption is the legal act by which our Father receives us; regeneration is that spiritual deed by which we receive the nature of our Father. Every man that is really adopted into the family of God also really becomes a son of God by being begotten again unto a lively hope. I want to put it to you whether you can on this double ground join in these inspired words, and say, "*And we are.*"

Let us work out the question. Are we really the children of God? We must answer that question by another: Do we truly believe in the Lord Jesus Christ? I have already quoted the inspired declaration: "But as many as received him, to them gave he power to become the sons of God, even to them that believe on his name" (John 1:12). We *can* answer that question. Are we believing in the Lord Jesus Christ with all our heart? Is he our confidence? Do we trust in his blood and righteousness? If so, if we believe in him, he has given us the right and the power to become the sons of God.

ILLUSTRATION

Learning to Trust Like a Child

If I am a child of God, I learn to *trust* my Father. I do not know a more delightful act of childhood than trustfulness in a parent. And how often if we trust God we shall be rewarded! Yesterday, I received a note from one of the trustees of the orphanage to say that the running account was so low that, when the checks were paid on Friday morning, we should have overdrawn our banking account. I did not like that state of things, but I did not fret about it. I breathed a prayer to God that he would send money to put into the bank to keep the account right. Last night, at nearly ten o'clock, I opened a letter that had in it a check for £200. That amount put the account square for the time being. At the moment when I opened the letter and found the £200, I felt as if my hair stood on end, because of the conscious nearness of the Lord my God.

If I were to tell my own personal experience of the way in which God hears prayer, it would seem to you as if it could not be true; it would appear too romantic. But it is a blessed thing to take everything to God, little or big, and leave all with him!

---

2 **Beloved, now are we the sons of God** All the blessings of the new covenant are spoken of in the present tense, because with the exception of eternal glory in heaven, they are all to be enjoyed here. I know that I shall be one day, if I am a believer in Christ, more sanctified than I am today—if not in the sense of consecration, yet still in the sense of purification—but at the same time I know this for sure: that when I stand at God's right hand, amid the lamps of eternal brightness, and when these fingers move with vigor across the golden strings, and when this voice is filled with the immortal songs, I shall not be one bit more a child of God than I am now.

it doth not yet appear what we shall be This is not the place where the Christian is to be seen. This is the place of his veiling; heaven is the place of his manifestation. Some of the reasons why "it doth not yet appear what we shall be" may be as follows. First, *our Master was, to a great extent, concealed and hidden, and we must expect to be as he was*. Is it not written, in this very epistle, "as he is, so are we in this world" (1 John 4:17)? Jesus said to his followers when he was here on earth, "The disciple is not above his master, nor the servant above his Lord. It is enough for the disciple that he be as his master, and the servant as his lord" (Matt 10:24–25). See that man wearing a seamless coat, "woven from the top throughout" (John 19:23)—the carpenter's son, the heir of poverty, the companion of the humblest classes of mankind. Can you see in him God over all, blessed forever? If you can, you are not looking with the eyes of your flesh, I am sure.

I may also remark that *we are not yet fit to let it appear what we shall be*. You and I, if we are believers in the Lord Jesus Christ, are kings—not only sons of God, but kings who are to reign with him forever. Then why are we not treated like kings? In some earthly royal families it is thought best for the prince, the heir apparent to the throne, that he should be a soldier or a sailor and serve his country in that capacity so that, when he comes to the throne, he may understand how to wield his scepter for the good of all classes of his subjects. So it is with you, Christian. You are so childish at present. You have so recently begun to learn the nature of divine things; you are so uninstructed. You know only in part, and you know that part so badly that it would not be fitting that your greatness should be revealed to you at present. You must be held back for a while until you have been better trained in the Holy Spirit's school, and then it will appear what you shall be.

A third reason why it does not yet appear what we shall be is, I think, because *this is not the world in which the Christian is to appear in his glory*. If he did, his glory would be lost in this world. The multitudes climbed to the tops of the trees, or the roofs of the houses, from which they might see Caesar or Pompey returning with the spoils of war. The multitudes still clap their hands when a warrior has overcome his country's enemies and so become a great man. But the world cares little or nothing about self-denial, about Christian love, about consecration and devotion to Christ and his cause; yet these things are the glory of a Christian. That moral excellence, that spiritual worth which flashes from the eyes of the holy angels and of the saints in glory, is almost unappreciated here.

And, to close this subject, "What we will be has not yet been revealed" because *this is not the time for the display of the Christian's glory*. If I may use such an expression, time is not the time for the manifestation of a Christian's glory. Eternity is to be the period for the Christian's full development and for the sinless display of his God-given glory. Here, he must expect to be unknown; it is in the hereafter that he is to be discovered as a son of the great King. "To every thing there is a season, and a time to every purpose under the heaven" (Eccl 3:1). But this is not the time for the full manifestation of Christians.

ILLUSTRATION

Going Incognito in This World

When a king is journeying through a foreign country, he does not wear his crown or the rest of his regalia; he often travels incognito. Even when he reaches his own country, he does not put on his royal robes for fools to admire at every village fair. He is not a puppet king, strutting upon the stage to show himself to the common people; he reserves his grandeur for great public occasions and grand court ceremonies.

In this poor sinful world, you Christians would be out of place if you could be what you shall yet be. You also must go incognito through this world to a large extent. But by and by, you shall take off the travel-worn garments that you have worn during your earthly pilgrimage, and put on your beautiful array, and be manifested to the whole universe as a son or a daughter of "the King eternal, immortal, invisible" (1 Tim 1:17).

We know that, when he shall appear It is quite certain that Christ will appear. John does not stop to prove it. He speaks of it as though it were perfectly understood that Christ would again appear, and he mentions what is to be the nature of that appearing.

Christ will appear in person. This is what the two angels declared to the disciples after his ascension: "This same Jesus, which is taken up from you into heaven, shall so come in like manner as ye have seen him go into heaven" (Acts 1:11); that is, he will come back from heaven as the incarnate God.

When he comes, *he will appear full of happiness*. There will be no more sorrow to wrinkle his brow, no more furrows to be plowed on his back, no fresh wounds to be made in his hands or his feet, no more offering of a sacrifice for sin. He will come to rejoice with his people forever.

Further, when he comes, *he will appear in his glory*—not as the man of Nazareth, to be despised and spat upon, but as the "mighty God, The everlasting Father, The Prince of Peace" (Isa 9:6). If you are tempted to ask, "When will he come?" I give you his own assurance: "Surely I come quickly" (Rev 22:20). So go your way and pray, as John did, "Amen. Even so, come, Lord Jesus" (Rev 22:20), yet do not forget Paul's inspired sentences, "But of the times and the seasons, brethren, ye have no need that I write unto you. For yourselves know perfectly that the day of the Lord so cometh as a thief in the night. For when they shall say, Peace and safety; then sudden destruction cometh upon them, as travail upon a woman with child; and they shall not escape" (1 Thess 5:1–3). Christ is coming, literally coming—not figuratively, and by his Spirit, but literally, actually, really.

we shall be like him We are to be like Christ, first, *as to our body*. Here, we are like the first Adam: of the earth, earthy. But we shall, one day, have a body like that of the second Adam, a heavenly body. Like the first Adam, we are mortal now; like the second Adam, we shall be immortal by-and-by. Christ's body is not now subject to any pains, or to any decay or disease; neither shall our body be. It is quite true that "flesh and blood cannot inherit the kingdom of God " (1 Cor 15:50); yet it will be this very body of ours that will inherit the kingdom of God. Only that which is corruptible in it, that which is mere flesh and blood, will then have been removed.

But, far more important than that, *we shall also be like Christ in soul*. Have the eyes of your spiritual understanding or sanctified imagination ever looked upon Christ's spotless, perfectly developed soul—that equably adjusted spirit in which no one power or passion was too prominent or predominant, but in which his whole being was beautifully molded and rounded according to the perfect pattern of moral excellence and beauty? You are to be just like that—not quick in temper, as perhaps you now are, but meek and lowly as he was; not haughty and prone to pride, but humble and gentle as he was;

not selfish and self-seeking, but as disinterested and as tender to others as he was; in fact, perfection's own self.

ILLUSTRATION

This Life Is Our Winter

At present, it is with us as it is with the world during the winter. If you had not seen the miracle wrought again and again, you would not guess, when you look upon those black beds in the garden, or when you walk over that snowy and frosty covering, crisp and hard beneath your feet, that the earth will yet be sown with all the colors of the rainbow, and that it will be gemmed with flowers of unspeakable beauty. No, the winter is not the time when the beauty of the earth is to be best seen.

Christian, you also must pass through your winter season. I might almost say that gray hairs come on your head, like the snowdrops appear upon the earth, as the harbingers of spring and of summer. Your soul shall yet blossom "with joy unspeakable and full of glory" (1 Pet 1:8), and all the graces and excellences of the Christian shall be revealed in you. It is winter with you now, but the summer comes.

I ought to add that *we shall be like Christ,* not only in body and in soul, but *also in condition.* We shall be with him where he is, and we shall be as happy as he is, as far as our capacity for happiness goes. We shall be crowned even as he is crowned, and we shall sit upon thrones even as he sits upon his Father's throne. He shall lead us to living fountains of water, and be our constant Companion, never going away from us again. He shall call us his brothers, and we shall share in his honor and glory. The joy of which we shall partake shall be his joy, and it will be in us that our joy may be full.

for we shall see him Our eyes shall see *him* and not another. We shall be sure it is him, for when we enter heaven we shall know him by his *manhood and Godhead*. We shall find him a man, even as much as he was on earth. We shall find him man and God too, and we shall be quite sure there never was another Man-God; we never read or dreamed of another. Don't suppose that when you get to heaven you will have to ask, "Where is the man Christ Jesus?" You will see him straight before you on his throne.

Take this thought with you: "we will see *him*," despite all the changes in his position. It will be the same person. We shall see the same hands that were pierced, the same feet that were weary, the same lips that preached, the same eyes that wept, the same heart that heaved with agony. He will be positively the same, except as to his condition. "We will see *him*."

How is it that we shall be like him because of seeing him? Partly, *by reflection*. When a man looks into a bright mirror, it makes him bright also, for it throws its own light upon his face. In a much more wonderful fashion, when we look at Christ, who is all brightness, he throws some of his brightness upon us. When Moses went up to the mountain to commune with God, his face shone because he had received a reflection of God's glory upon his face.

Further, we get to be like Christ by seeing him *in type and symbol*, as through a glass darkly. The Lord's supper is one of the glasses; believers' baptism is another; the preaching of the Word is another; the Bible itself is another of these glasses. It is only a partial reflection of Christ that we get from all these glasses, yet, as we look at it, as Paul writes to the Corinthians, "But we all, with open face, beholding as in a glass the glory of the Lord, are changed into the same image from glory to glory, even as by the Spirit of the Lord" (2 Cor 3:18).

ILLUSTRATION

Singing Like a Bird in a Cage

In some of the houses not far from here, I noticed some linnets in cages, in which there were tufts of grass or small branches of trees as perches for the poor prisoners; yet they were singing away right merrily. I suppose that grass and those fragments of trees were meant to remind them, in this great, dirty, smoky Babylon, that there are green fields and wide forests somewhere. I thought, as I looked upon them, "You poor birds are very like what I myself am! My Master has put me in a little cage, and bidden me wait here for a while, and he has given me my little tuft of grass as an earnest of my inheritance. He graciously sends me a few comforts on the way. But that poor little tuft of grass, what is it in comparison with the fields and the hedges that are the proper home of the singing birds that have their liberty?"

Christian, you do not know what it will be for you to have your cage door opened, that you may fly away to that blessed land where the true birds of Paradise forever warble, from their joyful throats, the loudest praises to the great King who has set them free forever.

---

as he is Our minds often revert to Christ as he was, and we have desired to see him as such. How often have we wished to see the babe that slept in Bethlehem! How earnestly have we desired to see the man who talked with the woman at the well! How frequently too have our thoughts retired to Gethsemane, and we have wished our eyes were strong enough to pierce through the years that part us from that wondrous spectacle, that we might see him as he was! We will never see him this way. We cannot, must not, see him as he was. Nor do we wish to, for we have a larger promise: "We shall see him as he *is*." Look at that a few moments by way of contrast, and then I am sure you will prefer to see Christ as he *is*, rather than behold him as he was.

Consider, first of all, that we shall not see him *abased in his incarnation*, but *exalted in his glory*. We shall see the head, but not with its thorny crown. We shall see the hand, and the nail prints too, but not the nail. It has been drawn out once and forever. We shall see his side, and its pierced wound too, but the blood shall not issue from it. We shall see him not with a peasant's garb around him, but with the empire of the universe upon his shoulders. We shall see him, not with a reed in his hand, but grasping a golden scepter. We shall see him, not as mocked and spat upon and insulted, not bone of our bone in all our agonies, afflictions, and distresses, but we shall see him exalted. He is no longer Christ the man of sorrows, acquainted with grief, but Christ the Man-God, radiant with splendor, effulgent with light, clothed with rainbows, girded with clouds, wrapped in lightning, crowned with stars, the sun beneath his feet.

Again, we shall not see the Christ *wrestling with pain*, but Christ *as a conqueror*. We shall never see him tread the wine-press alone, but we shall see him when we shall cry, "Who is this, that cometh from Edom, with dyed garments from Bozrah? This that is glorious in his apparel, travelling in the greatness of his strength?" (Isa 63:1). We shall never see him as when he stood foot-to-foot with his enemy, but we shall see him when his enemy is beneath his feet. We shall never see him as the bloody sweat streams from his whole body, but we shall see him as he has put all things under him, and has conquered hell itself. We shall never see him as the wrestler, but we shall see him grasp the prize.

ILLUSTRATION

Recognizing Jesus by His Wounds

We have heard of some who on the battlefield have been seeking for the dead; they have turned their faces up and looked at them, but did not know them. But the tender wife has come, and there was some deep wound, some saber cut that her husband had received upon his breast, and she said, "It is he; I know him by that wound."

So in heaven we shall in a moment detect our Savior by his wounds.

---

3 **And every man that hath this hope in him** *The Christian has a hope peculiar to himself.* As for its object, it is the hope of being like Jesus Christ. "We shall be like him; for we shall see him as he is" (1 John 3:2). Now, some would not put it in that shape. They would say that their hope, as Christians, is to pass within the pearly gates, to tread the golden streets, to listen to the harpers harping with their harps, and, standing on the sea of glass, to be forever free from sorrow, toil, and pain. But those are only the lower joys of heaven, except so far as they indicate spiritual bliss. The real truth—the truth that is contained in these metaphors and figures and underlies them all—is that the heaven a true Christian seeks after is a spiritual one. It is the heaven of being like his Lord. I take it that, while it will consist in our sharing in the Redeemer's power, the Redeemer's joy, and the Redeemer's honor, yet, from the connection of the text, it lies mainly in our being spiritually and morally like him—being purified, even as he is pure.

All true hope is hope in Christ. If your hope lies in yourself, it is a delusion. If your hope rests on any earthly priest, and not on this one great Apostle and High Priest of our profession, your hope is a lie. If your hope stands with one foot on the work of Christ and the other foot on your own resolutions or merits, your hope will fail you. "Hope in him" is the only hope that can be acceptable to God, the only hope that will bear the stress of your weight, the only hope that will stand the test of your dying hour and of the day of judgment. Our hope, then, of being like Christ is a hope in Christ. We are trusting him; we are depending on him. If he does not make us like himself, our hope is gone. If we are ever to get to heaven, it will be through him, and through him alone. Our hope is in him from top to bottom; he is our Alpha and our Omega, the beginning and the end. There our hope begins, and there our hope ends. This, then, is the believer's hope: a hope to be made like Christ, a hope based on Christ.

purifieth himself, even as he is pure Hope does not puff him up; it purifies him. I know there are some who will say, "Well, if I had a hope, a sure hope, a full assurance and confident expectation that I should go to heaven, I think I should feel myself to be someone very great." Yes, very likely *you* would; but then you do not possess such a hope, and God does not intend to give it to you while you are in your present condition. But when the Lord makes a man his child, then he takes away the evil heart out of his flesh. When he shows a man his great love to him, he humbles him, he lays him low, and so the expectation of heaven and of absolute perfection never exalts a man. If any man can say, "I am secure of heaven, and I am proud of it," he may take my word for it that he is secure of hell! If your religion puffs you up, puff your religion away, for it is not worth a puff. He who grows great in self-esteem through the love of God does not know the love of God in truth, for the love of God is like the fish that the Lord put into Peter's boat: the more full the boat became, the more quickly it began to sink.

Now, let me notice that *the believer is here said to purify himself*. If we are very orthodox, we can afford to use language that does not look so, but people who are heterodox usually have to be extremely guarded in their expressions. Now we do not believe that any man actually purifies himself, yet the text says that "everyone who has this hope in him purifies himself." We believe that the Holy Ghost purifies sinners by applying to them the precious blood of Jesus. We look to God for all purity, believing that he is the Creator of it. Still, the text says that "everyone who has this hope in him purifies himself"; that is to say, God the Holy Spirit so works in every man who has a true hope that he labors to become purified, and uses all possible means to overcome sin, and to walk in righteousness.

4 **sin is the transgression of the law** I know that there are some people who understand by the word "sin" some offense against their fellow men, or the outward neglect of religion. They regard sin as if it were the same thing as crime—an offense against the prosperity of the nation or the welfare of their fellow men. I am inclined to think that even some of my brothers in Christ do not really understand what sin is when they say that they live without it. I suppose they mean by sin

something very different from what the Scripture means by that word; otherwise they would hardly talk as they do.

Sin is any lack of conformity to the perfect mind of God. According to our text, "sin is lawlessness," and every transgression of the law is sin. Therefore, we say that, first, *every sin breaks God's law*. It does not matter what sin is committed; it breaks the law at one point. There are ten great commandments of God. It may be that you think you have never broken numbers 1, 2, 3, 4, 5, or 6, but if you have broken numbers 7, 8, 9, or 10, you have snapped the chain apart as really as if you had broken all its links. If the chain is broken, it matters little to miners in a pit at what particular link it came apart. Any offense against the law of God breaks the whole law and spoils any hope of the sinner being saved by keeping it.

Then take the other side of this truth. *Every breach of the law is a sin*. If you do not do what God commands you—fully, heartily, always, without fail—you have sinned. And if you do at any moment that which God commands you not to do, you have sinned against him. Let it never be forgotten that what I am now saying about actions also applies to words; our Lord told his disciples that for every idle word anyone utters he must give an account on the day of judgment. Remember, too, that this rule applies to thoughts and imaginations and desires, and to those secret motives that hide away within the soul and never actually come into deeds. God shall bring these hidden things to judgment. Every thought, word, or deed that is not in perfect conformity with the law and will of God is a sin. Who among us can stand before the Lord in his own righteousness if this is true?

Let me further say that *sin is mainly sin because it is a transgression of the law*. Many people will say, "I did no harm to anyone." That is not the point. If you break the law of God, you sin. We must never judge sin merely by its consequences, or we may make great mistakes. Some sins men can see at once are sins because they bring disease of body on the one who commits them, or they leave him in rags, or cover him with shame. Then men say, "This course of conduct is wrong, for see what comes of it." But that is a very imperfect way of looking at the matter. The wrong of a thing consists in this: that it is a breach of God's law.

ILLUSTRATION

Do Not Judge Sin by Its Consequences

A switchman on the railway does not turn the switch the right way, and one train crashes into another, and a hundred lives are lost. He may say to himself, "What a crime I committed by my carelessness," and everybody denounces him for it. But suppose he forgot to turn the switch, and by a sort of miracle the two trains escaped collision. If by some extraordinary coincidence the two mighty masses of matter rushing onward were stopped in their progress, and no hurt came of it, the switchman would be just as guilty in that case as in the other.

It is not the amount of damage that results from it that makes the sin; it is the thing itself. If you are doing wrong, even though you should feed a nation by your wrongdoing, I say that you would still be committing sin. If you get rich by an unholy trick, it is nonetheless trickery and deception, and there is a curse on your wealth.

---

5 **he was manifested to take away our sins** This is the source of the Christian's hope, *God's appearance in human form*. If it is so that the great God himself deigned to come to earth, and to take the form of a man—if it is so that the ever-blessed Second Person of the Divine Trinity was actually born of the Virgin, that he might become man like us—if it is so that he came here to fight evil, and that he has put his foot down against the advance of the enemy, then I have hope for mankind; I have hope for myself; I have hope that sin may be overcome. As we know

and are sure that God has come down among us, and has taken on himself our nature, since this is the very fundamental truth of our holy faith, therefore we see how sin can be put away.

Next, our hope lies in *Christ's death*. We have already sinned, and by reason of our sin we have incurred the righteous anger of God and his just displeasure. God must punish sin. If a man stands in the track of an avalanche, he must be buried beneath it. If a man stands in the way of the laws of God, those laws must crush him. There was just one way of deliverance from the guilt of sin, and that was for God himself, in human form, to take the consequences of human sin on himself.

But then, we need *Christ's life in us by the gift of the Spirit*. Even if sin is pardoned, that is not enough for us. We need to have sin put away from us, from the heart of us, and from the life of us. I think that if we could be forgiven and yet not wholly sanctified, we could never be happy while sin was still creeping and crawling over us. Our Lord Jesus Christ was manifested in order that, after his death, when he had ascended to heaven, the Holy Spirit might descend and come and dwell in us to conquer every evil passion and to work in us all manner of holy desires, and so abide in us as to speak out of our mouths, to act through our lives, and to make us to live after God's manner of living, and not according to the way of the flesh, as we once did.

and in him is no sin I am unable fully to tell about my perfect Master, Christ Jesus my Lord. But I may say this: his enemies have looked at him from every side, and they have never been able to find a joint in his harness through which to shoot their poisoned darts. Men who have flung aside the great truth of the inspiration of the Scriptures, and have been prepared even to make light of heaven and hell, have nevertheless gazed with astonishment on the character of the Lord Jesus Christ. It is unrivaled among the sons of men; it is absolutely perfect. As one snow-white peak rises above its brother Alps, so does the life of Christ rise above that of all philanthropists, and all teachers, and the loftiest purity that is merely of earth. There is none like him. There is no defect in Christ, and there is no excess.

6 **Whosoever abideth in him sinneth not** Insofar as Christ comes into contact with us, and we yield ourselves to him, we are affected by his divine purity so that we become pure even as he is pure. They say sometimes of a Christian man who does something that is not right, "He did so-and-so; *that* is your religion!" No, it is not. That is the point where, as yet, his religion has not thoroughly saturated him. That is his defect and failing.

Whosoever sinneth hath not seen him, neither known him That is to say, if sin is the habitual course of our life, we do not truly know the Lord. He who walks with God tries with all his might to be free from sin, and he is sanctified by abiding in Christ.

7 **Little children, let no man deceive you** Children are very credulous. They will believe any idle tale if it is told them by a clever and attractive person. Little children, believe your Savior, but do not be ready to believe anybody else. Believe God's Word, and stand fast to that. But if sinners entice you, do not consent to them, and if antichrist would teach you false doctrine, close your ear to it. Be like the sheep of whom Jesus said, "And a stranger will they not follow, but will flee from him: for they know not the voice of strangers" (John 10:5).

he that doeth righteousness is righteous You must judge a tree by its fruit. If it brings forth good fruit, it is a good tree; if it brings forth evil fruit, it is an evil tree. Do not be deceived about that matter, for there have been some who have dreamed of being righteous and of being the children of God, yet they have lived in sin as others do. They have been self-deceived; it has been a mere dream on which they have relied. Practical godliness is absolutely needful to a true Christian character, and a man is not righteous unless he does that which is righteous.

8 **For this purpose the Son of God was manifested, that he might destroy** Note that word "*destroy*"—not limit, nor alleviate, nor neutralize, but destroy. The work of the devil was so clever, the foundations of it were so deeply laid, and the whole thing had such a semblance of omnipotence about it, and

was, indeed, in itself so strong, that no champion was found in heaven or on earth that could hope to destroy it. Uprising from his divine retreat in the silences of eternity, the Son of God appeared in human form and thereby scattered and utterly destroyed the works of darkness.

Let us see how this was done. First, Christ's manifestation, even *in his incarnation*, was a fatal blow to the works of Satan. Did God come down to men? Was he incarnate in the infant form that slept in Bethlehem's manger? Then the Almighty has not given up our nature to be the prey of sin.

Next, look to *the life of Christ on earth*, and see how he destroyed there the works of the devil. Evil spirits had taken possession of human forms. Legions of devils were established in men, but the Lord Jesus Christ had only to speak the word, and away they fled, glad to leap into swine and rush into the sea to escape from his presence. All our Lord's preaching, all his teaching, all his labor here below was in order to pull away the cornerstone from the great house of darkness that Satan had built up.

But it was in *his death* that Jesus chiefly overthrew Satan and destroyed his works. Satan built on this—that man had become offensive to God and God must punish him. That punishment was his hope for the continuance of alienation. Behold, the august Son of God takes the offender's place! Marvel of marvels, the Judge stands where the criminal should have stood and is "numbered with the transgressors" (Isa 53:12)! Behold, the wrath of God falls upon his Well-beloved, and Jesus suffers, that he may reconcile man to his God, and heal the breach that sin had caused. The deed was done. Man is no more offensive to heaven, for one glorious man's boundless merit has put away the demerit of the race.

Our Lord's *rising again*, his ascension into glory, his sitting at the right hand of the Father, his coming again in the latter days—all these are parts of the manifestation of the Son of God by which the works of the devil shall be destroyed. So also is *the preaching of the gospel*. If we want to destroy the works of the devil our best method is to manifest the

Son of God more and more; only let it be never forgotten that Jesus destroys the works of darkness *by his Spirit*. It is the Spirit of God who puts divine energy into the sacred Word. When the Spirit manifests Christ in a man then the works of darkness are destroyed in that man. When Christ is manifested in a nation then the works of Satan begin to fall in that nation. In proportion as the Holy Ghost shall more and more reveal Christ to hearts and consciences, bringing them into obedience to the faith, in that degree shall the works of Satan be destroyed.

Lastly, our blessed Lord is manifested in his eternal power and kingdom as *enthroned*, in order to destroy the works of the devil; for "the government shall be upon his shoulder: and his name shall be called Wonderful, Counseller, The mighty God, the everlasting Father" (Isa 9:6). He is such a Father, and the age is made to feel his forming hand. Kings, presidents, parliaments, poets, leaders, and such like—these are visible powers, but there is over them all an invisible power.

the works of the devil This very strong expression is descriptive of *sin,* for the preceding sentence so interprets it. This name for sin is first of all *a word of detestation*. Sin is so abominable in the sight of God and of good men that its various forms are said to be "the works of the devil." Men do not like the idea of having any connection with the devil, and yet they have a most intimate connection with him until they are made new by the Spirit of God.

Next, it is *a word of distinction:* it distinguishes the course of the ungodly man from the life of the man who believes in the Lord Jesus. For the one who is of God does the works of God—his life is the work of God. It is a life that has much that is Godlike about it, and he is upheld by the power of God, the ever-blessed Spirit. But the ungodly man's life is very different—he lives for himself, he seeks his own pleasure, he hates all that oppose him, he is up in arms against the Lord, and his truth, and all that is pure and good. His spirit is not the spirit of God, but of the evil one. There is a radical distinction between the gracious and the graceless, and this comes out in their works: the one works the works of God and the other the works of the devil.

The language before us is, next, *a word of descent*. Sin is "of the devil." It came from him; he is its parent and patron. Sin is not of the devil such that we can lay the blame of our sins on him, for that is our own. You must not blame the tempter for tempting you to do that which without your will he could not make you do. He may tempt you, but that would be no sin of yours if your will did not yield to it. The responsibility lies with your will. The devil has plenty of sin of his own to answer for, and yet he is often made a packhorse to carry loads of evil that are not his.

Next, we have here *a word of description*. The work of sin is the work of the devil because it is such work as he delights in. What are the works of the devil? They are such actions as are like himself and exhibit his nature and spirit. Open your eyes and you will surely see "the works of the devil"; they are everywhere in this poor world. The earth is defiled with his horrible productions. How delightful it is to take a survey of the works of God! The wise man says that the works of the Lord "are great, sought out of all them that have pleasure therein" (Ps 111:2).

ILLUSTRATION

Contemplating the Works of God

I heard of a good man who went down the Rhine, but took care to read a book all the way for fear he should have his mind taken off heavenly topics by the beauties of nature. I confess I do not understand such a spirit—I do not want to. If I go into an artist's house I do that artist a displeasure if I take no notice of his works under the pretext that I am quite absorbed in him.

Why not enjoy the objects in which our heavenly Father has set forth his wisdom and power? There is nothing in any of the works of God to defile, debase, or carnalize the soul. Delight yourself in all your heavenly Father's handiwork, and make it a ladder by which you climb to him.

---

9 **Whosoever is born of God doth not commit sin** That is to say, this is not the course, and habit, and tenor of his life. There is sin in much that he does, but he hates it, loathes it, and flees from it.

he cannot sin, because he is born of God The new nature that God puts in us never sins. It cannot sin, because it has been fathered by God. "What?" you say. "Does a Christian never sin?" Not with the new nature. The new nature never sins; the old nature sins. It is the darkness that is dark. The light is not darkness; the light is always light. It is not possible that the Christ who dwells in us could sin. What sin there is in the believer comes from the remnants of corruption. The Spirit that is implanted can never sin, can never have communion with sin, any more than light can have communion with darkness.

10 **the children of God ... and the children of the devil** John makes a sharp and clear division of mankind into two classes. He does not give even the slightest hint that there is, or ever was, or ever can be a third class. He describes men as being the children of God or the children of the devil, and tells us how the two classes are manifested. Now, this distinction would not have been drawn by John so sharply if it had not existed. He was a man of most loving heart and gentle spirit, and if he could somewhere or other have found a space for neutrals, or people who come midway between saints and sinners, I am sure he would have done it. No one could suspect John of lack of charity, and therefore since *he* was convinced that no middle position was possible, we may be quite clear on that point and at once dismiss every theory that is meant to flatter the undecided. To this day, the world is still divided into children

of God and children of the evil one. This distinction should never be forgotten, yet thousands of sermons are preached in which it is quite ignored, and congregations are commonly addressed as if they were all the people of God.

he that loveth not his brother An unlovely spirit is also self-condemnatory as being an unholy spirit; in fact, lack of love is lack of righteousness. There are some who profess to be so righteous that they condemn everybody else, and they have no compassion for those who are suffering as a result of their fault. But it is one thing to hate sin, and it is another thing to hate the sinner! Let your indignation burn against everything that is evil, but toward him who has done the wrong have ever the gentle thought of pity, and pray for him that he may leave his sin and turn unto his gracious God. It may be difficult to reach this point, but there should always be just that happy mixture in the mind and heart of the child of God—love to the sinner and hatred of his sin.

APPLICATION

How to Purify Yourself

How does the one who has hope in Christ purify himself? *He does it, first, by noting the example of Christ.* The hoping man reads Christ's life, and he says, "Here is my model, but I am far short of it; God, give me all that there was in Christ! Take off from my character all the excrescences, for they must be excrescences if they were not in Christ." Familiarizing himself with the life of his Savior, and getting to commune with Christ, he is thus helped to see what sin is, and where sin is, and to hate it.

Then *he asks God to give him a tender conscience.* It is a blessed thing to have a conscience that will shiver when the very ghost of a sin goes by—a conscience that is not like our great steamships that do not yield to every wave but, like a cork on the water that goes up and down with every ripple, sensitive in a moment to the very approach of sin. May God the Holy Spirit make us so! The Christian endeavors to have this sensitiveness, for he knows that, if he does not have it, he will never be purified from his sin.

He tries always to keep an eye to God, and not to men. That is a great point in purity of life. You will never be a holy man until you do not care a fig what anybody says except your God, for a thing that is right is right anywhere. If it is right before the Lord, it is right although all the world should hiss it down. If only we had more moral courage, for moral courage is essential to true holiness!

And then *he notes the lives of others, and makes them his beacons.* If you were sailing down the Thames and saw a boat ahead of you that had run upon a shoal, there would be no need for you to go there to find out where the true channel was. You would let other shipwrecks be your beacons. So the Christian, when he observes a fault in another, does not stand and say, "See how faulty that man is!" but he says, "Let me shun that fault." And when he sees the virtue of another, if his heart is right, he does not begin to pick holes in it, and say, "He is not as good as he looks," but he says, "Lord, there is a sweet flower in that man's garden. Give me some of the seed of it; let it grow in my soul." So other men become both his beacon and his example.

A wise Christian tries to purify himself by *hearing a heart-searching ministry.* If the ministry never cuts you, it is no use to you. If it does not make you feel ashamed of yourself—and sometimes half-angry with the preacher—it is not good for much. If it is all smoothing you the way the feathers go, and making you feel happy and comfortable, be afraid of it. But if, on the contrary, it seems to open up old wounds, and make the sores fester and the soul bleed before the living God, then you may hope it is a ministry that God is using for your lasting good.

I might continue thus to show you the way by which the Christian, who has a good hope, endeavors to purify himself, but I must just notice that *he sets before himself Christ as his standard.* He purifies himself, even as Christ is pure. We shall make a mistake if we make anyone our model save the Lord Jesus Christ. No man is fit to be a model for all men except the Savior who redeemed men.

The Death of Sin in the Christian's Life

It is the resolve, the intent, the prayer, the hope, the assurance, of every believer, that, *one day, he shall be perfectly in Christ, and then he will be perfect as Christ.* There is not a sin within us except must die.

There is not to be any wrong thought, or wrong desire, or wrong action spared; we must put all to death if we would become as perfect and pure as Christ is. I confess that it is impossible to us, but it is not impossible to him who undertakes it for us. He was manifested to take away our sins. Since the manifestation included the incarnation, and the bloody sweat, and the death upon the cross, what is there that it cannot accomplish? Believe that every sin in you will yet be slain, and that you shall stand before God, "not having spot, or wrinkle, or any such thing" (Eph 5:27).

Believing this, let us struggle and fight to attain it, and let us never rest satisfied until we get it. "Then," says one, "we shall never rest satisfied this side of heaven." Of course you will not. As long as you are here, you will have to fight. As long as you are here, you will have to strive and struggle. If already you have gained the victory to a large degree, go on, and get more and more of it. There are some overt sins that you can get rid of, and ought to get rid of; but there is a long, long way between a soul that has just begun to perceive the guilt of sin, and to break off outward evil habits and vices, and that same soul being absolutely perfect like God himself. There is so great a distance that you must have God to carry you across it, or you will never traverse it. You must cast yourself as a sinner at the feet of Jesus, or you may never hope for it. Let all of us begin at the cross; let us begin by believing in the Lord Jesus Christ, and then he will purify us even as he is pure; and, at last, when he shall appear, we shall be like him, for we shall see him as he is.

The Works of the Devil to Be Destroyed

Has the Son of God been manifested to you to destroy the works of the devil in you? At first there was in your heart an *enmity to God;* for "the carnal mind is enmity against God" (Rom 8:7). Is that enmity destroyed? Has the love of God in Christ Jesus appeared to you in such a way that you can truly say you no longer hate God, but love him? Though you do not love him as you wish to do, yet your heart is toward him and you desire to be like him, and to be with him forever. This is a good beginning; the Son of God has destroyed your enmity. You have seen the love of God in Christ, and your rebellion against God has ceased.

The next work of the devil that usually appears in the human mind is *self-righteous pride*. The man says, "I am no enemy to God; I am righteous. If I am not perfect, still I am tolerably good." This is our natural boasting, but the Son of God destroys it. Has the Son of God destroyed all your self-righteousness? It is a precious lot of rags, but we so constantly practice the art of patching and mending that we dream that we are clothed in royal apparel. Have all those rags gone from you? Has a strong wind blown them away? Have you seen your own natural nakedness? If I were to talk about my own righteousness, I would be a fool and a liar in one. I have no righteousness of my own; I dare not dream of such a thing. Is that your case? Then the Lord Jesus Christ has been manifested to destroy in you the works of the devil.

When the Lord has destroyed self-righteousness in us, the devil generally sets forth another form of his power, and that is *despair*. He says, "You see what a sinner you are—God will never be reconciled to you! There is no forgiveness for you!" But if the Lord Jesus Christ has been manifested to you, despair has gone, that work of the devil has been all destroyed, and now you have a humble hope in God, and a joy in his mercy. Though you speak sometimes with bated breath, yet your doubt is about yourself, not about your Lord. You know whom you have believed, and you know that he is a God who passes by transgression, iniquity, and sin.

Jesus has not come that he may lock up our sins, and keep them quiet, hidden away in a dark corner; he has come to *destroy* them. The day shall come when every child of God shall be transformed and transfigured into the likeness of Christ, and shall be without fault before the throne of God. Meanwhile, let us seek after sanctification. Let us labor after holiness, and let us abound in it to the glory of God. Despite our failures and mistakes let us pursue holiness! Taking it by the heel; let us keep close to it. So may the Lord enable us for Jesus's sake.

1 JOHN 3:11–18

11 For this is the message that ye heard from the beginning, that we should love one another. 12 Not as Cain, *who* was of that wicked one, and slew his brother. And wherefore slew he him? Because his own works were evil, and his brother's righteous. 13 Marvel not, my brethren, if the world hate you. 14 We know that we have passed from death unto life, because we love the brethren. He that loveth not *his* brother abideth in death. 15 Whosoever hateth his brother is a murderer: and ye know that no murderer hath eternal life abiding in him. 16 Hereby perceive we the love *of God*, because he laid down his life for us: and we ought to lay down *our* lives for the brethren. 17 But whoso hath this world's good, and seeth his brother have need, and shutteth up his bowels of compassion from him, how dwelleth the love of God in him? 18 My little children, let us not love in word, neither in tongue; but in deed and in truth.

EXPOSITION

11 **we should love one another** Love is the essential mark of the true child of God. "God is love"; therefore, he who is born of God must love. Hatred, envy, malice, lack of charity—these are not the things to be found in the children of God. If they are found in you, you are not one of his children.

12 **Not as Cain, who was of the wicked one** Some people try to deceive us with the notion that all men are the children of God. But John, writing under the inspiration of the Holy Spirit, shows how false that idea is. Holiness and love distinguish the children of God from the children of the devil.

and slew his brother There is no hate like that: the hate of a bad man toward a good one, not for doing him any wrong, but simply for rebuking him by the silent eloquence of his holy life. Men who love sin cannot endure the sight of virtue. If they cannot kill the good man, they will try to kill his reputation. They sneer, and say, "He is as bad as others, no doubt, if you could only find him out!" That is exactly the spirit of Cain.

Because his own works were evil, and his brother's righteous That was the real evil at the bottom of his great crime. It was the wickedness of Cain's character that made him hate the good that was in Abel. Therefore, after a while, he slew his brother. When you see a man filled with hate and envy and malice, it is because his own life is not holy. There is no exception to this rule: true holiness and love always go together. Where love is absent, holiness must be absent too.

13 **Marvel not, my brethren, if the world hate you** This hatred is too old for you to wonder at it. If it began with the first man who was born into the world, even with Cain, do not marvel if it should spend some of its fury on you. It is the very nature and spirit of the world to hate those who are not of the world.

14 **We know** I have heard it said, by those who would be thought philosophers, that in religion we must believe, but cannot know. I am not very clear about the distinction they draw between knowledge and faith, nor do I care to inquire, because I assert that, in matters relating to religion, we *know*. In the things of God, we both believe and know. If you will read this epistle through and draw a line under the word "know" wherever it occurs, you will be astonished to see how continually John asserts about the great verities of our faith, "We know, we know, we know, we know." He does not admit that any one of these things is a subject of conjecture, but he asserts it to be a matter of positive knowledge.

These philosophical gentlemen call themselves agnostics. That is a word derived from the Greek, and has the same meaning as the word "ignoramus," which comes from the Latin, and is the English equivalent for a "know-nothing." If they like to be called ignoramuses, I have not the slightest objection to their keeping the title, but they should never presume to argue with Christian men. They put themselves out of court directly, for we say, "*We know*." They cannot deny anything we choose to affirm after that, because they confess that they do not know. If we do know, and they cannot allege against us that we are deceivers—if, in any court of law, they will admit that our testimony would be taken quite as quickly as theirs, and that our general repute is that we are as upright and as honest as they are—then they ought, in modesty, never to contradict us in anything but to believe what we declare to be true. Since they do not know anything themselves, let them be guided by those who do know.

At any rate, whether they choose to agree with us or not, we shall always affirm that we do know what we do know. There are some things about God, and about the future, and about prayer, and about the work of the Spirit of God in our own souls, that we do not fancy, or imagine, or even make to be merely matters of faith. We know them; we are sure of them, for we have felt them, tasted them, handled them, and we know them as surely as we know the fact of our own existence.

that we have passed from death unto life From this text, first, we know that once we were dead in trespasses and sins. We could not have passed from death if we were not in death; neither would there have been a change in bringing us into life if we were in life before. Herein, I believe, lies the doctrine of the natural ruin of man—his original sin, the depravity of his heart. Let us look back with shame on our original. Let us remember the hole of the pit from which we were dug out, and then stand fast in this one certainty: we know that we were dead.

Secondly, we know that we have undergone a very singular change. That passage, "from death to life," is the reverse of the natural one. There has been such a change in us as is altogether supernatural, such a change as never would have occurred if we had been left to ourselves. One of the surest proofs to any man of the existence of a God consists in his dealings with that man in turning him from darkness to light, and from the power of sin and Satan to God. All the arguments that ever were written by Joseph Butler, or William Paley, or any of the defenders of religion, will never convince a man like coming into personal dealings with God. And when those dealings assume this form—that we have passed from death to life—they become indisputable proofs of the Godhead and of the power of the gospel of Jesus Christ.

Thirdly, we know that we live. *We have entered into a new state of being*. We have made the acquaintance of a great many things that we did not know anything of before. We have not merely to talk about God now, but to know him; not simply to speak about Christ, but to live on him; not now to dream or read about the Spirit of God, but to feel him working in us. We have come now to know the blood of Jesus as applied to our souls to make us clean. The promises are now our riches, and prayer is a reality to us. We never need anybody to tell us that there is a power in prayer; we have tokens from day to day that the Lord hears our petitions. We are living in a new world altogether; we know we are. These things were unknown and unperceived by us once, but they are perceived by us now.

ILLUSTRATION

The Radical Change of the New Birth

Suppose you had been a pig all your life, and that you were suddenly made into a man. Well, now you are a man, you look through a telescope; swine cannot do that. You look through a microscope; I never knew a pig to do that in my life. Swine do not talk, but you speak, you sing, you pray, you are quite a different creature from what you were before.

Do I compare you to swine? If you do not like the image, I cannot help it. I will take any other that is true, but there is as great a difference between a living Christian and a mere man as there is between a living man and a dog. He has another life, and a higher life, and he has entered another realm. I would not try to teach a dog astronomy, and it is impossible for an unrenewed man to know the things of God. I would not think of putting my dog into a chair, and beginning to explain theology to him—and until you are born again, you will never understand the meaning of God's grace. You must get a new life, pass from death to life, or you cannot know these things. But we who believe in Jesus know that we have this life.

---

because we love the brethren We know that we live because we love. If we can say that *we love God's people, as God's people, because they are God's people,* that is a mark that we have passed from death to life. Do you love them *for Christ's sake*? Do you say to yourself, "That is one of Christ's people; that is one who bears Christ's cross; that is one of the children of God; therefore I love him, and take delight in his company"? Then that is evidence that you are not of the world. If you were, you would love the world, but, belonging to Christ, you love those who are Christ's, and you love them for Christ's sake.

He that loveth not his brother abideth in death No matter though he may be outwardly religious, and may think that, by doing certain external actions, he will save himself, there is no truth at all in his religion, for the very essence of true religion is that a man lives not unto himself, but unto God, and for the good of his fellow men.

All this chapter deals with love, and teaches us that the possession of love is the supreme test of our state. The inquiry is: Do I love God? Do I love my brother also? Is my spirit that of love? For, if not, I am not a child of God.

15 **Whosoever hateth his brother is a murderer** What a warning this is against the evil spirit of hate, revenge, and all that kind of feeling! These things are not compatible with the

possession of the life of God. Where hatred lives, there is no life of God in the soul. That evil must be shot to the very heart, by the arrows of almighty grace, or else we are not free from the dominion of the devil. Every man who hates another has the venom of murder in his veins. He may never actually take the deadly weapons into his hand, and destroy life; but if he wishes that his brother were out of the way, if he would be glad if no such person existed, that feeling amounts to murder in the judgment of God. It is not the lifting of the dagger, nor the mixing of the poison, that is the essence of the crime of murder; it is the hate that prompts the commission of the deadly deed; so, if we never commit the crime, yet, if the hate be in our heart, we are guilty of murder in the sight of God, and eternal life cannot be abiding in us.

and ye know that no murderer hath eternal life abiding in him His action is Cain-like, he is not of the chosen seed, he does not have the life of God abiding in him.

16 **Hereby perceive we the love of God** True love cannot long be dormant. It is like fire; it has an active nature; it must be at work. Love longs for expression; it cannot be dumb. Command it to be without expression, and you command it not to live. And true love is not satisfied with expressing itself in words. It does use words, but it is painfully conscious of their feebleness, for the full meaning of love is not to be conveyed in any human language. It breaks the backs of words, and crushes them to atoms when it lays upon them all that it means. Love must express itself in deeds, as our old proverb says, "Actions speak louder than words." Love delights, too, in sacrifices; she rejoices in self-denials. The more costly the sacrifice, the better is love pleased to make it. She will not offer that which costs her nothing; she loves to endure pains, and losses, and crosses, and thus she expresses herself best.

This is a general principle, which is not only applicable to men, but it reaches even up to God himself; for "God is love" (1 John 4:8), and being love, he must display love, nor can he rest with merely speaking of his love. His love must manifest itself in action. More than that, God could not rest until he had made the greatest sacrifice that he could make, and had given up his only-begotten Son to die in the place of sinners. When he had done that, then he could rest in his love. God does not come to us, and say, "Men and women, I love you. You must believe that I love you, although I do nothing for you to prove my love." He does ask us to believe in his love, but he has given us abundant proof of it; and, therefore, he has a right to claim our belief in it. The apostle of love, who wrote the chapter from which our text is taken, tells us, "We have come to know love by this: that he laid down his life on behalf of us." Just as we learn the love of others by seeing what they are prepared to sacrifice for us, so is it even with God himself. We discover, discern, perceive, and are made to know, the love that he bears to us by the fact that "he laid down his life on behalf of us."

ILLUSTRATION

Jesus Had No Obligation to Us

When Queen Eleanor sucked the poison from her husband's wounds, at the risk of her own life, I can see reasons why she should do it. I say not that she was bound to do it, but I do say that the relationship of a wife accounts for what she did.

But Jesus Christ, the Son of God, had no relationship to us until he chose to assume the relationship which he did assume out of infinite compassion. There was no more relation between him and us than between the potter and the clay; and if the clay upon the wheel goes amiss, what does the potter do with it but take it, and throw it into a corner? And so might the great Creator have done with us; but, instead of doing so, he sheds his blood that he may make us into vessels of honor fit for his own use.

---

because he laid down his life for us Learn three lessons from the fact that he "laid down his life for us." The first lesson should be: Did Christ lay down his life for me? Then how great must have been my sins! I never saw sin till that hour when I saw it tear Christ's glories from his head—when it seemed for a moment even to withdraw the loving-kindness of God from him—when I saw him covered with his own blood, and plunged into the uttermost depths of oceans of grief. Then I said, "Now I know what you are, O sin, as never before I knew it!" Though other sights might teach me something of the dire character of evil, yet never, till I saw the Savior on the tree, did I understand how base a traitor man's guilt was to man's God.

Second, did the Savior lay down his life for me? Then how greatly he must have loved me! I may look back, I may look forward, but whether I look back to the decrees of eternity, or look forward to the pearl-gated city, and all the splendors that God has prepared for his own beloved children, I can never see my Father's love so beaming forth, in all its effulgence, as when I look at the cross of Christ and see him die on it. Christ laid down his life, his glorious life, for a poor worm; he stripped himself of all his splendors, then of all his happiness, then of his own righteousness, then of his own robes, till he was naked to his own shame; and then he laid down his life, that was all he had left, for our Savior had not kept anything back.

Third, did my Savior lay down his life for me? Then how safe I am! The doctrine of Holy Scripture is this: that God is just, that Christ died in the stead of his people, and that, as God is just, he will never punish one solitary soul of Adam's race for whom the Savior did thus shed his blood. The Savior did, indeed, in a certain sense, die for all; all men receive many a mercy through his blood, but that he was the Substitute and Surety for all men, is so inconsistent, both with reason and Scripture, that we are obliged to reject the doctrine with abhorrence. Believer, this is your security, that all your sin and guilt, all your transgressions and your iniquities, have been atoned for, and were atoned for before they were committed; so that you may come with boldness, though red with all crimes, and black with every lust, and lay your hand on that Scapegoat's head, and when you have put your hand there, and seen that Scapegoat driven into the wilderness, you may clap your hands for joy, and say, "It is finished, sin is pardoned."

we ought to lay down our lives for the brethren Such self-sacrifice as this is the very highest form of love to the brothers, and is a following of the example of Christ, who "laid down his life for us."

17 **Whoso hath this world's good, and seeth his brother have need** Zealous words will not warm the cold; delicate words will not feed the hungry; the freest speech will not set free the captive, or visit him in prison; the most adorned words will not clothe the naked, and the words that are most full of unction will not pour oil and wine into the wounds of the sick. Words! Words! Words! Chaff! Chaff! Chaff! If there is no act there is no sympathy.

how dwelleth the love of God in him? Perhaps he will do it on what he calls "principle." He thinks it is wrong to help his needy brother, so he says. But however he may put it, the Holy Spirit asks this searching question: "Whoever has the world's material possessions and observes his brother in need and shuts his heart against him, how does the love of God reside in him?"

18 **My little children** Truly we have some Christian children who have seen a truth, and some friend they meet with does not see it; therefore they have tried to knock his eyes out to make him see it. That is a faithful description of many Christian controversies. It is idle to attempt to compel another to think as I think by scolding him, and heaping wrath upon him. Let us never do that. Let us love. If you cannot expect anything else of a child you do expect love; and love never seems to be more suitably enshrined than in the heart and mind of a little child.

let us not love in word, neither in tongue; but in deed and in truth Actions speak louder than words, and we shall always be anxious to tell our love in deeds as well as by our lips.

> The true disciple asks continually, "Lord, what will you have me do?" He esteems it his highest honor to serve the Lord. "I had rather be a doorkeeper in the house of my God, than to dwell in the tents of wickedness" (Ps 84:10).

APPLICATION

Loving God's People Is a Mark of Grace

It is a sure mark of grace when *we love the company of God's people as a people*: when we are willing to go to the little prayer meeting to hear them pray; when we hear them groaning and feel, "That is just the kind of sorrow that I would like to feel"; when we hear them joyful and say, "That is the kind of joy I want to feel"; when we hear them tell about what the Lord has done for them, and though we have not felt quite the same joy ourselves, say, "I love them because the Lord has loved them. If he has not yet worked all this in me, I love them because he has worked it in them. I rejoice to see my Father's finger anywhere, on anyone, whoever he may be."

If that is your case, go your way in peace. It seems only a very small token of the inward life that we love the brothers, yet it is one of the surest in the world, and it is one of which even you high and mighty saints may be glad to avail yourselves in the cloudy and dark day that sooner or later may come upon you. God grant us all to have a share in this precious knowledge, for Christ's sake!

Do You Know the Love of God?

As the text says, "We have come to know love by this: that he laid down his life on behalf of us." *Have you and I known that love?* That is a very simple question, yet I take the liberty to press it upon you. I think it is Aristotle who says that it is impossible for a person to know that he is loved without feeling some love in return. I think, as a rule, that is true. If you really perceive that Christ loved you so much as to die for you, there will leap up in your heart something of love to him.

And you Christian people, who do love him, if you have somewhat known his love, try to know it still more, that you may love him more. And if you really love him more, try to show that you do.

Notice the rest of the verse: "and we ought to lay down our lives on behalf of the brothers." We ought to prove our love to our God by our love to our fellow men, and especially by our love to our fellow Christians, and to prove our love by our actions.

If we profess to be Christians, let us be Christians in deed, and let us especially show our love to Christ by loving our fellow Christians. If you see any of them in need, aid them to the uttermost of your power. If they need cheering and comforting, give them good cheer and comfort. If they need substantial aid, financial aid, let them have that too. In the old days of persecution, there were always some noble souls who tried to hide away the Christians from those who sought their lives, although they did so at the risk of their own lives, and many a Christian has given himself up to die in order to save the lives of his fellow Christians. Some of the old people came tottering before the judge because they thought that they would not be so much missed from the church as the younger ones would be. On the other hand, sometimes the young men would gently push back the fathers, and say to them, "No; you are old. You had better linger here awhile and teach the young. But we young people are strong, so we will go and die for Christ." There was much contention, in the church of God, in persecuting times, as to who should first die for Christ. They were all willing to lay down their lives for their brothers.

Where has this self-sacrificing love gone now? I would like to see some of it. I would even wear microscopes over my eyes if I thought that I could so discover it, but I am afraid I cannot. Why, if we loved each other now as Christians loved each other then, we should be the talk of the town, and even worldly people would say, "See how these Christians love one another." Yet this is only what we ought to do. So, brothers and sisters in Christ, let it be what we will do. God help you to do it, for Christ's sake!

1 JOHN 3:19–24

[19] And hereby we know that we are of the truth, and shall assure our hearts before him. [20] For if our heart condemn us, God
is greater than our heart, and knoweth all things. [21] Beloved, if
our heart condemn us not, then have we confidence toward God.
[22] And whatsoever we ask, we receive of him, because we keep
his commandments, and do those things that are pleasing in his
sight. [23] And this is his commandment, That we should believe on
the name of his Son Jesus Christ, and love one another, as he gave
us commandment. [24] And he that keepeth his commandments
dwelleth in him, and he in him. And hereby we know that he abideth in us, by the Spirit which he hath given us.

EXPOSITION

19 **And hereby we know that we are of the truth** This is the very evidence that God gives, that by our love to others our hearts will be assured before him, and we shall have confidence concerning our own relationship toward God. That is still the test. Truthful love proves that "we are of the truth," children of the God of truth, and so assures and tranquilizes our hearts before him. Our hearts shall be calm, confident, and happy before God when we know that true love flows within them.

20 **if our heart condemn us** The question before our heart is, are we Christians or not? Have we believed in Christ or not? Conscience takes note of all our imperfections, failings, and shortcomings, and conscience says, "No, the man is not a Christian; he is guilty of such-and-such sins." And many dear children of God have often had a verdict in the court of their

own conscience that has been adverse to their hopes because their conscience has been cognizant of only one side of the case, or they have forgotten some great and important truth that ought to have been mentioned before the court, and then its verdict would have been different. There is a blessedly comforting meaning in these words of the apostle John as well as a meaning that should arouse us all to earnest concern about our real standing in the sight of God.

God is greater than our heart If your heart condemns you, remember the verdict is not final; there is still a higher court. I love the way Peter put it once. He had denied his Master, denied him repeatedly with oaths, but he had bitterly repented. When his Lord said to him, "Simon, son of Jonas, lovest thou me?" (John 21:16), his heart did not condemn him on the question of loving his Master. But his heart did condemn him sorely for having denied his Lord; so, after pleading, "Yea, Lord; thou knowest that I love thee," he takes his case into the higher court, and says, "Lord, thou knowest all things; thou knowest that I love thee" (John 21:17). In moments of soul conflict it will be wise for you to carry this question beyond yourself up to the Omniscient One.

ILLUSTRATION

New Evidence Changes the Case

New evidence is sometimes brought into court that completely changes the aspect of the case. If you have been on a jury, you would not like to tell your fellow jurors how many times you have changed your mind while you have heard the evidence. If you have listened attentively, I expect you have had half a dozen different opinions during the trial. You have heard the whole case against the prisoner, and you have said to yourself, "He's certainly guilty." Then some evidence is brought that throws more light on the case, and then something else is said in favor of the prisoner, and you have said, "I was too much in a hurry." Before the whole case was finished, you were quite satisfied that the man was innocent.

It is just so with our heart. It condemns a man when it has only heard half the evidence. But, happily, "God is greater than our heart and knows all things." A man is tried for a certain crime, but his counsel assures the court that the man who committed that crime is dead, and that the prisoner at the bar is not that man at all. A reliable witness is produced who testifies that he knew the other man well, and that he saw him dead and buried. Another trustworthy person declares that the prisoner at the bar is a different man altogether. So it is with us today: every true believer in Christ can say, "I was guilty, but I died with Christ, and was buried with him, and now I am a new creature in Christ Jesus. 'Old things are passed away; behold, all things are become new'" (2 Cor 5:17).

---

and knoweth all things That is, he knows all about your sins of omission, the good things that you have not done, the righteous acts that you have failed to perform. He knows what your motives have been; he knows how that apparently good action of yours was based upon sheer selfishness—how your pretended religiousness was, after all, only varnished hypocrisy. There are some of you who are great fools, for, while you are condemning yourselves, you are calmly sitting down in prospect of the eternal judgment as if you thought that God would acquit you! You have lost the case in the lower court, where the judge is partial and would give a verdict in your favor if possible. How then will you dare to stand in the higher court, where the verdict *must* go against you if your case remains as it now is?

21 **Beloved** Carefully observe that this text is spoken to the people of God. It speaks to those who are called "beloved." These are the people who are especially loved by God and by his

people. It is a very sweet and endearing title, but it evidently in this case belongs only to those who are of the family of grace. These alone can remain uncondemned in their hearts and live in confidence toward God.

I want you to observe this because there are different ways of addressing different people, and these ways are instructive. To those who are not yet numbered among the "beloved," we preach the gospel of our Lord and Savior Jesus Christ. It is a gospel intended for the sinful, and it talks to them of pardon bought with blood. It is a gospel intended for the ungodly, and it speaks to them of the work of the Holy Spirit whereby their ungodly hearts may be renewed. Its tale is altogether of grace and free favor, and the passing-by of transgression, iniquity, and sin to all those who cast themselves believingly at Jesus's feet. That is the voice of Scripture to those who as yet are not "beloved."

But when we come to speak to those who are saved, to those who are the "beloved" of God, we do not deal with the pardon of criminals, but with the conduct of children. They are saved in the Lord with an everlasting salvation; therefore we do not so much urge them to saving faith as to the higher degree of boldness that grows out of faith, to that confidence toward God that is the right and privilege of the heirs of salvation. We want them not only to know that they have believed, but to be assured of it, and to enjoy that holy familiarity with God—that blessed boldness toward God, that sweet joy and restfulness of spirit that are their privilege as the dear friends of the Lord. They may have these enjoyments if they will be obedient to the directions of the Spirit of God that are laid down by the beloved apostle in this epistle.

if our heart condemn us not Think of the trial held in the inner court of man's nature, within his heart. A man may get an acquittal from this court of conscience, for the question laid before the heart can be settled. It can be ascertained whether I sincerely believe in Jesus Christ. It can be ascertained whether I sincerely love God and love his people. It can be ascertained whether my heart is obedient to the commands of the Lord

Jesus Christ. These are not hazy, mysterious problems that can never be solved. The case may be made clear one way or the other. The court has before it no difficulty beyond its faculty; it is quite competent to decide the question in the light of Scripture by the help of God.

Note that this verdict has to be given upon gospel principles. The question before the court of conscience is not, "Have I perfectly kept the law?" The answer to that is simple enough: "For there is not a just man upon earth, that doeth good, and sinneth not" (Eccl 7:20); "Therefore by the deeds of the law there shall no flesh be justified in his sight" (Rom 3:20). The question is, "Am I a believer in the Lord Jesus Christ? Am I resting in him for salvation, and do I prove the truth of that faith by loving God, and loving the brothers, and by doing those things that are pleasing to God, and avoiding those things that are displeasing to him?" The question is not concerning merit, but concerning grace and the fruit of grace.

This question in the court of the heart must never be settled by our feelings. If the heart is at all right in its judgments it will never say, "I am a child of God because I am so happy." Nor will it exclaim, on the other hand, "I cannot be a child of God because I am so sad." Holy feelings may be brought in as evidence, but they are hard to estimate. Feelings are as variable as the wind; feelings depend so much upon the body and outward surroundings, so much even upon the condition of the atmosphere. The question in hand is not, "Am I happy?" but, "Am I a sincere believer, and does my faith prove its sincerity by the effect that it produces on my life?" Sinners can rejoice as well as saints, and saints can mourn as well as sinners. The point is not what we feel, but what we believe and do.

ILLUSTRATION

The Right Amount of Self-Examination

When a ship first leaves the stocks it is well for it to go on a trial trip, but to have a ship always being tried would be very absurd. It is time that it took voyages in earnest, and was registered in the merchant service; there will be trial enough in the actual execution of service.

Some Christians, by a continual introspection, are always raising the point, "Am I a Christian?" Be a Christian. "Am I a child of God?" Be a child of God, and enjoy it; do not spend a lifetime searching for the family register. However, it is certain that the genuine Christian is not averse to self-examination, nor to any form of test through which he can be put.

---

have we confidence toward God These words are full of comfort. The man who has a clear conscience has confidence toward God in this way. He knows that he is the Lord's, and that God loves him. He knows that God will not do him any hurt, and will not allow the devil or anyone else really to harm him. He knows that God is blessing him and will continue to bless him. He knows that God is his Father and his Friend, and he therefore goes to God in great confidence about his troubles and tells them all to him. He has much confidence in prayer, and he may talk to God in prayer in a way that other people may think too familiar, but it will not be so. His heart is right with God, and therefore he has confidence toward God. He does not doubt God's faithfulness, or God's truth, or God's power, or God's veracity. He simply confides in God and lets things go as they will, for he knows that God is ruling over all. He walks through the world with a childlike, restful confidence, knowing that God will keep him and preserve him even to the end. When he has to die, he will die in confidence, and when he rises from the grave, he will rise in confidence. When the world is all ablaze, he will behold the last great conflagration without alarm. When he stands before the judgment seat of Christ, he will stand there without a tremor. He has confidence toward God, far he has peace within him.

ILLUSTRATION

Do Not Merely Hope the Door Is Locked

When I go to bed at night and say to myself, "Did I lock the door?" I am not content to lie there and say, "I hope and trust that I did." There may be a thief in the garden, so it will not be safe for me to "hope and trust" that all doors and windows are properly fastened.

We like to be sure about these less important matters; how much more ought we to be sure about the salvation of our souls!

22 **whatsoever we ask, we receive of him** There are some things that are essential to prevalence in prayer. God will hear all true prayer, but there are certain things that the people of God must possess, or else their prayers will fall short of the mark.

If you want power in prayer you must have purity in life. There is no promise in the Bible that whatever you ask God will give you; it is made to persons of a certain character. The unlimited promise is to the man of who is so sanctified that he will not ask, and does not think of asking, anything that is not in accordance with God's will. Remember this passage: "Delight thyself also in the Lord; and he shall give thee the desires of thine heart" (Ps 37:4). The desire of the man who delights in God is always in accordance with the mind of God; therefore he is the man that can get whatever he wants. When you do all things that please God, and your life is sanctified and holy, it is then that you abide in his love. Has not Jesus said, "If ye abide in me, and my words abide in you, ye shall ask what ye will, and it shall be done unto you" (John 15:7)? Unsanctified desires will be graciously refused, but the will of the sincerely obedient man is conformed to the will of God, and therefore it shall be fulfilled. "And this is the confidence that we have in him, that, if we ask any thing according to his will, he heareth us" (1 John 5:14).

ILLUSTRATION

What God Does and Does Not Grant in Prayer

If a hungry person were at your door and asked for bread, you would give it to him, whatever might be his character. You will also give your child food, whatever may be his behavior. You will not deny your child anything that is necessary for life; you will never proceed in any course of discipline against him so as to deny him food or a garment to shield him from the cold.

But there are many other things that your child may desire, which you will give him if he is obedient, but you will not give if he is rebellious to you. This illustrates how far the paternal government of God will push the matter of prayer, and where it will not go.

---

because we keep his commandments There are certain prerequisites and essentials for powerful prayer; the first is *childlike obedience:* "Whatever we ask we receive from him, *because we keep his commandments.*" If we are destitute of this the Lord may say to us as he did to his people Israel, "Yet ye have forsaken me, and served other gods: wherefore I will deliver you no more. Go and cry unto the gods which ye have chosen" (Judg 10:13–14). Any father will tell you that for him to grant the request of a disobedient child would be to encourage rebellion in the family and render it impossible for him to rule in his own house. It is often incumbent upon the parent to say, "My child, you did not listen to my word just now; therefore, I cannot listen to yours." Not that the father does not love, but that he does love the child; and because of his love, he feels bound to show his displeasure by refusing the request of his straying offspring.

and do those things that are pleasing in his sight Another essential to victorious prayer is *childlike reverence.* We receive what we ask "because we keep his commandments, *and do what* *is pleasing in his sight."* We do not allow children when they have a command from their father to question its propriety or wisdom; obedience ends where questioning begins. Good children say, "Father has told us to do so-and-so, and therefore we will do it, for we always delight to please him." The weightiest reason for a loving child's action is the persuasion that it would please his parents. The strongest thing that can be said to hold back a gracious child is to prove that such a course of action would displease his parents. It is precisely so with us toward God, who is a perfect parent, and therefore we may without fear of mistake always make his pleasure the rule of right, while the rule of wrong may safely remain that which would displease him.

23 **And this is his commandment: that we should believe** This text suggests the necessity of *childlike trust.* Everywhere in Scripture faith in God is spoken of as necessary to successful prayer. We "must believe that he is, and that he is a rewarder of them that diligently seek him" (Heb 11:6) or else we have not prayed at all; but the success of our prayer will be in proportion to our faith. It is a standing rule of the kingdom, "According to your faith be it unto you" (Matt 9:29). Remember how the Holy Spirit speaks by the mouth of the apostle James: "If any of you lack wisdom, let him ask of God, that giveth to all men liberally, and upbraideth not; and it shall be given him. But let him ask in faith, nothing wavering. For he that wavereth is like a wave of the sea driven with the wind and tossed. For let not that man think that he shall receive any thing of the Lord" (Ja 1:5–7).

ILLUSTRATION

Preaching Jesus by Accident

When the Moravian missionaries first went to Greenland, they were months and months teaching the poor Greenlander about the Godhead, the doctrine of the Trinity, and the doctrine of sin and the law, and no converts were forthcoming. But one day, by accident, one of the Greenlanders happened to read that passage, "Behold, what manner of love the Father hath bestowed upon us, that we should be called the sons of God" (1 John 3:1), and asked the meaning. The missionary, hardly thinking him advanced enough to understand the gospel, nevertheless ventured to explain it to him, and the man became converted, and hundreds of his countrymen received the Word. Naturally enough, they said to the missionaries, "Why did you not tell us this before? We knew all about there being a God, and that did us no good; why did you not come and tell us to believe in Jesus Christ before?"

This is God's weapon, God's method. This is the great battering ram that will shake the gates of hell; we must see to it that it be brought into daily use.

---

on the name of his Son To speak more at large of the things that are to be believed to be justified by faith, they all relate to the person and the work of our Lord Jesus Christ. We must believe him to be God's Son—so the text puts it—"his Son." We must grasp with strong confidence the great fact that he is God, for nothing short of a divine Savior can ever deliver us from the infinite wrath of God. He who rejects the true and proper Godhead of Jesus of Nazareth is not saved, and cannot be, for he does not believe in Jesus as God's Son.

Jesus We must accept this Son of God as "Jesus," the Savior. We must believe that Jesus Christ the Son of God became man out of infinite love to man, that he might save his people from their sins, according to that worthy saying, "Christ Jesus came into the world to save sinners" (1 Tim 1:15).

Christ We must look upon Jesus as "Christ," the anointed of the Father, sent into this world on salvation's errand, not that sinners might save themselves, but that he, being mighty to save, might bring many sons to glory. We must believe that

Jesus Christ, coming into the world to save sinners, did really accomplish his mission; that the precious blood that is shed on Calvary is mighty to atone for sin, and therefore, all manner of sin and blasphemy shall be forgiven, since the blood of Jesus Christ, God's dear Son, cleanses us from all sin.

and love one another, as he gave us commandment The next essential to continued success in prayer is *childlike love.* The great commandment after faith is love. As it is said of God, "God is love," so may we say that "Christianity is love." If each of us were incarnations of love, we should have attained to the complete likeness of Christ. We should abound in love to God, love to Christ, love to the church, love to sinners, and love to men everywhere. If God is to hear us we must love God and love our fellow men; for, when we love God, we shall not pray for anything that would not honor God, and shall not wish to see anything happen to us that would not also bless our brothers. Our hearts will beat true to God and to his creatures, and we shall not be wrapped up in ourselves. You must get rid of selfishness before God can trust you with the keys of heaven; but when self is dead, then he will enable you to unlock his treasuries, and, as a prince, you shall have power with God and prevail.

24 **he that keepeth his commandments dwelleth in him** We must have *childlike ways* as well. It is one of a child's ways to love its home. The good child loves no place so much as the dear old house where its parents live. Now he who loves and keeps God's commandments is said to dwell in him—he has made the Lord his dwelling place and abides in holy familiarity with God. In him our Lord's words are fulfilled, "If ye abide in me, and my words abide in you, ye shall ask what ye will, and it shall be done unto you" (John 15:7). Faith and love, like two cherubic wings, have borne up the believer's soul above the world and carried him near to the throne of God. He has become like God, and now it is that his prayers are such as God can answer. But until he is thus conformed to the divine mind, there must be some limit to the potency of his pleadings. Dwelling in God is necessary to power with God.

ILLUSTRATION

If a Child Treated a Parent as We Treat God

Suppose one of you had a boy who said, "Father, I do not like my home. I do not care for you, and I will not endure the restraints of family rule; I am going to live with strangers. But father, I shall come to you every week, and I shall require many things of you, and I shall expect that you will give me whatever I ask from you." Why, if you are at all fit to be at the head of the house, you will say, "My son, how can you speak to me in such a manner? If you are so self-willed as to leave my house, can you expect that I will do your bidding? If you utterly disregard me, can you expect me to support you in your cruel unkindness and wicked insubordination? No, my son; if you will not remain with me and own me as a father, I cannot promise you anything."

And so is it with God. If we will dwell with him, and commune with him, he will give us all things. If we love as he should be loved, and trust him as he ought to be trusted, then he will hear our requests; but if not it is not reasonable to expect it.

hereby we know that he abideth in us, by the Spirit which he hath given us What is this but the Spirit of adoption—the Spirit that rules in all the children of God? The willful who think and feel and act differently from God must not expect that God will come around to their way of thinking and feeling and acting. The selfish who are actuated by the spirit of pride, the slothful who are actuated by the love of ease, must not expect that God will indulge them. The Holy Spirit, if he rules in us, will subordinate our nature to his own sway, and then the prayers that spring out of our renewed hearts will be in keeping with the will of God, and such prayers will naturally be heard.

APPLICATION

The Trial by Your Conscience Is Not the Ultimate One

Remember that the trial by your conscience is not, after all, the ultimate and the decisive one. Your conscience may go to sleep, or make a mistake in your favor, or may become morbid, and may not take under its consideration all the facts of the case, and so may go against you. Since there may be an error of judgment you should make your appeal to the Most High, saying, "Search me, O God" (Ps 139:23).

Above all, if your conscience should now condemn you, remember that there remains the free, full gospel even for the chief of sinners. If you stand before God condemned in heart today, throw yourself on your face with that sense of condemnation upon you, and cry, "God be merciful to me a sinner" (Luke 18:13). Whichever verdict comes from an enlightened conscience, it will be exceedingly serviceable to you if you have regard to it. If it does not condemn you, then you have confidence toward God. And if it condemns you, the condemnation may drive you at once to flee for refuge to the hope that is set before the guilty in the gospel of our Lord Jesus Christ. May the Holy Spirit thus bless you!

You Ought to Know Whether You Love the Lord

Many people shun anything like a trying of their religion by examination. Multitudes of persons seldom think; they live the life of butterflies, flitting from flower to flower with careless wing. There is no real purpose in their lives. Many others think, and think deeply, but not about their souls or their God. They consider the matter of their relationship to their Creator to be a very secondary matter that can be taken up in the last few minutes of their lives. They leave the best things to the worst moments, and think that they are wise in doing so. This is a grave folly.

Certain professing Christians, too, who should know better, seldom examine themselves as to whether they are in the faith. They take it for granted that all is well with them. They made a profession a great many years ago; they have been decent sort of people ever since. In fact, they have been respected among their fellow Christians, possibly they have even taken office in the church. Are they to question their foundation? Is it necessary that they should put themselves into the scales and be weighed again? It is a very ominous sign for a man when he is afraid of discussing his spiritual state in the chamber of his own heart. I am persuaded that many Christians are the subjects of doubts and fears about their condition simply because they have never had the matter out. It is a great deal better to sift an affair to the bottom than it is to be always tormented by suspicion. If I must go to sea, and I suspect the soundness of the vessel, I shall demand that the ship be surveyed so I can know whether it is a rotten old coffin or a good substantial ship.

You ought to know whether you love the Lord or not. Your love must be very cold and feeble if it is a matter of question. Warmth of love proves its own existence in many ways. You should be anxious to take stock of your spiritual estate. Your desire should be to know the very worst of your case. If your condition should turn out to be horribly bad, you had better know it; certainly your knowing it will not make it any worse. If your case should turn out to be all right, then you will have the confidence that comes of this knowledge—the confidence of which this text speaks. If our hearts, after due, deliberate, and impartial trial, do not condemn us, then we have confidence toward God, and that confidence sweetens life. He who gets confidence through honest searching of heart shall be filled with delight and strength.

Are We Doing What Pleases God?

Are we doing that which is pleasing in God's sight? We cannot expect answers to prayer if we are not. Have you been doing lately that which you would like Jesus Christ to see? Is your household ordered in such a way that it pleases God? Suppose Jesus Christ had visited your house this week, uninvited and unexpected: what would he have thought of that which he would have seen? You might say, "I know so-and-so acts very inconsistently." I am asking you to think of yourself! That is the point. Correct yourself. Unless the members of God's church do that which is pleasing in his sight, they bar the door against prosperity; they prevent the prayers of the church from succeeding. Who wishes to be the man that stands in the way of the prosperity of God's church through inconsistency of conduct? Who would be so guilty? Though some profess to be the followers of Christ, they are so inconsistent that they are not friends, but enemies of the cross of Christ.

The Command to Believe

The blessings that flow from preaching Christ to sinners as sinners are of such a character as prove it to be right. Do you not see that it *levels us all*? We have the same warrant for believing, and no one can exalt himself above his fellow man. Then how it inspires men with hope and confidence; *it forbids despair*. No man can despair if this is true. If he does, it is a wicked, unreasonable despair, because if he has been ever so bad, yet God commands him to believe. What room can there be for despondency?

Again, how it *makes a man live close to Christ*! If I am to come to Christ as a sinner every day—and I must do so, for the Word says, "As ye have therefore received Christ Jesus the Lord, so walk in him" (Col 2:6)—if every day I am to come to Christ as a sinner, then how paltry all my doings look! What utter contempt it casts upon all my fine virtues, my preaching, my praying, and all that comes of my flesh! And though it leads me to seek after purity and holiness, yet it teaches me to live in Christ and not in them, and so it keeps me at the fountainhead.

Sinner, whoever you may be, God now commands you to believe in Jesus Christ. This is his commandment. He does not command you to feel anything, or be anything, to prepare yourself for this. Now are you willing to incur the great guilt of making God a liar? Surely you will shrink from that: then dare to believe. You cannot say, "I have no right"; you have a perfect right to do what God tells you to do. You cannot tell me you are not fit. There is no fitness needed; the command is given and it is yours to obey, not to dispute. You cannot say it does not come to you—it is preached to every creature under heaven. Now it is so pleasant a thing to trust the Lord Jesus Christ that I want to persuade myself you need no persuading. It is so delightful a thing to accept a perfect salvation, to be saved by precious blood, and to be married to so bright a Savior, that I want to hope the Holy Spirit has led you to cry, "I believe! Help thou mine unbelief!" (Mark 9:24).

1 JOHN 4

1 JOHN 4:1–11

[1] Beloved, believe not every spirit, but try the spirits whether
they are of God: because many false prophets are gone out into
the world. [2] Hereby know ye the Spirit of God: Every spirit that
confesseth that Jesus Christ is come in the flesh is of God: [3] And
every spirit that confesseth not that Jesus Christ is come in the
flesh is not of God: and this is that spirit of antichrist, whereof ye
have heard that it should come; and even now already is it in the
world. [4] Ye are of God, little children, and have overcome them:
because greater is he that is in you, than he that is in the world.
[5] They are of the world: therefore speak they of the world, and
the world heareth them. [6] We are of God: he that knoweth God
heareth us; he that is not of God heareth not us. Hereby know we
the spirit of truth, and the spirit of error. [7] Beloved, let us love one
another: for love is of God; and every one that loveth is born of
God, and knoweth God. [8] He that loveth not knoweth not God; for
God is love. [9] In this was manifested the love of God toward us, because that God sent his only begotten Son into the world, that we
might live through him. [10] Herein is love, not that we loved God, but
that he loved us, and sent his Son *to be* the propitiation for our sins.
[11] Beloved, if God so loved us, we ought also to love one another.

EXPOSITION

1 **believe not every spirit** A simpleton believes every word that he hears, but "the wise man's eyes are in his head" (Eccl 2:14). He examines what he sees and hears, and does not blindly accept whatever may be told to him.

try the spirits whether they are of God "Take heed therefore how ye hear" (Luke 8:18), and consider what you listen to;

we should not entrust ourselves to every person who professes to be a spiritual instructor. I will give you one good test: see whether they search and probe you. Rest assured that the Lord has not sent those that speak smooth words and never trouble your conscience or make you search yourselves. "If thou take forth the precious from the vile, thou shalt be as my mouth" (Jer 15:19), says the Lord to his prophets, but not otherwise.

many false prophets are gone out into the world It was so in John's day; it is so in these days. If there were only one false prophet, we should have need to be on our guard, but "many false prophets are gone out into the world." If false prophets were all shut up in a cage and we had to go to seek them, there might be some danger from them, but there is so much more danger now.

2 **every spirit that confesseth that Jesus Christ is come in the flesh is from God** Some say that Jesus Christ was not God. Others say that he was not man, while some talk as if everything about him was a mystery. Those who are truly sent by God declare plainly that Jesus Christ literally came in the flesh; such teachers are "from God." If the doctrine of the incarnation of God in Christ is denied, as it was by the first heretics, we may conclude that the Spirit of God is not in such teaching. Any doctrine that dishonors Christ—whether in his person, or his offices, or his atonement, or in any other way—you may at once conclude is not from God, for that which comes from the Spirit of God glorifies Christ. Did not our Lord himself say, concerning the Holy Spirit, "He shall glorify me: for he shall receive of mine, and shall shew it unto you" (John 16:14)?

3 **every spirit that confesseth not that Jesus Christ is come in the flesh is not of God** If there is any question raised about the deity and the humanity of Christ, do not listen any longer. When you taste the first morsel of meat from a joint, and you find that it is tainted, there is no need for you to eat all the rest to see if it is good. If any man questions the true divinity and the real humanity of Christ, have nothing to do with him, and give no heed to what he says. He "is not from God."

ILLUSTRATION

Would You Take Any Drug?

Especially at this present time it is incumbent upon Christians to learn how to use the discerning faculty with regard to what is, and what is not, truth. Would you eat all meat indiscriminately without tasting and testing its quality? If so, would you not soon be ill? Does a man take any drug that may happen to be upon the chemist's shelves? Does he not expect great care to be exercised in the doctor's dispensary, lest he should be taking poison where he hoped for a salutary medicine?

Remember what the apostle John says: "Beloved, believe not every spirit, but try the spirits whether they are of God" (1 John 4:1). And when you do know what the truth is, do not be ready to listen to that which is contrary to it, or you will regret the day in which you lent your ear to the deceiver.

---

this is that spirit of antichrist That was the form that antichrist took in John's day. It is constantly taking different forms, but it is always anti-Christ—against Christ.

4 **Ye are of God** You who are trusting in Jesus, and are born again of his Spirit, though you may have only a small influence with others, and are like little children in your own esteem, yet "you are from God."

little children Little children are frequently timid. They are sometimes terrified when left alone; they are generally afraid of strangers. You are very weak and feeble, but do not be dismayed because of that, for there is a power dwelling in you that is mightier than the power that dwells in the world. Satan dwells in the world, and he is mighty. But God dwells in you, and he is almighty; therefore do not be afraid.

and have overcome them If you have a childlike spirit, if God has made you teachable as little children, and his Spirit dwells within you, you will not be overcome by these false prophets, but you will overcome them.

greater is he that is in you, than he that is in the world If God's own Spirit is in you, you need not fear any of these enemies. If it were a conflict between you and others who had the Spirit of God within them, the conflict would be grievous, and the issue of it would be doubtful. But now that the struggle is between the Spirit of God that is in you and the spirit of error that is in the world, you need have no question about the ultimate result of the battle.

5 **They are of the world** They are the world's prophets. They preach the world's doctrines. They flatter the world, and the world likes that. They speak according to the fashion of the world, and therefore it is no wonder that the world listens to them.

and the world heareth them When people say to you, "Everybody says so-and-so," that is not the reason why you should believe it. "All the men of advanced thought, all the scholars of the age, speak this way." Yes, just so: "They are from the world; therefore they speak from the world and the world listens to them."

6 **We are of God** The apostles spoke as men sent from God, for the Spirit of God dwelt in them. There are some nowadays who say, "We accept the teaching of the Gospels, but we will have nothing to do with the apostles and their epistles." Thus they clearly show that they are not from God, for John says, writing under the inspiration of the Holy Spirit, "He that knoweth God heareth us; he that is not of God heareth not us."

Hereby know we the spirit of truth, and the spirit of error I read in a certain learned theologian the other day a declaration that the evangelical doctrine that we preach is not Christianity, but Paulinism. By that utterance this theologian condemned himself. He who does not hear the apostles does not hear their Master. He who dares say that Paul has not given us the gospel is not of Christ, for Jesus says, "He that receiveth you receiveth me, and he that receiveth me receiveth him that sent me" (Matt 10:40). The testimony of the Holy Ghost by apostolic lips is as sure as the testimony by the Son of God himself, and it is flat rebellion against the Holy Ghost to graduate his utterances, whether they are through prophets, apostles, or the Christ himself. He who makes this to be true and that to be false, or this true and that truer still, has disparaged the Spirit of God, who speaks as he pleases but is always infallible. He who questions what the Spirit says does not have the Spirit of Christ dwelling in him.

7 **let us love one another** From the abundance of love that was in John's heart, we might almost be startled at the very strong things that he writes against those who are in error, if we did not remember that it is only a false charity that winks at error. He is the most loving man who has honesty enough to tell the truth and to speak out boldly against falsehood. It is very easy to pass through this world believing and saying that everybody is right. That is the way to make a soft path for your own feet and to show that you only have love for yourself. But to speak sometimes as John the Baptist spoke, or as Martin Luther spoke, is the way to prove that you have true love for others.

for love is of God The spirit of love, kindness, self-sacrifice, holy charity—this is from God. This is the distinguishing mark of the Christian dispensation, the distinguishing mark of the Christian—that he abounds in love, not in malice, anger, revenge, bitterness.

every one that loveth is born of God, and knoweth God He who has the spirit of love within him "is born of God," "for love is of God." He who constantly seeks the good of others, whose heart beats with love to those who are not within the narrow confines of his own ribs, whose love goes forth to God and his people, and to the sons of men in general—this is the man who "is born of God, and knoweth God."

I have no right, therefore, to believe that I am a regenerated person unless my heart truly and sincerely loves God. It is vain for me, if I do not love God, to quote the register that records an ecclesiastical ceremony, and say that this regenerated me. It certainly did no such thing, or the sure result would have followed. If I have been regenerated I may not be perfect, but this one thing I can say, "Lord, thou knowest all things; thou knowest that I love thee" (John 21:17). When by believing we receive the privilege to become the sons of God, we receive also the nature of sons, and with filial love we cry, "Abba, Father." There is no exception to this rule; if a man does not love God, neither is he born of God. Show me a fire without heat, then show me regeneration that does not produce love to God; for as the sun must give forth its light, so must a soul that has been created anew by divine grace display its nature by sincere affection toward God.

ILLUSTRATION

God's Love the Source of the Fountain

You have seen a noble fountain in a city adorning a public square. See how the water leaps into the air; then it falls into a circular basin that fills and pours out its fullness into another lower down, and this again floods a third. Hear the merry splash as the waters fall in showers and cataracts from basin to basin! If you stand at the lower basin and look on it and say, "In this is water," that is true, and will be true of the next higher one, and so forth. But if you would express the truth as to where the water really is, you may have to look far away, perhaps upon a mountain's side, for there is a vast reservoir from which pipes are laid to bring these waters and force them to their height that they may descend so beautifully.

Thus the love we have to our fellow creatures drops from us like the descending silvery cataract from the full basin, but the first source of it is the immeasurable love of God that is hidden away in his very essence, which never changes, and never can be diminished.

---

8 **He that loveth not knoweth not God** He may be very orthodox, but if he does not love, he does not know God. And if he does not know God, what does he know? There is such a thing as holding the truth in bitterness, but those who know God, and are truly his children, hold the truth in love.

All you have ever been taught from the pulpit, all you have ever studied from the Scriptures, all you have ever gathered from the learned, all you have collected from the libraries—all this is no knowledge of God at all unless you love God. In true religion, to love and to know God are synonymous terms. Without love you remain in ignorance still, ignorance of the most unhappy and ruinous kind. All attainments are transitory, if love is not as a salt to preserve them. Tongues must cease and knowledge must vanish away; love alone abides forever. You must have this love or be a fool forever. All the children of the true Zion are taught of the Lord, but you are not taught of God unless you love God. See then that to be devoid of love to God is to be devoid of all true knowledge of God, and so of all salvation.

for God is love Where there is the spirit of enmity, of envy, of pride, of contention, there is not the Spirit of God. We may depend upon it that that which makes toward love came forth from love. But that which makes toward division, contention, emulation, and strife, is not of God, "for God is love."

9 **In this was manifested the love of God toward us** There is love in our creation; there is love in providence. But most of all there is love in the gift of Christ for our redemption. The apostle here seems to say, "Now I have found the great secret of God's love to us. Here is the clearest evidence of divine love that ever was or ever can be manifested toward the sons of men."

God sent his only begotten Son We never sent to him; he sent to us. Suppose that, after we had all sinned, we had fallen on our knees and cried, "Father forgive us!" Suppose that day after day we had been, with many piteous tears and cries, supplicating and entreating forgiveness of God. It would be great love then that he should devise a way of pardoning us. But no; it was the very reverse. God sent an ambassador of peace to us; we sent no embassy to him. Man turned his back on God, and went farther and farther from him, and never thought of turning his face toward his best Friend. It is not man that turns beggar to God for salvation; it is, if I may dare to say it, as though the Eternal God himself begged of his creatures to be saved. Jesus Christ has not come into the world to be sought for, but to seek that which is lost. It all begins with him.

that we might live through him Then we were dead: dead to all goodness, or thought or power of goodness, criminals shut up in the condemned cell. And yet God loved us with a great love even when we were dead in trespasses and sins.

Child of God, God's love to you today is wonderful. But think of his love to you when you were far gone in rebellion against him. When not a throb of holy, spiritual life could be found in your entire being, he loved you and sent his Son that you might live through him.

10 **Herein is love** To find love, you need to send a lover; one whose soul is full of love is the most likely to discover it. John, with love in his heart, soars aloft and, using his eagle eye, looks over all history and all space, and at last he poises himself over one spot, for he has found that for which he was looking, and he says, "Herein is love." He did not point to his own heart, and say, "Herein is love," for that was but a little pool filled from the great sea of love. He did not look at the church of God, and say of all the myriads who did not count their lives dear to them, "Herein is love." Their love was only the reflected brightness of the great sun of love. But he looked to God the Father, in the splendor of his condescension in giving his only Son to die for us, and he said, "Herein is love," as if all love were here—love at its utmost height, love at its climax, love outdoing itself.

ILLUSTRATION

A Fly on the Dome of St. Paul's

You never saw a fly on the dome of St. Paul's; it would have been too small an object for you to see when walking around the cathedral. Now, a fly on the dome of St. Paul's is a monstrous being, a marvelous individual, compared with you crawling about this world. It bears a much larger proportion to St. Paul's than you do to this globe! What an insignificant little creature you are!

Supposing you could love that fly—it would seem a strange thing. Or that an angel could love that fly—it would be stranger still. But that God should love us is much more a wonder. In this is love: that God should love so insignificant a creature.

not that we loved God The love of God is love to those who do not love him. When God loves those who love him, it seems to be according to the law of nature. But when he loves those who do not love him, this must be above even all laws; it is according to the extraordinary rule of grace, and grace alone. There was not a man on earth who loved God. There was none that did good—"no, not one" (Ps 14:3); yet the Lord fixed the eye of his electing love upon sinners in whom there was no thought of loving him. There is no more love to God in an unrenewed heart than there is life within a piece of granite.

This is the startling word: "*Not* that we have loved God." There is a negative put there. The positive assertion is that God did love us, even though there is also the negative that we did not love him. It is very easy for us to love those who love us. It is hard, sometimes, to love those who do not love us, especially if they are under great obligation to us; I am sure that was our case with regard to God. We were deeply in debt to him, and we ought to have loved him with all our heart, and mind, and soul, and strength, but we did nothing of the kind. Notwithstanding all that, he loved us. While we were his enemies, he loved us, and sent his Son to save us.

but that he loved us Meditate on each one of these words: "*He loved us*." Three words, but what weight of meaning! *He*, who is infinitely holy and cannot endure iniquity—"*He* loved us." *He*, whose glory is the astonishment of the greatest of intelligent beings—"*He* loved us." *He*, whom the heaven of heavens cannot contain—"*He* loved us." *He* who is God all-sufficient, and needs nothing from us, neither can indeed receive anything from our hands—"*He* loved us."

Now ring that second silver bell: "He *loved* us." I do not think the apostle is here so much speaking of God's special love to his own elect as of his love to men in general. He saw our race ruined in the fall, and he could not bear that man should be destroyed. He saw that sin had brought men into wretchedness and misery, and would destroy them forever, and he would not have it so. He loved them with the love of pity, with the love of sweet and strong benevolence, and he declared it with an oath: "As I live, declares the Lord ... I have no pleasure in the death of the wicked" (Ezek 33:11).

Note the third word. "He loved *us*"—"us"—the most insignificant of beings. What is more, he loved us though in our insignificance we dared to rebel against him. Had he only glanced at us and annihilated us, it would have been as much as we could merit at his hands. But to think that he should love us—*love us*, when we were in rebellion against him—this is marvelous.

ILLUSTRATION

Our Love Is Borrowed Brightness

A child might point us to a bright mirror reflecting the sun, and he might cry, "In this is light!" You and I would say, "Poor child, that is only borrowed brightness. The light is not there, but in the sun." The love of saints is nothing more than the reflection of the love of God. We *have* love, but God *is* love.

---

and sent his Son God "*sent*." Love caused that mission. If there was to be reconciliation between God and man, man ought to have sent to God. The offender ought to be the first to apply for forgiveness; the weaker should apply to the greater for help; the poor man should ask of him who distributes alms. But "in this is love," that God "sent." He was first to send an embassy of peace. Today "we are ambassadors for Christ, as though God did beseech you by us: we pray you in Christ's stead, be ye reconciled to God" (2 Cor 5:20).

Moreover, God "sent *his Son*." If men send an embassy to a great power they select a great one of their nation to wait upon the potent prince, but if they are dealing with a petty principality they think a subordinate person quite sufficient for such a business. Admire, then, the true love of the infinitely gracious God, that when he sent an embassy to men he did not commission an angel or even the brightest spirit before his throne. He sent his equal Son to rebels who would not receive him, would not hear him, but spat upon him, scourged him, stripped him, slew him! Yes, he "that spared not his own Son, but delivered him up for us all" (Rom 8:32).

to be the propitiation That is, to be not only a reconciler, but the reconciliation. His sacrifice of himself was the atonement through which mercy is rendered possible in consistency with justice. I have heard men say with scorn that God required a sacrifice before he would be reconciled, as if that were wrong on the part of the Judge of all. But let me whisper in their ears: God required it, it is true, for he is just and holy—but God found it himself. It was himself, his own Son, one with himself, who became the propitiation and the reconciliation. It was not that God the Father was unkind and could not be placated unless he smote his Son, but that God the Father was so kind that he could not be unjust. He was so supremely loving that he devised a way by which men could be justly saved. An unjust salvation would have been none at all.

for our sins That God should deal with us as to our virtues, if we had any; that he should deal with us as to our love, if we had any, might not seem so difficult. But that he should send his Son to dwell with us as sinners, and to come into contact with our sins, and thus to take the sword, not only by its hilt, but by its blade, and plunge it into his own heart, and die because of it—this is a miracle of miracles. Christ never gave himself for our righteousness, but he laid down his life for our sins. He viewed us as sinners when he came to save us. "Christ Jesus came into the world to save sinners" (1 Tim 1:15).

ILLUSTRATION

Letting the Guilty Escape Makes the Innocent Suffer

Think what an injury and injustice would be inflicted upon all the honest men in London if the thieves were never punished for their roguery. It would be making the innocent suffer if you allowed the guilty to escape.

God, therefore, not out of arbitrary choice, but from necessity of rightness, must punish us for having done wrong. But God's love thought out a plan, a wondrous plan, by which Jesus came to be a Substitute, to stand in our place that we might go free.

---

11 **Beloved, if God so loved us** Our love to one another is simply God's love to us, flowing into us, and flowing out again. That is all it is. "Herein is love, not that we loved God, but that he loved us," and then we love others. Observe, then, that since the love of God is the source of all true love in us, so a sense of that love stimulates us. Whenever you feel that you love God, you overflow with love to all God's people. It is when you get to doubt the love of God that you grow hard and cold, but when you are fired with the love of a dying Savior who gave himself for you, you feel as if you loved every beggar in the street, and you long to bring every harlot to Christ's dear feet; you cannot help it. If Christ baptizes your heart into his love, you will be covered with it, and filled with it.

we ought also to love one another Read the text: "we *ought* also to love one another." If you get to the highest point of self-sacrifice you will never be able to boast, for you have only done what it was your duty to have done. Thus you see the highest grade of Christianity excludes all idea of salvation by works, for when we come up to its utmost pitch, if we give our body to be burned for love, yet still we have done no more than it was our duty to have done, considering the tremendous obligations under which the love of God has laid us.

ILLUSTRATION

Don't Be a Clogged Pipe

If you had to manage waterworks for the distribution of water all over this city, and there was a certain pipe into which you poured water, and none ever came out at the other end, do you know what you would do? You would take it out and say, "This does not suit my purpose. I want a pipe that will give out as well as receive."

That is exactly what the Lord desires of us. Do not selfishly say, "I want to sit down and enjoy the love of God. I will never say a word to anybody about Christ. I will never give a poor creature so much as a brass farthing. I want to sit down and be solaced with the love of God." If you think this way, you are a plugged-up pipe. You are of no use. You will have to be taken out of the system of the church, for the system of love-supply for the world requires open pipes, through which love divine may freely flow.

APPLICATION

Bound to Love Our Fellow Christians

Christian, by the love that God has manifested to you, you are bound to love your fellow Christians. You are to love them though they have many infirmities. You have some yourself. If you cannot love one because he has a crusty temper, perhaps he may reply that he cannot love you because you have a lethargic spirit. Jesus loved you with all your infirmities, so love your infirm brothers. Shall Christ forgive you all your myriad offenses, and you not forgive your brother?

It is easy to be courteous to those who are better off than ourselves, and show deference to those who wear respectable attire, but the thing is to love the Lord's people who are poor—yes, and to love them all the more tenderly for their poverty, for they have in some respects more of the image of Christ than we do. Christ was poor, and so are they. And let us cleave close to God's persecuted ones. Some people always run away from a man as soon as anybody flings a handful of dirt at him, but if God so loved us when we were sinners, we ought to love our fellow Christians when they are under a cloud.

Love Because God Loved Us

If you go into the world and say, "I am to love my fellow men because I love God," the motive is good, but it is questionable, limited, and variable. How much better it is to argue that I am to love my fellow men because God loves me. When my love grows cold toward God, and when by reason of my infirmity and imperfection I am led even to question whether I love God at all, then my argument and my impulse would fail me if it came from my own love to God. But if I love the fallen because God loved me, then I have an unchanging motive, an unquestionable argument, and a forcible impulse not to be resisted: hence the apostle cried, "The love of Christ constraineth us" (2 Cor 5:14). It is always well for a Christian to have the strongest motive, and to rely upon the most potent and perpetual force, and hence the apostle bids us look to divine love, and not to our own. "Herein is love," says he, "not that we loved God, but that he loved us."

Our Love Follows the Love of God

Our love ought to follow the love of God in always seeking to produce reconciliation. It was to this end that God sent his Son. Has anybody offended you? Seek reconciliation. "But I am the offended party." So was God, and he went straight away and sought reconciliation. Do the same. "But I have been insulted." So was God. All the wrong was toward him, yet he sent. "But they are so unworthy." So are you, but "God loved you and sent his Son." I do not mean that this love is to come out of your own heart originally, but I do mean that it is to flow out of your heart because God has made it to flow into it. Love has poured into you from above; let it run over to those who are below. Go at once, and try and make reconciliation, not only between yourself and your friend, but between every man and God. Let that be your object. Christ has become man's reconciliation, and we are to try and bring this reconciliation near to every poor sinner that comes in our way.

God Gave His Son for You

Try, if you can, to realize that God did actually give up his only begotten Son that you might live through him. If you are a believer in that dear Son of God, and you do live through him, if he bore your griefs and carried your sorrows, if he was wounded for your transgressions and bruised for your iniquities, if he put away all your sin, then fall down at his dear feet and weep yourself away. No, rise and sing yourself away. And when you have done that, come back again and go forth to work for him with all your might, and try to love your fellow men at something like the rate at which God loved you. You will never reach that climax of love, but aim at getting as near it as you can, and God bless you in the effort!

It does seem to me so sad that there should be anybody in the world who does not believe in the Lord Jesus Christ, and that there should be any poor sinner who does not lay hold of eternal life as it is set forth in the gospel. You self-righteous people, you who never did any wrong, I do not expect you to take any notice of this. You are so wretchedly wrapped up in yourselves that you care nothing for my blessed Master. You are like the self-made man who adores his maker. But you who are poor and needy, burdened with sin, and full of guilt, this is the God for you. This is the Christ for you; come and have him, come and trust him, and then sing with all of us who have believed in him, "Herein is love, not that we loved God, but that he loved us, and sent his Son to be the propitiation for our sins."

1 JOHN 4:12–16

[12] No man hath seen God at any time. If we love one another, God dwelleth in us, and his love is perfected in us. [13] Hereby know we that we dwell in him, and he in us, because he hath given us of his Spirit. [14] And we have seen and do testify that the Father sent the Son to be the Saviour of the world. [15] Whosoever shall confess that Jesus is the Son of God, God dwelleth in him, and he in God. [16] And we have known and believed the love that God hath to us. God is love; and he that dwelleth in love dwelleth in God, and God in him.

EXPOSITION

12 **No man hath seen God at any time** We do not need to see him to love him. Love knows how good he is, though she has not beheld him. Blessed are those who have not seen God, yet who love him with heart, and mind, and soul, and strength.

If we love one another No man is a Christian who does not love Christians. He who, being in the church, is yet not of it heart and soul, is but an intruder in the family. But since love to our brothers springs out of love to our one common Father, it is plain that we must have love to that Father, or else we shall fail in one of the indispensable marks of the children of God. "We know that we have passed from death unto life, because we love the brethren" (1 John 3:14). But we cannot truly love the brothers unless we love the Father. Therefore, lacking love to God, we lack love to the church, which is an essential mark of grace.

ILLUSTRATION

Showing God's Love to Our Neighbors

A beautiful spirit worthy of a Christian was that of a man who found his horse in the pound one day. The farmer who put it in said, "I found your horse in my field, and I put it in the pound. If I ever catch it there again, I'll put it in again." "Well," replied the other, "I found six of your cows in my farmyard the other night eating my hay. I just drove them out, and put them into your farmyard. I didn't impound them, and if I ever catch them in my yard again, I'll do the same." The other farmer said, "You are a better man than I am," and immediately he went and paid the fees and let his neighbor's horse out of the pound, ashamed of himself.

Such a generosity of disposition becomes you, especially to your brother Christians. If God has such wonderful love to us, let us love those who offend us, and show compassion toward the Lord's poor people.

God dwelleth in us He is not far to seek. If you love one another, God is in you. He dwells in you; he is your nearest and dearest Friend, the Author of all other love. The grace of love comes from the God of love.

and his love is perfected in us We cannot see God, but we can love God. Love, therefore, takes the place of eyes to us. When we love God, it is because he dwells in us. That is better than seeing him—to have him resident within our spirit, although he is not discernible by these mortal eyes.

13 **Hereby know we that we dwell in him, and he in us** Just as the seal that comforted our Lord and made him to know in times of depression that he was indeed beloved by the Father was that he had the Spirit of God, so to you and to me the possession of the Spirit of God is our continuous encouragement. By this we may know beyond all question that we reside in God

and God resides in us. The seal answers a twofold purpose: it is on God's part a testimony, and to us an encouragement.

because he hath given us of his Spirit And his Spirit is the spirit of love. Wherever it comes, it makes man love his fellow man and seek his good. If you have that love in your heart, it came from God, and you dwell in God.

14 **we have seen and do testify** Doubtless John may be understood as referring to himself and his brother apostles when he says this. There are two things joined together in this text that must never be parted: "We have seen and do testify." In the first place, never let any man testify what he has not seen. If you are not personally aware of it, do not tell it; it is the personality of the testimony that is the power of the testimony. That truth which you have never experienced, you had better leave to somebody else to preach. This is the cause of the failure of a great many ministers. There is no personal conversion behind their ministry, and consequently no Christian life within them; their preaching is the testimony of a man who says that he heard such and such a thing.

ILLUSTRATION

Testify Only to What You Know

You know how a judge will stop a witness when he begins to say what others have told him: "No, no," he says, "what did you see yourself? What do you know about this business on your own account? I do not want to know what others said to you about it."

So is it with the message delivered from the pulpit. The preacher should bear testimony to what he has seen, and tasted, and felt, and handled. When you try to bring others to Christ, you must do it by bearing witness to what Christ has done for you. If he has never done anything for you personally, for *you*, you cannot testify for him, and must not pretend to do so.

In the next place, you should testify to what you have seen. If you have seen those things for yourself, do what Mary did when she had seen the risen Christ: she ran to bring his disciples word. What right do you have to see for yourself alone? If you have received light from God, "let your light so shine before men" that they may see it and glorify God for it (Matt 5:16).

the Father sent the Son The apostles' seeing was eminently conclusive as to the mission of Christ. What they saw was not only Christ, but "that the Father sent the Son." This was seen in Christ's miracles. It is especially recorded of our Lord's first miracle, when he turned the water into wine, "This beginning of miracles did Jesus in Cana of Galilee, and manifested forth his glory; and his disciples believed on him" (John 2:11). It was rather a simple miracle, the turning of water into wine, but Jesus did it in such a marvelous manner that the thought flashed upon the apostles as he did it, "This is the Son of God. This is the Messiah." If you had been with Christ during his earthly life and had been spiritually enlightened, you would have seen, in his walking the waves, or in his opening the eyes of the blind, or in his healing all manner of sick folk who were brought to him, something of his glory, and you would have felt that the evidence as to his mission was very conclusive.

to be the Savior of the world What the apostles saw was eminently conclusive as to his being sent to save. There was nothing about Christ's life that was contrary to that declaration. He cursed no man; he called no fire from heaven upon any man. Even when wicked men had nailed him to the tree, he breathed a prayer for them. Every way, he was not a destroyer, but a Savior. These men were themselves saved—saved from known sin, saved from groveling occupations, saved from themselves—and they knew it. They knew that the Father must have sent the Son to be the Savior of the world, for he had saved them.

But they knew it better still after they had seen him die, after they had beheld his empty tomb, after they had felt the descending Spirit on the day of Pentecost. Then, when the tongues of fire were given to them, and they went out to speak in his name, and three thousand felt the mighty touch of grace, they knew that the Father had sent the Son to be the Savior of the world.

15 **Whosoever shall confess that Jesus is the Son of God, God dwelleth in him, and he in God** Let Christ be God to you, and you are saved. If you take him to be the Son of God, and consequently rest your eternal hopes on him, God dwells in you, and you dwell in God.

16 **we have known** You will observe the distinction that the apostle makes. It struck my mind as being a very beautiful description of the Christian's twofold experience. Sometimes he *knows* the love that God has to him, and at other times he *believes* it. There is a difference here. Sometimes he knows it by seeing it. He goes to his house and he finds it stored with plenty—"bread shall be given him; his waters shall be sure" (Isa 33:16). Another time he sees it after coming out of affliction.

Besides what Christians see there is something that they *feel*. John could say, "We have known," for he had laid his head on Jesus's bosom. He had been with him in the garden of Gethsemane; he had been with him on the mount of transfiguration; he had been with him, too, when he worked his special miracles. Therefore, from the fact that he had communion with Christ at the supper and in his sufferings and his miracles, John might say, "We have known" the love that he has for us.

and believed the love that God hath to us The first position, that of knowing God's love, is the sweetest, but that of believing God's love is the grandest. To feel God's love is very precious, but to believe it when you do not feel it is the noblest. He may be only a little Christian who knows God's love, but he is a great Christian who believes it when the visible contradicts it and the invisible withholds its witness.

he that dwelleth in love dwelleth in God, and God in him Is anyone full of anger, enmity, malice, and envy? If so, let him know that God does not dwell in the heart that harbors such abominations. Until these base passions are expelled, and we

> feel love to all mankind for Christ's sake, God is not in us, for "the one who resides in love resides in God, and God resides in him." The old method, according to Jewish tradition, was, "Thou shalt love thy neighbor, and hate thine enemy" (Matt 5:43). But Christ's new rule is, "Love your enemies, bless them that curse you, do good to them that hate you, and pray for them which despitefully use you, and persecute you; that ye may be the children of your Father which is in heaven" (Matt 5:44–45). This is the point in which our likeness to God will be seen, for he loved us when we were his enemies, and he expects his children to love their enemies. May he graciously teach us that sacred art!

APPLICATION

Apostolic Testifying and Ours

Many of you can join in what the apostle John said, "We have seen that the Father has sent the Son to be the Savior of the world." Now let us bear our testimony concerning it as the apostles did.

First, *we should do it in the same manner*. What was the apostolic manner of testifying? It was very fervent and ardent. Those first preachers of the gospel never preached cold sermons. Some sermons hang like icicles upon the lips of the speaker, but the apostles preached as if they were on fire. The apostles also proclaimed their message very simply. I do not believe there ever was an apostolic sermon in which the preacher tried to show himself off; there is no record of any display of oratorical fireworks. Tell the people the way to heaven, and point it out to them as plainly as you can. We need speech that can be easily understood by the people, the plain speech of the common folk of our day. So the apostles spoke, and so should we. But they also spoke very boldly. You never meet with any timidity in them. The apostles spoke boldly in the name of Jesus Christ of Nazareth, and Jesus Christ of Nazareth backed up their words. If God has not sent you, go home. But if he has, in God's name, do not apologize for his message. There is an honor put upon you by your Lord who sent you, and you must put honor upon your Master by being faithful to him.

Thus, like the apostles, we have to bear testimony for Christ, and *we should do it in the same power*. What was the source of their power? Their only power was the Holy Ghost. We also must come to see that there can be no power in us to win a soul for Christ but the supernatural energy of God the Holy Spirit. If we have that, the work will be done. If we are without it, we shall be like "sounding brass, or a tinkling cymbal" (1 Cor 13:1).

Then again, if we are to testify as the apostles did, *we should do it with the same message*. What was that message? "The Father has sent the Son to be the Savior of the world." There is salvation; there is a Christ ready to save. Look to him, blind eyes; look to him, dead souls; look to him.

Know and Believe the Love of God

There are doubtless some who are saying, "I cannot think that God would have mercy on such a sinner as I am." Another one says, "Though I know my guilt, I cannot conceive that the love of God can blot out such iniquity as mine." Now I take your hand and I say, "We have come to know and have believed the love that God has in us," and *we* are the very chief of sinners ourselves. Will you honor God by believing that he is able to save you through the blood of Christ? For if the Lord now enables you to honor him in believing, depend upon it, he has begun a good work in you and has set his heart upon you. Sinners, believe that God is love. Trust him who gave his Son to die. He will deny you nothing. If you ask with humble faith, you shall assuredly receive.

1 JOHN 4:17–21

[17] Herein is our love made perfect, that we may have boldness in
the day of judgment: because as he is, so are we in this world.
[18] There is no fear in love; but perfect love casteth out fear: because fear hath torment. He that feareth is not made perfect in
love. [19] We love him, because he first loved us. [20] If a man say, I love
God, and hateth his brother, he is a liar: for he that loveth not his
brother whom he hath seen, how can he love God whom he hath
not seen? [21] And this commandment have we from him, That he
who loveth God love his brother also.

EXPOSITION

17 **that we may have boldness in the day of judgment** According to some, the saints will not be in the day of judgment. Then what is the use of "boldness in the day of judgment"? As I read my Bible, we shall all be there, and we shall all give an account to God. I shall be glad to be there, to be judged for the deeds done in my body. Not that I hope to be saved by them, but because I shall have a perfect answer to all accusations on account of my sin. "Who is he that condemneth? It is Christ that died, yea rather, that is risen again, who is even at the right hand of God, who also maketh intercession for us" (Rom 8:34).

because as he is, so are we in this world If we can be to the world, in our poor feeble measure, what God is to it—fountains of love, dispensaries of goodness—then we do not need to be afraid of the verdict even on the great day of judgment. If you live among men as Christ lived among men, if you are a savior to them in your measure, if you love them, if you try to exhibit the lovely traits of character that were in Christ, happy are you!

ILLUSTRATION

Not Giving Christ What We Ought To

I am afraid that many of us are like the children at school, who have a good, fair copy set them at the top of the page, and the next line is written to imitate the copy, and the next imitates the imitation of the copy, and as it gets to the bottom of the page—alas! poor writing—how unlike it is to the perfect copy at the top!

So what is due to Christ stands at the top: what I believe about Christ in my best moments stands next: what I actually give to Christ comes next to that: and then far down the page how badly do I write, and how far do I fall short of what my love knows I ought to give to him!

18 **There is no fear in love** If a man is conscious that he intends no harm to anyone, that he wishes good to all mankind, that he loves his God, and loves his fellow men for God's sake, what does he have to fear? He becomes the bravest of the brave, and often finds himself safe and unharmed in places where others do not dare to go.

perfect love casteth out fear There is a loving, holy fear that is never cast out. Filial fear grows as love grows. We must always cultivate that sacred dread, that solemn awe of God, but we are not afraid of him. God is your best Friend, your choicest love. You long to approach him. Though he is a consuming fire, you know that he will only consume what you want to have consumed. He will purify you and make your gold to shine more brightly because the consumable alloy is gone from it. He will not consume you, but only that which would work for your hurt if it were left within you.

because fear hath torment That is a servile fear, of course, for there is a fear that has no punishment in it—the holy fear that even angels feel when they veil their faces in the presence of the Most High. There is no punishment in that reverent awe. The more we have love toward God, the more of that filial fear we shall have. But that slavish dread, that awful terror that begets dislike within itself, cannot live where true love is planted within the soul.

He that feareth is not made perfect in love Questioning, mistrust, unbelief, doubt—all these die when we come truly and heartily to love our Lord. In proportion as our love to him burns like a flame of fire, it burns up all this wood, hay, and stubble of trembling, slavish fear.

19 **We love** Now, if you are a child of God, you will say, "We love him." As sure as you have passed from darkness to light, whether you are an Episcopalian, or a Presbyterian, or a Baptist, or whatever you may be, you will agree with this utterance of the one mouth of the one church. We all, without exception, who have believed in him, love him. When we believe, know, and feel that God loves us, we, as a natural result, love him in return. And in proportion as our knowledge increases, our faith strengthens, and our conviction deepens that we are really beloved by God. We, from the very constitution of our being, are constrained to yield our hearts to God in return.

But we do not love him at all as we ought to love him, and not at all as we wish to love him. Our conception of what is due to Christ is, no doubt, very short of what is due to him, but we fall short even of our own conception. But for all that, in the next place, *we do really love him*. The devil tells us we do not, but when it comes to close quarters we can turn to one who knows better than the devil, and we can say, "Lord, thou knowest all things; thou knowest that I love thee" (John 21:17). What a mercy it is that Jesus Christ does not believe our actions, for they very often say, "Jesus, we do not love you." But he reads our hearts, and our hearts still beat with this: "In my very soul I love Christ, and if it were possible I would never sin against him." Yes, we do really love him.

ILLUSTRATION

Action Is More Interesting Than Mere Doctrine

If you have visited the picture galleries at Versailles, where you see the wars of France from the earliest ages set forth in glowing colors upon the canvas, you cannot but have been struck with the pictures and interested in the terrible scenes. Upstairs in the same palace there is a vast collection of portraits. I have traversed those galleries of portraits without much interest, only here and there pausing to notice a remarkable countenance. Very few persons linger there; everybody seems to walk on as quickly as the polished floors allow. Now, why is it that you are interested by the portraits downstairs and not by those upstairs? They are the same people; very many of them in the same dress. Why do you not gaze upon them with interest? The reason lies here: the portrait in still life, as a rule, can never have the attraction that surrounds a scene of stirring action. There you see the warrior dealing a terrible blow with his battle axe, or the senator delivering an oration in the assembly, and you think more of them than of the same bodies and faces in repose. Life is impressive; action awakens thought.

It is just so with the text, "We love him, because he first loved us." Look at it as a matter of doctrinal statement; and if you are a thoughtful person you will consider it well. But feel the fact itself, feel the love of God, know it within our own souls, and manifest it in our lives, and how engrossing it becomes.

because he first loved us We love God, not because we felt that we ought to love him, but "because he first loved us." A sense of duty is a very proper thing concerning many matters, and I do not deny that it is our duty to love God with all our heart, and mind, and soul, and strength, for this is the very essence of the law of the Lord, but no man ever loves as a mere matter of duty. You love even an earthly object because you cannot help yourself, and you love God because he is infinitely lovely, and because he has so completely won your heart as to engross your whole affection. Because he first loved us, and that love of his has been shed abroad in our hearts, we have loved him in return as a matter of course. We could not help doing so. The mighty deeps of his immeasurable love, high up on the eternal hills, flow down into the inmost recesses of our empty hearts. When, afterward, a fountain of love is seen springing up out of them, the secret of its action is to be traced to that great reservoir away up on the everlasting hills.

ILLUSTRATION

Loving God on Equal Terms

There are two gentlemen of equal rank in society, and the one is not at all obliged to the other. They, being equal, can easily feel a disinterested admiration for each other's characters, and a consequent disinterested affection.

If the love of disinterested admiration were required from a sinner, I do not see how he could readily render it. But I, a poor sinner, by nature sunk in the mire, full of everything that is evil, condemned, guilty of death, so that I deserve to be cast into hell, am under such obligations to my Savior and my God that it would be idle for me to talk about a disinterested affection for him, since I owe to him my life, my all.

---

20 **he is a liar** This is a very strong expression. John was not one of those oily, sugary sorts of people who cannot speak the truth. There is no real love in that kind of man; he only has the mere pretense of love. John speaks sharply because he loves ardently. True love hates that which is unlovely. It is

inevitable that a man who is full of love should feel intense indignation against that which is contrary to love. Some people think that, if you love, you will never use strong language, but that is not the case. Sometimes, because a surgeon loves the patient, he cuts more deeply.

he that loveth not his brother The word "brother" is to be understood in the widest possible sense. We are all brothers, springing from the same common parent. Therefore we ought to be philanthropists, lovers of man, loving even the guilty and the worthless, having an earnest desire to do good even to those who do us ill. If we have not yet reached that spirit, we need to begin our true Christian life at the foot of the cross by trusting and loving him who died there out of love for sinners. Only there can we learn, in the person of Christ Jesus our Lord, this divine philosophy of love to God and men.

whom he hath seen If you could see God, it is clear that you would not love him. If you talk about your love to him whom you have not seen, it is utterly false if you do not love men like yourself whom you have seen.

how can he love God whom he hath not seen God looked on us with an eye that saw all our sin and misery, yet he loved us. And he wants us to have a love that, while it sees all the imperfection and all the undeserving in our fellow men, still loves them. If we do not love those whom we see, the apostle says that we lie when we talk of loving God whom we have not seen.

21 **this commandment have we from him** This is the "new commandment" that our Lord gave to his apostles, and through them to his whole church, "That ye love one another, as I have loved you" (John 15:12). John was, in a special sense, "that disciple whom Jesus loved" (John 21:7). It was appropriate, therefore, that he should be the apostle to be inspired by the Holy Spirit to bring this commandment to the remembrance of any who had forgotten it.

He who loveth God love his brother also If you do not live in love, you do not live in God. If you are harboring any animosities, ill feelings, and unkindnesses, get rid of them; get rid of them at once. Remember the Apostle Paul's injunction, "Let not the sun go down upon your wrath" (Eph 4:26). As God has forgiven you, forgive all others for Christ's sake, and dwell in a loving-hearted Christlike spirit toward all mankind.

APPLICATION

How to Love God from This Text

I trust that there are some who, although they do not love God now, yet desire to do so. Well, this text tells you how to love God. You say, perhaps, "I will love God when I have improved my character, and when I have attended to the external duties of religion." But are you going to get love to God out of yourself? Is it there, then? "No," you say. How, then, will you get it from where it is not? You may go often to an empty iron safe before you will bring a thousand pound note out of it, and you may look a long time to your own heart before you will bring out of it a love to God that is not there.

What is the way by which a heart may be made to love God? The text shows us the method of the Holy Spirit. He reveals the love of God to the heart, and then the heart loves God in return. If, then, you desire to love God, use the method that the text suggests: meditate on the great love of God to man, especially upon this, "For God so loved the world, that he gave his only begotten Son, that whosoever believeth in him should not perish, but have everlasting life" (John 3:16). See clearly that you have to trust your soul with Christ by faith. Perceive that it is vast love which sets before you such a way of salvation in which the only thing required of you is that you be nothing, and trust Christ to be everything, and even that faith he gives you as a gift of his Spirit, so that the plan of salvation is all of love. If you want to repent, do not so much consider your sin as the love of Jesus in suffering for your sin. If you desire to believe, do not so much study the doctrine as study the person of Jesus Christ on the cross. If you desire to love, think over perpetually, until it breaks your heart, the great love of Jesus Christ in laying down his life for his worthless foes. The love of God is the birthplace of holy love. It is not there in your hearts where you are attempting an absurdly impossible feat, namely, to create love in the carnal mind that cannot be reconciled to God, but love must be born in the heart of Jesus and then it shall come down to you.

Love to God Is an Argument That God Loves

Wherever there is love to God in the soul it is an argument that God loves that soul. I remember meeting once with a Christian woman who said she knew she loved God, but she was afraid God did not love her. That is a fear so preposterous that it ought never to occur to anybody. You would not love God in deed and in truth unless he had shed abroad his love in your heart.

On the other hand, our not loving God is not a conclusive argument that God does not love us; otherwise the sinner might be afraid to come to God. Loveless sinner, with heart unquickened and chill, the voice of God calls even you to Christ. Even to the dead in sin his voice says, "Live." His mighty sovereignty comes forth dressed in robes of love, and he touches you the unlovable, the loveless, the depraved, degraded sinner, at enmity with God. He touches you in all your alienation and he lifts you out of it and makes you to love him, not for your own sake, but for his name's sake and for his mercy's sake. You had no love at all to him, but all the love lay in him alone. Therefore he began to bless you, and will continue to bless you world without end, if you are a believer in Jesus. In the bosom of the Eternal are the deep springs of all love.

Believing in His Love Melts You

This is the personal point: he loves me, an insignificant nobody, full of sin, who deserved to be in hell, who loves him so little in return—God loves ME. Does this not melt you? Does this not fire your soul? I know it does if it is really believed. It must.

And how did he love me? He loved me so that he gave up his only begotten Son for me, to be nailed to the tree, and made to bleed and die. And what will come of it? Because he loved me and forgave me, I am on the way to heaven. Within a few months, perhaps days, I shall see his face and sing his praises. He loved me before I was born. He loved me before a star began to shine, and he has never ceased to do so all these years. When I have sinned he has loved me. When I have forgotten him he has loved me. When in the days of my sin I cursed him, still he loved me. And he will love me when my knees tremble, and my hair is gray with age; "even to your old age" (Isa 46:4). He will bear and carry his servant. He will love me when the world is ablaze, and love me forever and forever.

Chew the cud of this blessed thought; roll it under your tongue as a dainty morsel. Sit down, if you have leisure, and think of nothing but this—his great love with which he loves you. And if you do not feel your heart bubbling up, if you do not feel your soul yearning toward God, and heaving big with strong emotions of love to God, then I am much mistaken. This is so powerful a truth, and you are so constituted as a Christian as to be wrought upon by this truth, that if it is believed and felt, the consequence must be that you will love him because he first loved you. God bless you, brothers and sisters, for Christ's sake.

We Love Him on Earth

Children of God, if Christ were here on earth, what would you do for him? If it should be rumored tomorrow that the Son of Man had come down from heaven, as he came at first, what would you do for him?

I can conceive that there would be a tumult of delighted hearts—a superabundance of liberal hands—that there would be a sea of streaming eyes to behold him. One might say, "If he were hungry, I would give him meat, even if it were my last crust. If he were thirsty, I would give him drink, even if my own lips were parched with fire. If he were naked, I would strip myself and shiver in the cold to clothe him. I would hurry away, and I would cast myself at his dear feet. I would ask him, if it would only honor him, to tread on me, and crush me in the dust, if he would only be raised one inch the higher by it. If he wanted a soldier, I would enlist in his army. If he needed that someone should die, I would give my body to be burned, if he stood nearby to see the sacrifice and cheer me in the flames." Would you not go forth to meet him? We would dance, like David before the ark, exulting for joy, if Christ came.

We think we love him so much that we would do all that. But there is a grave question about the truth of this matter: Do you not know that Christ's wife and family are here? And if you love him, would it not follow as a natural inference that you would love his bride and his offspring? You might say, "Christ has no bride on earth." Doesn't he? Has he not espoused to himself his *church*? Is not his church, the mother of the faithful, his own chosen wife? And has he not declared that he never will be divorced from her, and that he will consummate the marriage in the last great day, when he shall come to reign with his people on the earth? And does he have no children here? The daughters of Jerusalem and the sons of Zion, "who hath begotten me these?" (Isa 49:21). Are they not the offspring of the everlasting Father, the Prince of Peace, the Child born, the Son given? Surely they are.

If we love Christ as we think we do, as we pretend we do, we shall love his church and people. Do you love his church? Perhaps you love the part to which you belong. You love the hand. It may be a hand that is garnished with many brilliant rings of noble ceremonies, and you love that. You may belong to some poor, poverty-stricken denomination—it may be the foot—and you love the foot. But you speak contemptuously of the hand, because it is garnished with greater honors, while perhaps you of the hand are speaking lightly of those who are of the foot. It is a common thing with us all to love only a part of Christ's body, and not to love the whole. But if we love him we should love all his people.

1 JOHN 5

1 JOHN 5:1–5

[1]Whosoever believeth that Jesus is the Christ is born of God: and every one that loveth him that begat loveth him also that is begotten of him. [2]By this we know that we love the children of God, when we love God, and keep his commandments. [3]For this is the love of God, that we keep his commandments: and his commandments are not grievous. [4]For whatsoever is born of God overcometh the world: and this is the victory that overcometh the world, even our faith. [5]Who is he that overcometh the world, but he that believeth that Jesus is the Son of God?

EXPOSITION

1 **Whosoever believeth** *The believing intended here is that which our Lord and his apostles exhorted men to exercise*, and to which the promise of salvation is always attached in the word of God. It is, for instance, the faith that Peter inculcated when he said to Cornelius, "To him give all the prophets witness, that through his name whosoever believeth in him shall receive remission of sins" (Acts 10:43), and that our Lord commanded when he came into Galilee, saying, "Repent ye, and believe the gospel" (Mark 1:15).

Furthermore, *the faith here intended is the duty of all men.* It can never be less than man's duty to believe the truth. Jesus Christ is the truth, and it is the duty of every man to believe it. I understand here "believes" means confidence in Christ. It is surely the duty of men to confide in that which is worthy of confidence. Since it is certain that Jesus Christ is worthy of the confidence of all men, it is therefore the duty of men to confide in him.

At the same time, *this faith, wherever it exists, is in every case, without exception, the gift of God and the work of the Holy Spirit.* A man has never believed in Jesus with the faith here intended unless the Holy Spirit led him to do so. He has wrought all our works in us, and our faith too. Faith is too celestial a grace to spring up in human nature until it is renewed; faith is in every believer "the gift of God" (Eph 2:8).

ILLUSTRATION

The Passover Was a Type of Faith

It was an eminent type of faith when the Hebrew father in Egypt slew the lamb and caught the warm blood in the basin, then took a bunch of hyssop and dipped it in the blood and marked the two posts of his door, and then struck a red mark across the lintel.

That smearing of the door represented faith. The deliverance was wrought by the blood, and the blood availed through the householder's own personally striking it upon his door. Faith does that. It takes the things of Christ and makes them its own. It sprinkles the soul, as it were, with the precious blood, accepts the way of mercy by which the Lord passes over us, and exempts his people from destruction.

---

that Jesus is the Christ The faith intended in the text *evidently rests upon a person*—Jesus. It is not belief about a doctrine, or an opinion, or a formula, but belief concerning a person. Translate the words, "Everyone who believes that Jesus is the Christ," and they stand like this: "Everyone who believes that the Savior is the Anointed." It is assuredly not meant by this whoever professes to believe that he is so, for many do that whose lives prove that they are not regenerate. But whoever believes it to be the fact, as truly and in very deed to receive Jesus as God has set him forth and anointed him, is regenerate.

is born of God You are born again if you believe that Jesus is the Christ. If you are relying upon a crucified Savior, you are assuredly begotten again unto a lively hope. Mystery or no mystery, the new birth is yours if you are a believer. Have you never noticed that the greatest mysteries in the world reveal themselves by the simplest indications? The simplicity and apparent easiness of faith is no reason why I should not regard its existence as an infallible indication of the new birth within.

ILLUSTRATION

Faith and the Telegraph Needle

Go into a telegraph office at any time, and you will see certain needles moving right and left with unceasing click. Electricity is a great mystery, and you cannot see or feel it, but the operator tells you that the electric current is moving along the wire. How does he know? "I know it by the needle." How is that? I could move the needles easily. Yet he who is taught the art sees before him in those needles, not only electric action, but a deeper mystery still. He perceives that a mind is directing the invisible force and speaking by means of it. Not to all, but to the initiated is it given to see the mystery hidden within the simplicity.

The believer sees in the faith, which is as simple as the movements of the needle, an indication that God is operating on the human mind. The spiritual man discerns that there is an inner secret intimated by it that the carnal eye cannot decipher. To believe in Jesus is a better indicator of regeneration than anything else, and in no case has it ever misled. Faith in the living God and his Son Jesus Christ is always the result of the new birth, and can never exist except in the regenerate. Whoever has faith is saved.

---

and every one that loveth him that begat loveth him also that is begotten of him Those who are born of God ought to love all those of the same household. And who are they? All those who have believed that Jesus is the Christ, and are resting their hopes where we rest ours, namely, on Christ the Anointed One of God. We are to love all such. We are to do this because we are of the family. We believe, therefore we have been begotten of God. Let us act as those who are of the divine family. Let us count it our privilege that we are received into the household, and rejoice to perform the lovely obligations of our high position.

2 **By this we know that we love the children of God** Do you love God? Do you love his children? Listen to another word from the same apostle: "We know that we have passed from death unto life, because we love the brethren" (1 John 3:14). That may appear to be a very small evidence, but I can assure you it has often been a great comfort to my soul. I know I love the brothers; I can say to my Lord, "Is there a lamb among your flock I would disdain to feed?" I would gladly cheer and comfort the least of his people. Well, then, if I love the brothers, I love the Elder Brother. If I love the babies, I love the Father, and I know that I have passed over from death to life.

when we love God, and keep his commandments Love is a practical thing; love without obedience is a mere pretense. True love shows itself by seeking to please the one who is loved. May God the Holy Ghost work in us perfect obedience to the commands of God, that we may prove that we really do love him!

3 **For this is the love of God, that we keep his commandments** A man who is not obedient to God's commandments is evidently not a true believer. Although good works do not save us, yet, being saved, believers are sure to produce good works. Though the fruit is not the root of the tree, yet a well-rooted tree will bring forth its fruits in season. So, though the keeping of the commandments does not make me a child of God, yet, being a

child of God, I shall be obedient to my heavenly Father. But I cannot be this unless I love God. A mere external obedience, a decent formal recognition of the laws of God, is not obedience in God's sight. He abhors the sacrifice where the heart is not found. I must obey because I love, or else I have not obeyed at all in spirit and in truth. See then, that to produce the indispensable fruits of saving faith, there must be love for God. Without it, they would be unreal and indeed impossible.

And his commandments are not grevious Anything that makes us think that God's will is burdensome is of the spirit of the world against which we have to fight. If, for instance, we are tempted to think that the restrictions of God's law—his commandments and precepts—are too stringent, it is the spirit of the world that tempts us to think so, for "his commandments are not burdensome" to those who truly love him. It is only to the rebellious world that the restrictions of God appear to be too stringent, or that the commands of Christ become burdensome.

4 **For whatsoever is born of God** Being born again makes us something more than God's creatures; we are God's children. You know that blessed truth of adoption, by which God takes men and adopts them into his family, but regeneration is a great deal more than adoption. We are not only God's adopted children; if we are indeed born from above, we are God's newborn children. The divine nature is actually put into us when we are born of God; is that not a wonderful thing? And that miracle of mercy must be wrought in all of us who are ever to conquer the world.

overcometh the world How is it that the same gospel that always speaks of peace here proclaims warfare? How can it be? Simply because there is something in the world that is antagonistic to love. There are principles that cannot bear light; therefore, before light can come, it must chase the darkness. Before summer reigns, it has to do battle with old winter and to send it howling away in the winds of March, shedding its tears in April showers. So also, before any great or good thing can have the mastery of this world, it must do battle for it.

What is this "world" that we have to overcome? Did God not make the world, and did he not see "every thing that he had made, and, behold, it was very good" (Gen 1:31)? Yes, he did. But after sin entered this world, men came under its power, and now by "the world" is meant all mankind who remain under the power of sin and are enemies to God. "The world" means the whole corrupt mass of human society out of which God has taken a people whom he has chosen for himself, whom he quickens by his Divine Spirit, and whose business it is to overcome the world. They will find that the world—the power of evil—will war against them, and they also must war against it, and the issue of the battle must not long be doubtful. There remains for us only one of two courses: either the world must overcome us and we must yield to it, or else we must overcome the world and cause it to submit to us.

ILLUSTRATION

What Conquering the World Is Not

Alexander the Great, when he was master of the whole world, was the greatest slave in it, for he was discontented even with his victories. The pride of conquest held him in captivity by its iron chain.

He who aims at the highest greatness in this world may only be more greatly selfish than the rest of mankind, and what is that but to be really little? He is truly great who is the most unselfish, and he is the least of all who lives for himself alone.

And this is the victory that overcometh the world, even our faith The instrument with which this new nature fights against the world is faith. Faith conquers, first, *by regarding the unseen reward that awaits us*. The world comes and offers pleasure as the reward of sin, but faith says,

"There are greater pleasures to be had by abstaining from sin." The world says, "Take this gain today," but faith says, "No, I will put what I have out at interest. There is something infinitely better to be had after this." In its beginning, faith generally works in that way; it despises all the treasures of Egypt and values far more the eternal rewards that Christ has laid up for it in heaven.

But as faith grows, it attains to something better than that, for *it recognizes the unseen Presence that is with us*. The world says, "Come with us, and go our way. We will pat you on the back and say that you are a good fellow, and you will have a fine time if you come with us." But faith says, "I do not care how I appear to your eye, for there is another eye that I can see, but you cannot see. God is looking at me, and I am most of all concerned to be right in his sight." Faith realizes that the newborn nature is in the divine presence, and thus makes God's presence to be just as real and just as vivid as the presence of men. That presence of God altogether outweighs the presence of men. That is a higher position than the one I first mentioned, for faith not only regards the unseen reward that awaits the believer, but faith recognizes the unseen presence of God and is moved by an all-constraining desire to please him.

ILLUSTRATION

Hitting the Center

I once saw a colonel shooting at a target. There were two targets near each other, and he hit the center of one of them. The attendant called out, "Which target was that gentleman shooting at?" "The one on the left," was the answer. "I thought so," said the man, "for he hit the one on the right."

There are some people who are always shooting at the world, and it seems to be their great aim to hit it, but the Christian man is always aiming at Christ. If he has not hit the center yet, he will shoot again and again until he does, for his great desire is that he may live for Christ alone, and be found in him, not having his own righteousness "that is of the law, but that is through faith in Christ, the righteousness from God on the basis of faith" (Phil 3:9).

---

5 **Who is he that overcometh the world** What is it to conquer the world? The first thing that is necessary with many who are seeking to overcome the world is *to cut themselves loose from the world's customs*. Every man, sooner or later, finds himself in a world of sin. There are ungodly companions with whom he is linked—evil associations to which he is bound. There are some men who, in their unconverted state, give themselves up entirely to the pleasures of the world, the amusements and frivolities of what is called "society." Now, if such men ever expect to overcome the world, the very first thing they must do is to cut their old connections altogether, to sever all the bonds that unite them to those who lead them into sin.

But that emancipation is merely a beginning. Overcoming the world further consists in *maintaining that freedom*. That fight is the difficulty, and nobody can be victorious in that fight unless he is one of a peculiar race—those who are born of God, born from above. This is a stern battle: when the world surrounds us everywhere, when pleasure tempts us, when gain tries to corrupt us, when poverty assails us, when evil company seeks to sway us. It is hard for us to come out of all our former associations and then to keep out, remaining conquerors over the world throughout the whole of the rest of our life, and being conquerors even in death, having vanquished the world even on our dying bed.

but he that believeth that Jesus is the Son of God It is faith in Jesus that is, first of all, the evidence of the new birth, and that is, afterward, the weapon wielded by the newborn soul with which it fights until it gains the victory over the world.

APPLICATION

Love All Who Are Fathered by God

We look around us and see many others who have believed in Jesus Christ; let us love them because they are of the same kindred. "But some of them are unsound in doctrine; they make gross mistakes as to the Master's ordinances." We are not to love their faults, nor should we expect them to love ours, but we are nevertheless to love them. First I love God, and therefore I desire to promote God's truth and to keep God's gospel free from taint. But then I am to love all those whom God has begotten despite the infirmities and errors I see in them, being also myself "compassed with infirmity" (Heb 5:2). Life is the reason for love. The common life that is indicated by the common faith in the dear Redeemer is to bind us to each other.

Let me beg the members of the church to exhibit mutual love to one another. Are there any feeble among you? Comfort them. Are there any who need instruction? Bring your knowledge to their help. Are there any in distress? Assist them. Are they backsliding? Restore them. "Love one another" is the rule of Christ's family; may we observe it. May the love of God that has been "shed abroad in our hearts by the Holy Ghost which is given unto us" (Rom 5:5) reveal itself by our love to all the saints. And remember, he has "other sheep ... which are not of this fold" (John 10:16); he must bring them in also. Let us love those who have yet to be brought in and lovingly go forth at once to seek them. In whatever other form of service God has given us, let us with loving eyes look after our prodigal brothers. Who knows? We may bring into the family this very day some for whom there will be "joy in the presence of the angels of God" because the lost one has been found (Luke 15:10).

Overcoming the World

Do you not see that you must overcome the world, or else you will perish? But you cannot overcome the world as you are. You must, therefore, be born again. Your only hope lies in your being born of God. This, if it is ever to take place, must be God's work. It is God alone who can do it. You are like ships on their beam-ends; you cannot right yourselves. Cry, therefore, with your whole heart unto God, and ask him to work this miracle in you. He can save you.

He can take away the heart of stone out of your flesh and give you a heart of flesh. He can breathe on the dry bones and make them live. He, the mysterious Father of our spirits, can create in us a new spirit that shall be begotten by himself and be like himself. We must have this, or we can never overcome the world.

We Must Be Born Again for Faith to Conquer

If faith is the conquering weapon, and we intend to be conquerors, we must become believers in the invisible God. In order to exercise faith in the invisible God in Christ Jesus, we must be born again. Until that new nature comes into us, we never do believe in Christ. We may believe a great deal in ourselves; we may believe in worldly society, in its threats or in its bribes, but we do not believe in Christ. Whether you know it or not, that is salvation—to be saved from sin and from self. There is no getting salvation from the groveling meannesses of selfishness except by being born again, for self clings to every man until he is born again, and it is not always gone even then. Satan spoke the truth when he said to the Lord, "Skin for skin, yea, all that a man hath will he give for his life" (Job 2:4). He will not be ready to part with life itself until he gets a higher life, and a better one, imparted to him by the Spirit of God.

If we are to be saved, we must look to God. We must seek salvation at his hands. We must ask him for faith; what a mercy it is that he waits to give it! Be nothing, and God will be everything to you. Get to the end of yourself, and that will be a proof that God has already begun with you. Cease to believe in your own merits or your own virtues. Put away all trust in yourself and come and trust in God as he is revealed in his Son Jesus Christ, and you have received that salvation which will keep on progressing until all sin shall be driven out of you, and you shall dwell forever where Jesus is—as unselfish as Jesus is; as pure, as blessed, as glorious as he is. God grant this to us all, for Christ's sake!

1 JOHN 5:6–12

[6] This is he that came by water and blood, even Jesus Christ; not by water only, but by water and blood. And it is the Spirit that beareth witness, because the Spirit is truth. [7] For there are three that bear record in heaven, the Father, the Word, and the Holy Ghost: and these three are one. [8] And there are three that bear witness in earth, the spirit, and the water, and the blood: and these three agree in one. [9] If we receive the witness of men, the witness of God is greater: for this is the witness of God which he hath testified of his Son. [10] He that believeth on the Son of God hath the witness in himself: he that believeth not God hath made him a liar; because he believeth not the record that God gave of his Son. [11] And this is the record, that God hath given to us eternal life, and this life is in his Son. [12] He that hath the Son hath life; and he that hath not the Son of God hath not life.

EXPOSITION

6 **This is he that came by water and blood, even Jesus Christ**
By the terms "water" and "blood" I understand the purifying and the pardoning effects of Christ's work for his people. He came to purify them from the power of sin that they might no longer live in it; this is indicated by the declaration that he "came by water." He came also to put away the guilt of their sin that they might not be condemned for it; this is set forth by the intimation that he also came "by blood."

The two ordinances of our holy religion were intended, I take it, to sum up the teaching of Christ. The one is baptism, which represents the cleansing of the conscience as the body is washed with water, the death of the soul to the old carnal life, its burial with Christ, and its resurrection to a life of holiness.

Then comes the ordinance of the Lord's Supper, which sets forth, in the broken bread and the poured-out wine, the great truth of Christ's atonement: the fact that he has, by his death, perfected forever all those who have been set apart unto him.

It is very important that we should always carry in our minds the remembrance of these two truths: first, *that Jesus Christ "came by water,"* that is, it was his divine purpose to purify his people and make them holy; and, secondly, *that Jesus Christ "came by blood,"* that is, it was his grand aim and object to deliver his people from the guilt of sin.

not by water only, but by water and blood We might say that all the Lord's prophets who came before Christ in a certain sense "came by water." That is to say, they all sought the purification of the Lord's people. Whether it was Isaiah, whose lips had been touched with the live coal from the altar; or Jeremiah, whose eyes were fountains of tears as he wept over sinners; or Amos, who spoke as a herdsman; or Ezekiel, whose message was one of grandeur and sublimity, the object of every one of them was to purge the people from their sins. It was against sin that they all lifted up their voices, yet none of them could pardon sin, and none of them ever professed to be able to do so. Of all of them it must be said that they came by water only, and not by blood.

Jesus Christ does what the prophets could not do. It is true that he does seek to make his people holy, but it is by his blood that all their sins are forever put away. John the Baptist was the last and the greatest of all the prophets who came before Christ, yet he had to say, "He that cometh after me is mightier than I, whose shoes I am not worthy to bear" (Matt 3:11). John never spoke of his own blood having any power to take away sin, but he pointed to Christ and said, "Behold the Lamb of God, which taketh away the sin of the world" (John 1:29). So far as our Lord's first disciples were concerned, he certainly "came by water," for contact with his unique personality must have tended to purify their lives. Yet he also came "by blood" as well as by water, for it was by virtue of his atoning sacrifice that their sins were blotted out and that they became "accepted in the beloved" (Eph 1:6).

And it is the Spirit that beareth witness, because the Spirit is truth Now the Spirit of God, wherever he abides upon a man, is *the* mark that that man is accepted by God. We do not say that where the Spirit merely strives at intervals there is any seal of divine favor, but where he abides it is assuredly so. The very fact that we possess the Spirit of God is God's testimony and seal in us that we are his and that, as he has sent his Son into the world, even so he sends us into the world.

7 **For there are three that bear record** Our Lord himself was attested by these three witnesses. If you will carefully read in Exodus 29 or in Leviticus 8, you will see that when a priest was ordained (and a priest was a type of Christ) three things were always used: he was washed with water, a sacrifice was brought, and his ear, his thumb, and his toe were touched with blood. Then he was anointed with oil, in token of that unction of the Spirit with which the coming High Priest of our profession would be anointed. Thus every priest came by the anointing Spirit, by water, and by blood, as a matter of type. If Jesus Christ is indeed the Priest that was to come, he will be known by these three signs.

Godly men in the olden times also understood that there was no putting away of sin except with these three things. For proof of this we will quote David's prayer, "Purge me with hyssop"—that is, the hyssop dipped in blood—"and I shall be clean. Wash me"—there is the water—"and I shall be whiter than snow" (Ps 51:7). Then, "Restore unto me the joy of thy salvation; and uphold me with thy free spirit" (Ps 51:12). Thus the blood, the water, and the Spirit were recognized of old as necessary to cleanse from guilt. If Jesus of Nazareth is indeed able to save his people from their sins, he must come with the triple gift—the Spirit, the water, and the blood.

8 **the spirit** Our Lord was attested by *the Spirit*. The Spirit of God bore witness to Christ in the types and prophecies—"holy men of God spake as they were moved by the Holy Ghost" (2 Pet 1:21)—and Jesus Christ answers to those prophecies as exactly as a well-made key answers to the wards of a lock. By the

power of the Holy Spirit our Lord's humanity was fashioned and prepared for him, for the angel said to Mary, "The Holy Ghost shall come upon thee, and the power of the Highest shall overshadow thee: therefore also that holy thing which shall be born of thee shall be called the Son of God" (Luke 1:35). When our Lord in due time commenced his public ministry, the Spirit of God descended on him like a dove and rested on him, and a voice was heard from heaven saying, "This is my beloved Son, in whom I am well pleased" (Matt 3:17). This was indeed one of the surest seals of our Lord's Messiahship, for it had been given by the Spirit of prophecy unto John as a token: "Upon whom thou shalt see the Spirit descending, and remaining on him, the same is he which baptizeth with the Holy Ghost" (John 1:33). The Spirit abode in our Lord without measure, throughout his whole public career, so that he is described as full of the Spirit and led by the Spirit. Hence his life and ministry were full of power. How truthfully he said, "The Spirit of the Lord is upon me, because he hath anointed me to preach the gospel to the poor; he hath sent me to heal the brokenhearted, to preach deliverance to the captives, and recovering of sight to the blind" (Luke 4:18). Peter said, "How God anointed Jesus of Nazareth with the Holy Ghost and with power: who went about doing good, and healing all that were oppressed of the devil; for God was with him" (Acts 10:38). Mighty signs and miracles were the witness of the divine Spirit to the mission of the Lord Jesus. The Spirit abode with our Lord all his life long. And to crown all, after he had died and risen again, the Holy Ghost gave the fullest witness by descending in full power upon the disciples at Pentecost. The Lord had promised to baptize his disciples with the Holy Ghost, and they tarried at Jerusalem in expectation of the gift. They were not disappointed, for all of a sudden "they were all filled with the Holy Ghost, and began to speak with other tongues, as the Spirit gave them utterance" (Acts 2:4). Those cloven tongues of fire and the "rushing mighty wind" (Acts 2:2) were sacred tokens that he who had ascended was Lord and God. The apostles said, "And we are his witnesses of these things; and so is also the Holy Ghost, whom

God hath given to them that obey him" (Acts 5:32). The word of the apostles, through the Holy Spirit, convinced men "of sin, of righteousness, and of judgment" (John 16:8), as the Master had foretold. Then the Spirit comforted the penitents, and they believed in the exalted Savior, and were baptized the same day. The words of Jesus were abundantly fulfilled: "When the Comforter is come, whom I will send unto you from the Father, even the Spirit of truth, which proceedeth from the Father, he shall testify of me" (John 15:26). Thus from our Lord's birth, throughout his life, and after his ascension, the Holy Ghost bore conspicuous witness to him.

and the water It is also manifest that our Lord came with *water* too. He was not unclean, and therefore one would have thought he might dispense with this, but to "fulfill all righteousness" (Matt 3:15). His first step was to be washed in the Jordan by the hands of John the Baptist. He came to the door of his ministry by that baptism in water which indicates that by death, burial, and resurrection, he was about to save his people.

As soon as that baptism had been accomplished—indeed, and before that—you could see that he had come with water, for by water is signified that clean, pure, hallowed life which the outward washing was meant to typify. His first years of obscurity were years of holiness and his years of service were spotless. "In him is no sin" (1 John 3:5). He did not come by water merely as a symbol, but by that which the water meant—by unsullied purity of life. His doctrine was as pure as his example. He was the friend of sinners, but not the apologist for their sins. His tenderness to sinners was that of a physician whose aim is to remove the disease. His whole doctrine is comparable to purifying and life-giving water, and it operated upon men's hearts in that manner. In this last sense especially he came by water.

It is very remarkable how John's Gospel is both the exposition and the text of John's first epistle, for if you turn to it you find our Lord Jesus coming by water at the outset of his teaching. He says to Nicodemus that a man must be "born of water and of the spirit" (John 3:5), to the woman of Samaria he speaks of "living water" (John 4:10), and on the great day of the feast he cries, "If any man thirst, let him come unto me, and drink" (John 7:37). In his ministry he not only issued the invitation, but to all who believed in him he gave of the water of the fountain of life freely. Thus our Lord came by water in the sense of communicating a new, pure, and purifying life to men. The water is the emblem of the new life that springs up within the soul of believers, a life fresh and sparkling, leaping up from the eternal fountains of the divine existence. This life will flow on forever, and widen and deepen like Ezekiel's river, and increase in fullness of power and joy until it unites with the ocean of immortal bliss.

Our Lord closed his life with washing his disciples' feet, a fit conclusion to a life that had by its example been cleansing throughout, and still remains as the grandest corrective of the corrupt examples of the world. Even after death our Lord retained the instructive symbol by giving forth from his pierced heart water as well as blood. John evidently thought this very significant, for when he wrote concerning it he said, "And he that saw it bare record, and his record is true: and he knoweth that he saith true, that ye might believe" (John 19:35). From the Jordan to the cross both the symbol and the substance were with our great Master, while his own personal purity and his gift of life to others proved his mission to be from above.

and the blood With Jesus also was *the blood*. This distinguished him from John the Baptist, who came by water, but Jesus came "not by water only, but by water and blood" (1 John 5:6). We must not prefer any one of the three witnesses to another, but what a wonderful testimony to Christ was the blood! From the very first he came with blood, for John the Baptist cried, "Behold the Lamb of God, which taketh away the sin of the world" (John 1:29). Now, the lamb that takes away sin is a slaughtered lamb, a bleeding lamb, so that John saw that he must bleed for human sin at the time when the baptismal waters were upon him.

Then at last, taking all our sins upon his shoulders in the agony of Gethsemane, the blood bore witness that he was indeed the Lamb of God, and on the tree where he disinterestedly died for his enemies, unselfishly suffering an ignominious doom that he might redeem those who had rejected and scoffed at him, his invincible love triumphed over death itself. However pure the life he led, if he had never died he could not have been the Savior appointed to bear the iniquity of us all. The blood was needed to complete the witness. The blood must flow with the water, the suffering with the serving. The most pious example would not have proved him to be the divine Shepherd if he had not laid down his life for the sheep. Take away the atonement and Jesus is no more than any other prophet. The essential point of his mission is gone. It is evident that he who was to come was to "finish the transgression" and to "make reconciliation for iniquity" (Dan 9:24). This could not be done except by an expiation, and as Jesus has made such an expiation by his own blood, we know him to be the Christ of God. His blood is the seal of his mission, the very life of his work.

and these three agree in one Therefore every true believer should have the witness of each one, and if each one does not witness in due time, there is cause for grave suspicion. For instance, persons have arisen who have said the Spirit of God has led them to do this and that. We inquire of them, what are your lives? Does the water bear witness? Are you pardoned? Does the blood testify for you? If these questions cannot be answered, they may rave as they like about the Spirit of God, but the witness to their salvation is open to the gravest suspicion.

ILLUSTRATION

The Inner Witness Stands Against Flimsy Arguments

When they bring out a new book to disprove Genesis, and another to evaporate the atonement, do not be afraid. As long as the gospel is in the world the devil will find somebody to write books against it. Take no notice of them; they cannot stand against facts. A philosopher once wrote a book to prove that there is no such thing as matter, and a certain reader believed it until he happened to knock his head against the bedpost, and then he abandoned the theory.

When a man feels the power of the Holy Spirit, or the power of the inner life, he does not care to argue. He has a homespun philosophy of facts that answers his purpose better.

---

9 **If we receive the witness of men** We are accustomed to receive the testimony of people. David said, "All men are liars" (Ps 116:11), but he spoke in haste. There would be no history if we did not receive the testimony of people. If we neglected human evidence there could be no courts of law, no trading except for ready money, confidence would cease, and the bands that unite the social fabric would be snapped. We do and must believe the testimony of people as a general rule, and it is only right that we should account witnesses honest until they have proved themselves false. The principle may be pushed too far very readily, and we may take the testimony of people and find ourselves deceived. Still, for all that, the evidence of honest men is weighty, and "in the mouth of two or three witnesses every word may be established" (Matt 18:16; 2 Cor 13:1).

Now God has been pleased to give us a measure of the testimony of people with regard to his Son, Jesus Christ. We have the witness of such men as the four evangelists and the twelve apostles. These men saw Jesus Christ. Some of them were familiar with him for years. They saw evidence of his deity, for they saw him walk the waters and heard him say to the winds and the waves, "Peace, be still" (Mark 4:39), and there was a great calm. These witnesses say that they saw him heal lepers with a touch and open blind men's eyes, and even raise the dead. Three of them tell us that they were on the mountain of transfiguration with him and saw his glory, and heard a voice out of heaven, saying, "This is my beloved Son, in whom I am well pleased; here ye him" (Matt 17:5).

ILLUSTRATION

The Importance of Human Testimony to the Things of God

Some years ago there went into a Methodist class meeting a lawyer who was a doubter, but at the same time a man of candid spirit. Sitting down on one of the benches, he listened to a certain number of poor people, his neighbors, whom he knew to be honest people. He heard some thirteen or fourteen of these persons speak about the power of divine grace in their souls, and about their conversion, and so on. He jotted down the particulars, went home, sat down, and said to himself, "These people all bear witness; I will weigh their evidence." It struck him that if he could get those people into the witness box to testify on his side in any question before a court, he could carry anything. They were persons of different degrees of intellect and education, but they were all persons whom he would like to have as witnesses, persons who could bear cross-examination and by their very tone and manner would win the confidence of the jury. "Very well," he said to himself, "I am as much bound to believe these people about their religious experience as about anything else." He did so, and that led to his believing in the Lord Jesus Christ with all his heart.

You see, the testimony of God to us does in a measure come through people, and we are bound to receive it.

---

the witness of God is greater God is to be believed if all men contradict him. "Let God be true, but every man a liar" (Rom 3:4). One word of God ought to sweep away ten thousand words of men whether they are philosophers of today or sages of antiquity. God's word is to be trusted against them all, for he knows infallibly. He knows his own Son as no one else can; he knows our condition before him; he knows the way to pardon us. There is nothing in God that could lead him to err or make a mistake, and it would be blasphemy to suppose that he would mislead us. It would be an insult to him to suppose that he would willfully mislead his poor creatures by a proclamation of mercy that meant nothing, or by presenting to them a Christ who could not redeem them. The gospel, with God for its witness, cannot be false. Whatever may be the witness against it, the witness of God is greater! We must believe the witness of God.

for this is the witness of God which he hath testified of his Son What is the testimony of God with regard to Christ? How does he prove to us that Jesus Christ really came into the world to save us? He proves it in three ways, according to the context. God's witnesses are *the Spirit*, the water, and the blood. Whenever God the Holy Ghost is pleased to work, whether in revivals or by individual conversions (the wonderful phenomena wrought by him that are miracles in the world of mind as astonishing as the miracles of Christ in the world of matter), God is saying by them, "I declare Christ to be my Son and your Savior, for I have sent the Holy Ghost to prove it."

Then *the water*—that is to say, the purifying power of the gospel is also God's witness to the truth of the gospel. If it does not change men's characters when they receive it, it is not true. If it does not purify and produce virtue and holiness, do not believe it. But because God everywhere—among the most savage tribes or among the most refined of mankind—makes the gospel to be a sacred bath of cleansing to the hearts and lives of men, he gives another witness that his Son is really divine and that his gospel is true.

The blood also witnesses. Does believing in Jesus Christ do what the blood was said to do, namely, give peace with God through the pardon of sin? Does it or not? Hundreds and thousands all over the world affirm that they had no peace of conscience until they looked to the streaming veins of Jesus. Then they saw how God can be just and yet forgive sin. Wherever God gives peace through the blood, that blood witnesses with the Spirit and the water on God's behalf.

10 **He that believeth on the Son of God** Believing in the Son of God comes before the inner testimony. No one can read these words without seeing that a man must be a believer before he has the testimony in himself. *The basis of faith is the testimony of God concerning his Son*—the testimony of God as we find it in holy Scripture. I do not believe Christ Jesus to be the Son of God because of anything I feel within myself, but because God himself declares him to be such. Neither do I trust my soul with Jesus because of certain emotions felt within, but because God, in the book that I accept as his testimony, declares that he has set forth Jesus to be the propitiation for sin. In the Bible I see that God himself witnesses that everyone who trusts Jesus is thereby forgiven, accepted, and saved, and therefore I trust him. We have no other foundation for our faith to rest upon than the witness of God.

Now, *this basis of faith is abundantly sufficient*. Has God said it? Then to ask any confirmation of it is a direct insult to him, a gratuitous impertinence against the majesty of heaven. Has God said it? Then we are more bound to believe than if all the scientific men in the world for centuries had witnessed to it. Has God said it? We are surer of it than if all the traditions of all nations had handed it down to us. Has God said it? Then we are surer of it than if our reason proved it by mathematical demonstration. Has God said it? Then we are more certain of it than if we saw it with our eyes, for they might be deceived, or than if we heard it with our ears, for they might be imposed upon. Our senses are deceivable, but God is not deceivable. He must be true, and we may wisely cast the weight of our souls upon his faithfulness, and take all the consequences, fully assured that what the Lord has promised he is able also to perform.

ILLUSTRATION

Expecting the Cure Before Taking the Medicine

We may not ask for any witness to begin with beyond the testimony of God, nor will any other witness be given. I charge you not to say, "I will believe in God when I obtain the inward witness." No, you are bound to believe in God first, on the sure testimony of his Word. If you believe his Word you shall know the sweets of grace.

To ask for more evidence first is as though a man should say, "Here is a medicine prepared by a physician of great repute, and it is said to be very powerful for driving out the disease from which I suffer. I will take it as soon as I see that I am improving by its means." The man has lost his reason, has he not? He cannot expect even a partial cure until he has taken the medicine. He cannot expect the result to come before the cause. You must take the good Physician's medicine as a matter of faith, and afterward your faith will be increased by the beneficial result.

---

hath the witness in himself The inner witness naturally follows upon faith. And you cannot have this witness apart from faith, because the Holy Ghost never sets his seal to a blank sheet of paper. There must first of all be the writing of faith upon the heart, and then the Spirit of God puts his attesting seal to it. Would you have God the Holy Ghost witness to a falsehood? And yet it would be witnessing to a lie if he gave an inner witness of salvation to a man who is still an unbeliever, and who consequently is condemned already. If you refuse to believe God's Word, how can you think that the Spirit will bear witness of anything in you unless it is to your condemnation? There must be faith going before, and then the witness will follow after.

The inward evidence lies very much this way. First, *a wondrous sense of change* comes over the believer. Having believed in Jesus Christ on the simple evidence of God, there is a work of regeneration performed on him and he feels himself altogether transformed.

Then there is a *wondrous power that goes with the Word of God*—not always, but often. Are you not conscious of often feeling when you are reading the Word, or hearing it, as you never did feel when listening to any other form of speech? Get to the foot of the cross, for instance, and look up, and view the flowing of your Savior's precious blood. Do you not feel then as nothing else can make you feel? You are reading a religious book and it has a holy effect on you, but if you reflect you will see that it is only powerful because it is borrowed from the Word of God.

A similar witness is borne by *a sense of being put into our right place*. You were all out of place before, but having believed in Jesus Christ you are put in your right position. You stand in harmony with the divine system, and this you feel could only be effected by the truth, for a lie works to disorder and not to right.

The *deep feeling of peace* that comes to us through believing in Jesus makes us feel quite sure again that he can save and that we are secure in him. We took God at his word when we had no feeling, but having believed in Jesus Christ we are now conscious of a wonderful rest—"The peace of God, which passeth all understanding" (Phil 4:7). We see that we are forgiven, justly forgiven, saved by mercy, but still not to the violation of the justice of God, and therefore we are perfectly at ease.

ILLUSTRATION

Not Having the Inner Witness

You might be the possessor of a large estate, and an adversary might contest your right to it, and you might not be able to find your title deeds. The estate might be yours clearly enough, but those deeds of yours might be mislaid and locked up in a forgotten drawer, and perhaps you might be sorely put to it until the day of trial settled the dispute as to whether it is yours or not.

I believe that many children of God have plenty of witness in their own soul, but they do not have the wisdom to perceive it. They have plenty of witness, but through ignorance or carelessness they do not collect it and refresh themselves with it. They believe they have the witness within themselves, and they will be comforted if they have light enough to know what the witness is, but often through negligence in searching the Word of God they have the witness, but cannot discover it.

He that believeth not God hath made him a liar They are guilty of this sin who deny that Jesus is the Messiah, the promised Savior, the Son of God. Out of heaven God himself declared, "This is my beloved Son, in whom I am well pleased" (Matt 3:17; 17:5). Peter truly said at Pentecost that Jesus of Nazareth was "a man approved of God among you by miracles and wonders and signs, which God did by him in the midst of you" (Acts 2:22). God says in many ways, "He is my beloved Son," and if you say he is not you make God a liar. That is clear enough.

If you continue to say you cannot believe God and that Christ is not to be trusted, what will happen to you? It is written, "He that believeth not shall be damned" (Mark 16:16). May you never know what that means, but you will know it as sure as you live if you continue in unbelief. God is not a liar, but if he does not damn the man who dies an unbeliever he will be. Therefore depend upon it that he will do it. If he is false he may let you escape, but if he is true he will cast you into hell. There is nothing else before you.

because he believeth not the record that God gave of his Son There are some who deny his deity. Over and over in Scripture we are told that Jesus Christ is God "manifest in the flesh" (1 Tim 3:16). "The Word was God" (John 1:1). "For by him were all things created, that are in heaven, and that are in earth, visible and invisible" (Col 1:16). He is "called Wonderful, Counseller, The mighty God" (Isa 9:6). The miracles that Christ wrought, and especially his resurrection from the dead, all prove his deity, the Father bearing witness that he is his equal.

I will pass on. A poor trembling, weeping sinner comes to me, and among other things he says, "My sins are so great that I do not believe they can be pardoned." I meet him this way:

God says, "Though your sins be as scarlet, they shall be as white as snow; though they be red like crimson, they shall be as wool" (Isa 1:18).

"But my sin is very great indeed."

"The blood of Jesus Christ his Son cleanseth us from all sin" (1 John 1:7).

"But my transgressions have been exceedingly aggravated."

"Let the wicked forsake his way, and the unrighteous man his thoughts: and let him return unto the LORD, and he will have mercy upon him; and to our God, for he will abundantly pardon" (Isa 55:7).

"I cannot believe it."

Stand up, then, and tell the Lord so in the plainest manner, "God, you have said you will abundantly pardon, but it is a lie." I challenge you to make that avowal outright, for you are making it in your hearts. It is idle to deny it, for it is so. God says, "I will and I can pardon," and you say he cannot—what is that but accusing the Lord of falsehood?

ILLUSTRATION

Seeing According to Your Eyes

When a dove flies over a landscape it sees the clear streams and the fields of corn, but when a vulture passes over the same landscape what does it see? A dead horse here and there, a carcass, or a piece of carrion. Everybody sees according to his eyes. A graceless, impure-minded man cannot see purity.

Christ said to the proud Pharisees, "How can ye believe, which receive honour one of another, and seek not the honour that cometh from God only?" (John 5:44).

Their pride stood in the way. In every case in which a man declares concerning the Lord Jesus, "I cannot believe," the difficulty is in himself, not in the facts to be believed or in the evidence of those facts.

---

11 **And this is the record, that God hath given to us eternal life, and this life is in his Son** Our only hope lies in Christ. There is life for us in Christ, and life eternal, if we only believe in him. That is the gospel in brief, what Luther would have called a little Bible, containing a condensation of the whole revelation of God.

12 **He that hath the Son hath life** Of course, by "life" here is meant not mere existence or natural life, for we all have that whether we have the Son of God or no. We are all created living souls in the image of the first Adam, and continue in life until the Lord recalls the breath from our nostrils. The life here intended is spiritual life, the life received at the new birth, by which we perceive and enter into the heavenly kingdom, come under new and spiritual laws, are moved by new motives, and exist in a new world.

By the term "has the Son" we understand possessing the Lord Jesus Christ. Faith appropriates the finished work of Jesus. We trust in Christ, and Christ becomes ours. As the result of grace in our souls, we choose the Lord Jesus as the ground of our dependence, and then we accept him as the Lord of our hearts, the guide of our actions, and supreme delight of our souls. The one who has the Son, then, is a man who is trusting alone in Jesus, in whom Jesus Christ rules and reigns. Such a man is most surely the possessor of spiritual and eternal life at the present moment. It is not said "shall have life"—he *has* it, he enjoys it now, he is at this hour a quickened spirit. God has breathed into him a new life, by which he is made a partaker of the divine nature and is one of the seed according to promise, and he has this life by virtue of his having received the Son of God to be his all.

ILLUSTRATION

Faith Is the Mark on the Battlefield

See the battlefield, strewn with men who have fallen in the terrible conflict! Many have been slain; many more are wounded. There they lie in ghastly confusion, the dead all stark and stiff, covered with their own crimson, and the wounded faint and bleeding, unable to leave the spot where they have fallen. Surgeons have gone over the field rapidly, ascertaining which are corpses beyond the reach of mercy's healing hand and which are men who are faint with loss of blood. Each living man has a paper fastened conspicuously on his breast, and when the soldiers are sent out with the ambulances to gather up the wounded, they do not need to stay and judge which may be living and which may be dead. They see a mark on the living, and they bear them to the hospital where their wounds may be dressed.

Now faith in the Son is God's infallible mark, which he has set upon every poor wounded sinner whose bleeding heart has received the Lord Jesus. Though he faints and feels as lifeless as though he were mortally wounded, yet he most surely lives if he believes, for the possession of Jesus is the token that cannot deceive. Faith is God's mark witnessing in unmistakable language—"this soul lives."

It is a great mercy that having the Son is abiding evidence. "The one who has the Son *has* the life." I know what it is to see every other evidence I ever gloried in go drifting down the stream far out of sight. It is frequently my inward experience to see sin and unworthiness marked upon everything I have ever done for God. As far as he has done any good thing by me or in me, it lives, but often as I look back on my years of ministry and see multitudes of sermons, and prayers, and other efforts, I have thought of them all as being less than nothing and vanity, tainted, and marred, and spoiled by my personal imperfections. I could not depend on them to make so much as a feather's weight toward my salvation. When you begin to doubt your inward graces and to judge all your past life and find it wanting, it is sweet even then to say, "One thing I know: I rest in Jesus."

he that hath not the Son of God hath not life That is, he does not have spiritual life. The sentence of death is recorded against him in the book of God. His natural life is spared him in this world, but he is condemned already and is in the eye of the law dead while he lives. The unbeliever has no spiritual life; he neither laments his soul's need nor rejoices that it may be supplied. He lives without prayer and he knows nothing of secret fellowship with God because he has no inward life to produce these priceless things.

APPLICATION

By Water and By Blood

Jesus Christ must come to you "by blood" or else he will never come to you "by water." Christ never gives a man holiness of life unless that man accepts him as the great propitiation for sin. If you ask how Christ can come to you by water and by blood, the only way that I know is the one that I have pointed out to you over and over again. It is this: You are a sinner, lost and undone; Jesus Christ came to seek and to save the lost. To do this, he had to take the sinner's place, bear the sinner's guilt, and suffer the penalty that the sinner deserved to suffer. "He was wounded for our transgressions, he was bruised for our iniquities: the chastisement of our peace was upon him; and with his stripes we are healed" (Isa 53:5).

And rest assured that there never was a sinner who trusted Christ and then was told that he had no right to trust him. He himself said, "Him that cometh to me I will in no wise cast out" (John 6:37), and he will not cast you out if you come to him. Can you believe that his blood was shed for you? Do you dare to rest your soul's salvation on the great work of which he said, "It is finished," before he bowed his head and gave up the ghost (John 19:30)? Will you now trust Christ as your Substitute and Savior?

If you have received Christ in this way as coming to you by blood, I feel sure that you will also believe that he has come to you by water, to purify you from all defilement. Therefore, you will not any longer knowingly and willfully continue in sin. The gratitude that you must feel in your heart for all that Christ has done for you will constrain you to walk before him in holiness and humility and to seek to obey his will at all times.

Never Substitute the Inner Testimony for the Word's Testimony

Excellent as the inner witness is, it must never be put in the place of the divine witness in the Word. Why not? Because it would insult the Lord and be contrary to his rule of salvation by faith. Moreover, it is not always with us in equal clearness; or rather, we cannot equally discern it. If the brightest Christian begins to base his faith upon his experience and his attainments, he will be in bondage before long.

Build on what God has said, not on your inward joys. Accept these precious things not as foundation stones but as pinnacles of your spiritual temple. Let the main thing be to believe because God has spoken. If any other evidence comes to your net, accept it, but go you on fishing by faith: faith in God, in God's naked Word.

Then, if the Lord's hand should turn, and in providence you should be stripped bare like Job so that you sit on a dunghill covered with sore boils, you will be able to say, "I believed that God loved me when he gave me children; I believed God loved me when I had sheep and oxen; I believed that God loved me when I had camels and donkeys; still these were not the grand reasons of my faith, but God himself. Therefore I still believe that he loves me, now that every child is dead and all my property is swept away, and I myself am sick. 'Though he slay me, yet will I trust in him'" (Job 13:15). That is faith. God grant you to have faith that can sing, "Although the fig tree shall not blossom ... and there shall be no herd in the stalls: yet I will rejoice in the LORD" (Hab 3:17–1 8). Though there are no evidences of grace in me, though there are no joys, though there is a broken peace, though there is sin to mourn over, though there is hardness of heart to stagger me, yet still I took the Lord Jesus as a sinner's Savior at first, and I take him as a sinner's Savior still. I did not trust him at first because I was a saint, and now I will not doubt him because I find out more and more that I am a sinner. But I will still go to him just as I am and rest on the great salvation that God has provided for me.

The Unbeliever Lost Because of Unbelief

Not only will the unbeliever be lost, but he will be lost by his unbelief. Thus says the Lord, "The one who does not believe has already been judged." Why? "Because he hath not believed in the name of the only begotten Son of God" (John 3:18). Has he not committed a great deal else that will condemn him? Yes, a thousand other sins are upon him, but justice looks for the most flagrant offense to write it as a superscription over his condemned head. It selects this monster sin and writes, *"Judged, because he has not believed in the name of the one and only Son of God."*

When the Spirit of God came into the world to convince men of sin, he began by convincing them of the greatest of all. Which did he choose as the most glaring? "Of sin, because they believe not on me" (John 16:9). I am only telling you what I find in the Scriptures. His word is sharper than a two-edged sword, and I ask him to make it cut to your very marrow—to wound and kill, so that afterward Christ may make alive. By your reason that is yet left to you, by your love for yourselves, by heaven and by hell, by the bleeding wounds of Jesus, and by the truth of God, I entreat you accept Jesus. May the Holy Ghost go with my entreaties that your souls may relent, that your stony hearts may melt before the cross, and you may receive Jesus Christ to be your all in all this day.

The Living Among the Dead

Since the living are constrained to live among the dead, since the children of God are mixed up by providence with the heirs of wrath, what manner of persons should they be? In the first place, let us take care that we do not become contaminated by the corruption of the dead. You who have the Son of God, take care that you are not injured by those who do not have the Son. I have heard of some professed Christians wanting to see the ways of the ungodly, going into low places of amusement to judge for themselves. Such conduct is dangerous and worse. I would feel very much afraid to go into hell, to put my head between the lion's jaws for the sake of looking down his throat. I would think I was guilty of a gross presumption if I went into the company of the lewd and the profane to see what they were doing. I would fear that perhaps it might turn out that I was only a mere professing Christian, and so should taint myself with the dead matter of the sin of those with whom I mingled and perish in my iniquity. "Wherefore come out from among them, and be ye separate, saith the Lord, and touch not the unclean thing" (2 Cor 6:17). The resort of the ungodly is not the place for you. "Follow me," said Christ, "and let the dead bury their dead" (Matt 8:22).

If we must in this life, in a measure, mingle with the dead, let us take care that we never allow the supremacy of the dead to be acknowledged over the living. It would be a strange thing if the dead were to rule the living. Yet sometimes I have seen the dead have the dominion of this world. They have set the fashion, and living Christians have followed. The carnal world has said, "This is the way of trade!" and the Christian man has replied, "I will follow the custom." Christian, this must not be. You might say, "I must do as others do, for you know we must live." This also is not true, for there is no necessity for our living. There is a very great necessity for our dying sooner than living, if we cannot live without doing wrong. Christian, you must never permit corruption to conquer grace. By God's grace, if you get at all under the power of custom, you must cry out, "O wretched man that I am! Who shall deliver me from the body of this death?" (Rom 7:24). You must wrestle until you conquer, and cry, "I thank God through Jesus Christ our Lord!"

What I think we should do toward dead souls is this—we should pity them. When the early Christians dwelled in the catacombs where they could not go about without seeing graves, they must have had strange thoughts arising in their minds. Now, you are in a similar plight. You cannot walk through London without thinking, "Most of those I meet are dead in sin." Some of these dead souls live in your own house. When you go out to work, you have to stand at the same bench with spiritually dead men. You cannot turn aside from your daily labor to enter the house of God without meeting the dead even there. Should this not make us pray for them: "Eternal Spirit, quicken them! They cannot have life unless they have the Son of God. Bring them to receive the Son of God"?

In connection with such prayer, be diligent to deliver the quickening message. The quickening message is, "Believe and live." "Whosoever believeth that Jesus is the Christ is born of God" (1 John 5:1). Should you living ones not be perpetually repeating the great life-word, depending on the Holy Spirit to put energy into it? Seek to win souls, and from this day, separating yourselves from the world as to its maxims and its customs, plunge into the very thick of it where you can serve your Master, plucking brands from the burning and winning souls from going down to the pit.

1 JOHN
5:13–21

13 These things have I written unto you that believe on the name of the Son of God; that ye may know that ye have eternal life, and that ye may believe on the name of the Son of God. 14 And this is the confidence that we have in him, that, if we ask any thing according to his will, he heareth us: 15 And if we know that he hear us, whatsoever we ask, we know that we have the petitions that we desired of him. 16 If any man see his brother sin a sin which is not unto death, he shall ask, and he shall give him life for them that sin not unto death. There is a sin unto death: I do not say that he shall pray for it. 17 All unrighteousness is sin: and there is a sin not unto death. 18 We know that whosoever is born of God sinneth not; but he that is begotten of God keepeth himself, and that wicked one toucheth him not. 19 And we know that we are of God, and the whole world lieth in wickedness. 20 And we know that the Son of God is come, and hath given us an understanding, that we may know him that is true, and we are in him that is true, even in his Son Jesus Christ. This is the true God, and eternal life. 21 Little children, keep yourselves from idols. Amen.

EXPOSITION

13 **These things have I written unto you that believe** This epistle, and this particular text in it, were written for all those who believe in the name of the Son of God. All the epistles are so written. They are not letters to everybody; they are letters to those who are called to be saints. No person, young or old, is excluded from this text, unless he is an unbeliever.

If you inquire why it is not addressed to unbelievers, I answer: simply because it would be preposterous to wish men to be assured of that which is not true. John never wished that a man who had not believed in Jesus Christ should think that he had eternal life; it would be a fatal error. If "he that believeth not shall be damned" (Mark 16:16), how could he have an assurance of possessing it? Faith is a necessary preliminary to assurance. Do not dream of being sure that you are saved apart from making sure that you have trusted yourselves with the crucified Savior. The atonement presented by Jesus Christ, the Son of God, gives assurance of salvation to all who trust in it, but to no one else.

ILLUSTRATION

Faith Naturally Develops Assurance

Take pure and unadulterated milk, and let it stand, and you will soon get cream. Faith is the milk, and full assurance is the cream upon it. When faith has stood long enough, you may see the rich cream of holy confidence on the top of it.

---

on the name of the Son of God Do you believe that Jesus is the Anointed One of God? Is he so to you? Is he anointed as your prophet, priest, and king? Have you realized his anointing so as to put your trust in him? Do you receive Jesus as appointed by God to be the Mediator, the Propitiation for sin, the Savior of men? If so, you are born of God. "How may I know this?" Our evidence is the witness of God himself. We need no other witness. Suppose an angel were to tell you that you are born of God; would that be a more sure testimony than the infallible Scripture? If you believe that Jesus is the Christ, you are born of God. John has thus positively declared the truth that you may know that you have eternal life. Can anything be more clear than this?

so that you may know that you have eternal life A large number of Christ's people who may be perfectly sound in the doctrinal view of the nature of eternal life do not know that they possess it at this present moment. John would not have our assurance vary with the thermometer or turn with the weather vane. He says, "These things have I written unto you ... that ye may *know* that ye have eternal life." He would have us certain that we are partakers of the new life, and so know it as to reap the golden fruit of such knowledge, and be filled with joy and peace through believing.

I find even the commentators, when they try to write on this text, and most of the preachers who have left us printed sermons upon it, read the text as if it said, "that you may know that you *shall have* eternal life." They speak about the full assurance that we shall one day enter into glory. I beg their pardon, the text does not say anything of the kind. It is "that ye may know that ye *have* eternal life," even here, at this present hour. The spiritual life that is in the believer at this moment is the same life that shall be in him in heaven. The grace-life is the glory-life in the bud: the same life, only less developed.

When he says, "that ye may know that ye have eternal life," I think his first meaning is *that you may know that everybody who believes in Jesus Christ has eternal life*. This is not a fact about you and a few others only, but it is a general truth—everyone who believes in the name of the Son of God has eternal life. We may not doubt this. It is not a matter of inference and deduction, but a matter of revelation from God. You are not to form an opinion on it, but to believe it, for the Lord has said it.

I think that John in this passage meant something more—namely, *he would have us know that we personally have eternal life by having us know that we do personally believe in Jesus*. It is one thing to know that every believer has eternal life, but it is quite another thing to know that I am a believer so as to have eternal life myself. The largest provisions of grace are useless to us unless we have a personal interest in them. It is true that every believer has eternal life, but what if I am not a believer?

ILLUSTRATION

Reading a Will in Two Ways

You begin to read a will, but you do not find it interesting. It is full of words and terms that you do not take the trouble to understand because they have no relation to yourself. But if you should, in reading that will, come upon a clause in which an estate is left to you, the nature of the whole document will seem changed to you. You will be anxious now to understand the terms, and to make sure of the clauses, and you will even wish to remember every word of the clause that refers to yourself.

May you read the Testament of our Lord Jesus Christ as a testament of love to yourself, and then you will prize it beyond all the writings of the sages.

14 **And this is the confidence that we have in him, that, if we ask any thing according to his will, he heareth us** From the assurance of our interest in Christ, the next step is to a firm belief in the power of prayer, in the fact that God does regard your prayer. You can hardly get this unless you have attained to an assurance of your own interest in him, for my belief in the prevalence of my prayer to a great extent must depend upon my conviction of my interest in Christ. For instance, here is Paul's argument: "He that spared not his own Son, but delivered him up for us all, how shall he not with him also freely give us all things?" (Rom 8:32). I must therefore be sure that God has given me Christ. If he has given Christ to me, then I know that he will give me all things. But if I have any doubt about Christ's being mine, and about my being the receiver of God's unspeakable gift in Christ, I cannot reason as the apostle did, and I cannot therefore have that confidence that my prayer is heard.

15 **we know that we have the petitions that we desired of him** Let me commend the habit of expecting an answer to prayer, and looking for it, for many reasons. I will give you an outline of them.

By this means, *you honor God's ordinance of prayer*. He who prays without expecting to receive a return mocks the mercy seat of God. By not expecting to receive anything from God, you in effect despise the throne of grace. Of what use can the mercy seat be if God has said, "Seek ye my face" (Ps 27:8), in vain? If no answers come to supplication, then supplication is a vain waste of time. You play with prayer when you do not expect an answer. The truly prayerful man is resolved in his own soul that he must have the answer. He feels his need of it; he sees God's promise; his heart is stirred to earnestness, and he cannot be satisfied to go away without some token for good.

Such a spirit, in the next place, having honored prayer, also *honors God's attributes*. To believe that the Lord will hear my prayer is honor to his truthfulness. He has said that he will, and I believe that he will keep his word. It is honorable to his power. I believe that he can make the word of his mouth stand fast and steadfast. It is honorable to his love. The larger things I ask, the more I honor the liberality, grace, and love of God in asking such great things. It is honorable to his wisdom. If I ask what he has told me to ask, and expect him to answer me, I believe that his word is wise and may safely be kept.

Again, to believe that God hears prayer, and to look for an answer, is truly *to reverence God himself*. If I stand with a friend, and I ask him a favor, and when he is about to reply to me I turn away and open the door and go to my business, what an insult this is! It is not always considered courteous if you do not answer a person, but it is always discourteous if, after having asked a question, you do not stop to have it answered. Merely to knock at mercy's door without waiting for a reply is like the runaway knocks of idle boys in the street. You cannot expect an answer to such prayers. Stand on your watchtower and "hear what God the Lord will speak: for he will speak peace unto his people, and to his saints: but let them not turn again to folly" (Ps 85:8).

Furthermore, to believe in the result of prayer this way *tries and manifests faith*. When we pray and expect the answer, this is a sure token that our prayer has not been a mere formality.

Then Faith lays hold of God, and she waits, Patience standing by her side, knowing that the windows of heaven, however fast they may be closed, will open soon, and God's right hand will scatter his liberality upon waiting souls. So Faith waits and watches, and waits and watches again.

Such a habit, moreover, helps *to bring out our gratitude to God*. None sing so sweetly as those who get answers to prayer. Some of you would give my Master sweet songs if you only noticed when he hears you. But perhaps the Lord may drop an answer to your prayer, and you merely cry, "It is a fortunate circumstance," and God gets no praise for it. If, instead, you had been watching for it, and seen it come, you would fall on your knees in holy gratitude.

ILLUSTRATION

Not Caring about the Response to a Petition

If I send a petition to a man's door, and then having earnestly asked, or pretended to ask earnestly, I am utterly careless about the answer, I have not treated the man respectfully. If that person should send me a letter in return to my request, and I should not even take the trouble to open it, how could I provoke him worse?

So you first ask God to grant you a favor, and then you do not stop to get it. And when he sends it, you receive it as a matter of course and do not praise it as a gracious answer to your supplication. Let me commend to you the gracious art of believing in the success of your prayer, because in this way you will help to ensure your own success.

---

16 **If any man see his brother sin a sin which is not unto death** What then? He should run all over the place and tell everybody about it? No! That is not what the apostle

says, yet I have seen something like that carried into practice. But when I look into the Bible, I do not see anything about talking of this sin to our fellow men. Something is said about talking of it to God, and this is what every true Christian should do. If you see any man sin, mind that you ask for pardon for the erring one.

he shall ask, and he shall give him lifc for them that sin not unto death He who has committed the sin that leads to death has no desire for forgiveness. He will never repent; he will never seek faith in Christ, but he will continue hardened and unbelieving. He will from this point on never be the subject of holy influences, for he has crossed over into that dark region of despair where hope and mercy never come.

Perhaps some of you think that you have committed that unpardonable sin, and are at this moment grieving over it. If so, it is clear that you cannot have committed that sin, or else you would not grieve over it. If you have any fear concerning it, you have not committed the sin that leads to death, for even fear is a sign of life. Whoever repents of sin and trusts in Jesus Christ is freely and fully forgiven; therefore it is clear that he has not committed a sin that will not be forgiven. There is much in this passage to make us prayerful and watchful, but there is nothing here to make a single troubled heart feel anything like despair. He who is born again, born from above, can never commit this unpardonable sin. He is kept from it. "The wicked one toucheth him not" (1 John 5:18), for he is preserved by sovereign grace against this dreadful damage to his soul.

There is sin leading to death "What is it?" someone asks. Wouldn't you like to know? If you did know that, you could go and commit all other sins except that one, could you not? But would that be any help to your piety? Certainly not. Your business is to keep as far away from all sin as you can, whether it is leading to death, or not leading to death.

ILLUSTRATION

Not Knowing Where the Traps Are Set

You may sometimes have seen a notice put up on certain estates in the country, "Mantraps and spring guns set here." If so, did you ever go around to the front door of the mansion and say, "Will you tell me where the mantraps are, and whereabouts the spring guns are set?" If you had asked that question, the answer would have been, "It is the very purpose of this warning not to tell you where they are, for you have no business to trespass there at all."

So "all unrighteousness is sin" (1 John 5:17), and you are warned to keep clear of it. "There is a sin unto death" (1 John 5:16), but you are not told what that sin is on purpose that you may, by the grace of God, keep clear of sin altogether.

I do not say that he shall pray for it John does not in such a case forbid our prayers, neither does he encourage them, but I take it that he gives us a permit to pray on. We do not know for certain that the most guilty person has indeed passed the boundary of mercy, and therefore we may intercede with hope. If we have a horrible dread upon us that possibly our erring relative is beyond hope, if we are not commanded to pray, we are certainly not forbidden. It is always best to err on the safe side, if it is erring at all. We may still go to God, even with a forlorn hope, and cry to him in the extremity of our distress. We are not likely to hear the Lord say to us, "How long wilt thou mourn for Saul?" (1 Sam 16:1) We are not likely to hear him say, "How long will you pray for your boy? How long will you mourn over your husband? I do not intend to save them." We do not have such depressing revelations, and we ought to be very thankful that we do not, for now we may go on hopefully pleading for all who come in our way. We may continue, and should continue, as Samuel did, to wrestle in prayer as long as we live.

17 **All unrighteousness is sin** If a thing is not right—if it is not right all around—it is sin, be sure of that. I heard the other day of a man who was said to be a splendid Christian Godward, but a wretched creature manward. There cannot be such a monstrosity as that. Such a man as that was not a Christian at all. Our righteousness, if it is real and true, must be an all-around righteousness, toward men as well as toward God.

and there is a sin not unto death There are multitudes of such sins. But there is a place, beyond which, if a man passes in sin, he becomes dead from that point, and utterly insensible. He will never be quickened and never be saved.

18 **We know that whosoever is born of God sinneth not** How can it be true that "whosoever is born of God sinneth not," yet men who are fathered by God do sin? That question has puzzled many, but we must remember that every man of God is two men in one. That new part of him, which is fathered by God—that new nature which was implanted in regeneration—cannot sin because it is fathered by God. It is the imperishable seed that lives and endures forever (1 Pet 1:23). But, as far as the man is still in the flesh, it is true that "the carnal mind is enmity against God: for it is not subject to the law of God, neither indeed can be" (Rom 8:7). The old nature sins through the force of nature, but the new nature does not sin because it is fathered by God.

but he that is begotten of God keepeth himself, and that wicked one toucheth him not We are so one with Christ that while the Head lives the members cannot die. We are so one with Christ that the challenge is given, "Who shall separate us from the love of Christ?" (Rom 8:35). A list is added of things that may be supposed to separate, but we are told that they cannot do so, for "in all these things we are more than conquerors through him that loved us" (Rom 8:37). Is it not clear, then, that we are quickened with a life so heavenly and divine that we can never die?

I entreat you to keep a hard and firm grip on this blessed doctrine of the perseverance of the saints. How earnestly do I long "that ye may know that ye have eternal life" (1 John 5:13)! Away with your doctrine of being alive in Christ today and dead tomorrow. Hold fast to eternal salvation through the eternal covenant carried out by eternal love unto eternal life.

19 **And we know that we are of God, and the whole world lieth in wickedness** Doubts may arise when we are being instructed. Doubts may still trouble us when we apprehend and understand. But when we come to be acquainted with Jesus, they are less likely to haunt us. Out of fellowship with Jesus springs the higher state of absolute certainty as to divine things.

John himself was very certain. He allows no force to the evidence even of a contradicting world, because one man abiding in the truth has more weight in his witness than millions under the power of the father of lies. This is a blessed state to get into—that of certainty. I am utterly amazed at hearing it continually asserted that the thoughtful public teacher must make great allowances for "the spirit of the age, which is one of earnest skepticism." I do not believe it. The spirit of the age is that of thoughtlessness and trifling. But what do I or any other Christian man have to do with the spirit of the age? The spirit that is in us by which we ought to speak is the Spirit of God and not the spirit of the age.

20 **And we know that the Son of God is come** We know the great facts of the gospel, and this is no small blessing. Myriads of our fellow creatures are unaware of the first principles of the faith, scarcely knowing that there is a God, and altogether ignorant of the wondrous plan of redemption by the blood of Jesus. Even in this (so-called) Christian country there is much ignorance about these things. I wish that Christian people would more frequently question others about what they know of Christ. No book is less read, in proportion to its circulation, than the Bible, and certainly no book is less understood. With all the preaching we have—and some of it is very excellent—there is everywhere a great ignorance of the rudimentary truths of the gospel of Jesus Christ. The language that is used in the pulpit is not understood at all by most people. The

preacher is somewhere up in the clouds; they learn nothing from his big words. They suppose it is all right, and very good, and they listen to it, but as far as instruction is concerned many a preacher might almost as well speak in Syriac.

It is a happy thing to know that Jesus Christ, the Son of God, has come in the flesh, that he took upon himself the sins of his people, that he bore the wrath of God on their behalf, that by believing in him men are justified from all things from which they could not be justified by the law of Moses. It is a blessed thing to know that in him "we have redemption through his blood" (Eph 1:7) and sanctification and eternal life. It is a blessed thing to know the Holy Ghost, to know that he converts the soul, and comforts, and illuminates, and guides, and sanctifies. It is well to know something of the future life, to know the doctrine of election, the doctrine of effectual calling, and the doctrine of the eternal security of the saints. There are many who have not found out these truths. If we have done so, it is not a thing to boast of, but a matter to be very thankful for.

and hath given us an understanding, that we may know him that is true No one knows the true God in the real sense of knowledge except through Jesus Christ, for "no man cometh unto the Father" except by the Son (John 14:6). But even if he could know God, in a measure, apart from the revelation of him in Christ Jesus, it would be a knowledge of terror that would make him flee away and avoid God. It would not be life to our souls to know God apart from his Son, Jesus Christ. We must know the Christ whom he has sent or our knowledge does not bring eternal life to us. But when we see God in Christ meeting us, demanding a penalty and yet providing it himself, decreeing the punishment most justly and then bearing it himself, when we see him to be both Judge and expiation, both Ruler and sacrifice, then we see that "herein is love, not that we loved God, but that he loved us, and sent his Son to be the propitiation for our sins" (1 John 4:10). It is in the knowledge of God in Christ and God through Christ that we find that we have entered into eternal life.

ILLUSTRATION

Knowing God, Not Just Knowing about Him

A friend comes to you and he says, "Do you know such and such a person?" You say first, "I know there is such a person"—that is instruction. Being further asked, "But do you know him?" you answer, "Well, I know that he was a fine tall man, a soldier in the infantry, and that he went to the Crimea." That is a sort of knowing him by apprehension, but does not fully answer the question, "Do you *know* him?" You say, "Well, I cannot say that I *know* him, for if I were to see him I could not recognize him. I have never even spoken to him."

To be acquainted with a man is a higher order of knowledge than this. In that sense believers know God, and know Jesus Christ, and know the Holy Spirit. They are acquainted with God.

and we are in him that is true, even in his Son Jesus Christ There is nothing like life in Christ. Life in heaven is only life in Christ; if he were gone from the realms of bliss, there would be no life in heaven itself. The center, the core, the soul of the everlasting joy of the redeemed lies in the fact of Christ being with them and their knowing him. "This is life eternal" (John 17:3): to know Jesus Christ whom God has sent, and to know God in him.

This is the true God, and eternal life It would not be eternal life to know Jesus Christ if he were not God—if, as some say, he was only a good man. It is impossible that he was only a good man, for he was the worst of impostors if he was not God. He spoke of himself as God, and if he was not divine then he imposed on men. If he were nothing but a mere man, how could he give us eternal life? And what help would it be to trust in him? But if he who bled on Calvary was "very God of very God," as well as man, then the sacrifice he offered has an infinite value about it, and I dare trust my soul to him with the full assurance that there must be, in such a Savior, ability to "save them to the uttermost that come unto God by him" (Heb 7:25).

21 **Little children** I do not think that John meant literally to address little children, nor do I think he merely referred to a certain class of believers who are very little in grace. I think he addressed himself to the whole body of believers to whom he was writing and, through them, that he addressed the whole church of Christ.

This is, first, *a title of deep affection*. The Christian church is the home of Christian love. When it is what it should always be, it is a family, it is "the household of faith" (Gal 6:10) of which God himself is the Father, the Lord Jesus is the Elder Brother, and all the members are brothers—all equal, all one in Christ Jesus, all seeking to serve the rest, laying themselves out to be servants to the whole band of brothers and sisters in Christ. It seems most appropriate that an aged apostle, such as John doubtless was when he wrote this epistle, should have looked around on the younger members of the Lord's family and should have called them "little children."

The title "little children" also *indicates the humility of those who are rightly called by that name*. A little child is not proud. He does not meddle with high things; he is content to sit at his father's feet or to lie in his mother's bosom. And Christians, being born again—born from above—become like little children; otherwise they could not enter the kingdom of heaven. They were very great people once, but they are very little now.

Moreover, *this title denotes teachableness*. A little child will go to school. A little child is not above learning his letters. We cannot often get men to do this, especially in spiritual things. They are so crusted over with prejudice that they think they know all they need to know. It is little that they do know, and even that little is wrong, yet it is enough to keep them from being willing to be taught what they really need to learn. Truly blessed is the man who is a little child in relation to God.

And little children, too, have *faith*. What a great deal of faith they usually have, and how wicked it is for anyone ever to trifle with the faith of little children! It is really scandalous when nurses and others tell little children idle tales and foolish stories that the children believe to be true. We should be very careful and jealous concerning the faith that little children repose in their elders and never do or say anything to weaken their belief. Little children have a very beautiful faith, especially when the word of their father is concerned. Let us be little children of that sort toward God: unquestioningly believing whatever he says to us, not asking how or why it is so, but being quite prepared to be told that we cannot yet understand everything and that all we have to do is implicitly believe all that our Heavenly Father says.

So far, we see that it is a good thing to be called little children, but I think there is another view of the matter that we must not forget: *the title also implies weakness*. Little children are very apt to be led astray, and so are we. Surrounded as we are by hosts of idolaters, we are all too apt to be swayed by their example.

Little children also have this weakness: they need, as a rule, something to see. You cannot teach them so well in any other way as you can by pictures and models. That tendency is also manifest in us spiritually; we have a craving for signs and symbols. The great mass of people—even Christian people—want something or other that they can see.

Little children also have a very bounded range. Put a little child down with a few broken platters and a little dirt, and he will amuse himself by the hour. It does not seem to strike him that he may grow up to be a man and have to work for his living, or manage a big business like his father does. It is, under some aspects, a great blessing to be such a child as that, but it is a pity that we are so prone to be thus childish spiritually. We are so much engrossed in the present that, if we have a little trouble, we fret over it as if that trouble would last for years. Little children, it is because of this special weakness of yours that the apostle has said, "Keep yourselves from idols."

keep yourselves from idols I do not need to say, *Guard yourselves from all sorts of visible idols*, for I trust that you abhor them as much as I do. But I must speak concerning other idols.

First, *keep yourselves from worshiping yourselves*. Some fall into this sin by indulgence at the table. How much eating, and especially drinking, is nothing better than gluttony and drunkenness! There are others who worship themselves by living a life of indolence. They have nothing to do, and they seem to do it very thoroughly. They take their ease, and that is the main thing in which they take any interest. Do not worship yourselves by trifling as these indolent people do. Some worship themselves by decorating their bodies most elaborately; their first and their last thought is, "Wherewithal shall we be clothed?" (Matt 6:31). Do not fall into that idolatry.

Then *there are some people who make idols of their wealth*. Getting money seems to be the main purpose of their lives. Now, it is right that a Christian man should be diligent in business. He should not be second to anybody in the diligence with which he attends to the affairs of this life, but it is always a pity when we can be truthfully told, "So-and-so is getting richer every year, but he has gotten stingier also. He gives less now than he gave when he had only half as much as he now has."

ILLUSTRATION

A Guinea Purse and a Shilling Heart

We meet occasionally with people like the man who, when he was comparatively poor, gave his guinea, but when he grew rich, he only gave a shilling. His explanation was that when he had a shilling purse, he had a guinea heart; but when he had a guinea purse, he found that he had only a shilling heart. It is always a pity when hearts grow smaller as means grow greater.

Remember that it will be only a little while before you must leave all that you have. What is the use of your having it at all unless you really enjoy it? And how can you so truly enjoy it as you can when you lay it at your Savior's feet and use it for his glory?

> *Some worship the pursuit that they have undertaken.* They give their whole soul up to their art, or their particular calling, whatever it may be. In a certain sense, this is a right thing to do. But we must never forget that the first and great commandment is, "Thou shalt love the Lord thy God with all thy heart, and with all thy soul, and with all thy mind" (Matt 22:37). This must always have the first place.
>
> Let me here touch a very tender point. *There are some who make idols of their dearest relatives and friends.* Some have done this with their children. Make no idol of your child, or your wife, or your husband. By putting them into Christ's place, you really provoke him to take them from you. Love them as much as you please—I would that some loved their children, their husbands, or their wives more than they do—but always love them in such a fashion that Christ shall have the first place in your hearts.

APPLICATION

Our Duty to Obtain Assurance

It is our duty to obtain full assurance. We should not have been commanded to give diligence to make our calling and election sure if it were not right for us to be sure. I am sure it is right for a child of God to know that God is his Father and never to have a question in his heart as to his sonship. I know it is right for a soul that is married to Christ to know the sweet love of the Bridegroom and never to tolerate a cloud of suspicion to come between the soul and the full enjoyment of Christ's love. For this reason, I would urge you onward to know that you have eternal life. John, being dead, yet speaks out of the Bible: he calls on you to know that the Son of God is come, and has given us an understanding that we may know him that is true, and that we are in him that is true, even in his Son Jesus Christ. He bids us as believers firmly repose our souls upon the promise of our faithful God.

Try to Get Assurance

If John wished us to know that we have eternal life, let us try to know it. The Word of God was written for this purpose; let us use it for its proper end. The whole of these Scriptures were written that we "might believe that Jesus is the Christ, the Son of God; and that believing ye might have life through his name" (John 20:31). This Book is written to you who believe so that you may know that you believe. Will you allow your Bibles to be a failure to you? Will you live in perpetual questioning and doubt? If so, the Book has missed its mark for you. The Bible is sent that you may have full assurance of your possession of eternal life. Do not, therefore, dream that it will be presumptuous on your part to aspire to it. Our conscience tells us that we ought to seek full assurance of salvation. It cannot be right for us to be children of God and not to know our own Father. How can we kneel down and say, "Our Father which art in heaven" (Matt 6:9), when we do not know whether he is our Father or not? Until the spirit of adoption enables you to cry, "Abba, Father," where is your love to God? Can you rest? Do you dare rest while it is a question whether you are saved or not?

I ask you, make sure work for eternity. If you leave anything in uncertainty, let it concern your body or your estate, but not your soul. Conscience bids you seek to know that you have eternal life, for without this knowledge many duties will be impossible to perform. Are you not bidden to make your calling and election sure? Are you not a thousand times over exhorted to rejoice in the Lord, and to give thanks continually? But how can you rejoice if the dark suspicion haunts you that perhaps, after all, you do not have the life of God? You must get this question settled or you cannot rest in the Lord and wait patiently for him. I ask you, as you would follow Scripture and obey the Lord's precepts, get the assurance without which you cannot obey them.

Reasons to Believe in God's Answering Prayer

Let us believe in God's answering prayer because *we have God's promise for it*. Hear what he says: "Thou shalt make thy prayer unto him, and he shall hear thee" (Job 22:27); "But know that the Lord hath set apart him that is godly for himself: the Lord will hear when I call unto him" (Ps 4:3); "He shall call upon me, and I will answer him" (Ps 91:15); "Call upon me in the day of trouble: I will deliver thee, and thou shalt glorify me" (Ps 50:15); "And it shall come to pass, that before they call, I will answer; and while they are yet speaking, I will hear" (Isa 65:24); "And all things, whatsoever ye shall ask in prayer, believing, ye shall receive" (Matt 21:22); "For every one that asketh receiveth; and he that seeketh findeth; and to him that knocketh it shall be opened" (Matt 7:8; Luke 11:10); "And whatsoever ye shall ask in my name, that will I do, that the Father may be glorified in the Son" (John 14:13); "And whatsoever we ask, we receive of him, because we keep his commandments, and do those things that are pleasing in his sight" (1 John 3:22). How is it possible after this that God should refuse to hear us? Do we have promise upon promise, and will he break them all? God forbid. If there is a God, and if this Book is his Word, if God is true, prayer must be answered.

Again, prayer must be answered because *of the character of God our Father*. Will he let his children cry and not hear them? He hears the young ravens, and will he not hear his own people? He is a God of love. Remember his loving-kindness, and you cannot, I think, doubt that he hears prayer. A God who hears prayer, this is his memorial throughout all generations. Do not rob him of his character by distrusting him.

Then think of the *efficacy of the blood of Jesus*. When you pray it is the blood that speaks. Every drop of Jesus's blood cries, "Father, hear him! Father, hear him! Hear the sinner's cry!" That blood was sprinkled on the mercy seat that the mercy seat might be an efficacious mercy seat for you. Do not doubt the blood of Christ. Can he die, and yet that blood have no more efficacy in it than the blood of bulls or of goats? You would not think this; then do not doubt that prayer prevails.

Think, again, that *Jesus pleads*. He points to the wound upon his breast and spreads his pierced hands. Shall the Father deny the Son? Shall prayers offered by Christ be cast out from heaven's register? These things must not—cannot—be.

Besides, *the Holy Spirit* himself is the author of your prayers. Will God incite the desire and then not hear it? Shall there be a schism between the Father and the Holy Spirit? You will not dream of such a thing. Believe me, when I review my own personal experience during the fifteen years that I have known something of the Savior, it leads me to feel that it is as certain that God hears prayer as that twice two make four. It is as certain as that the rock, falling by the law of gravitation, seeks the earth.

I ask you by the love you bear to Jesus, do him the honor of believing in the prevalence of his plea. By the light and life you have received from the Holy Ghost, do not discredit him by thinking he can teach you to pray a prayer that will not be accepted before God. Let us stand on our watchtower and look. Let us meet again and again at special meetings, and let us cry mightily unto the Most High, pouring out our hearts like water before him. He will open the windows of heaven and give us greater blessings than we have ever had before, great as those already received have been. Let the season of prayer begin, and let it be sustained. It is to believers that these words are spoken. May God lead you who are not believers to trust in Jesus.

Guard Yourselves from Idols

I do not need to say to you that we must carefully preserve our integrity in the matter of worshiping anything that can be seen. No child of God may dare to worship a picture, an image, or anything that is visible. But keep yourselves from all other idols: from the idols of your own brain, from creeds of your own making, from thoughts of your own imagining. Keep yourselves from letting anything but God rule you. Keep yourselves from the love of fame; keep yourselves from the adoration of human science. Keep yourselves from allowing anything but God to get the upper hand of you. Do not make gods of yourselves, your own persons. Do not make gods of your families; do not make gods of your children. It must be God first, God last, God in the middle, and God without end. May he make it so with us that, from now on, we shall have this eternal life, which consists in knowing the only true God and Jesus Christ whom he has sent (John 17:3)!

In the matter of your faith, be sure to keep yourselves from the idol of the hour. Some of us have lived long enough to see the world's idols altered any number of times. Just now, in some professedly Christian churches, the idol is "intellectualism," "culture," "modern thought." Whatever name it bears, it has no right to be in a Christian church, for it believes very little that appertains to Christ. Now, I have some respect for a downright honest infidel, like Voltaire or Tom Paine; but I have none for the man who goes to college to be trained for the Christian ministry and then claims to be free to doubt the deity of Christ, the need of conversion, the punishment of the wicked, and other truths that seem to me to be essential to a full proclamation of the gospel of Christ.

Keep yourselves from this idol of the times, for it is the precursor of death to any church that gives it admittance. Unitarianism, to which this so-called liberality of thought always goes, is a religion of a parasitical kind. It flourishes by feeding on the life of other churches, just as the ivy clings to the oak, and sucks the life out of it. Let us tear this ivy down wherever we find it beginning its deadly work. Believe me that the church of Christ, if not the world, shall yet learn that the highest culture is a heart that is cultivated by divine grace, that the truest science is the science of Jesus Christ and him crucified, and that the greatest thought and the deepest of all metaphysics are found at the foot of the cross. The men who will keep on simply and earnestly preaching the old-fashioned gospel and the people who will stand fast in the old paths are the ones who will most certainly win the victory.

Sources

1 John 1:1–4

"Expositions by C. H. Spurgeon: Genesis 24:1–16; 1 Samuel 30:1–13; 1 John 1:1–3." In *The Metropolitan Tabernacle Pulpit Sermons*, 61:237–40. London: Passmore & Alabaster, 1915.

"Exposition by C. H. Spurgeon: 1 John 1, and 2:1–6." In *The Metropolitan Tabernacle Pulpit Sermons*, 50: 503–4. London: Passmore & Alabaster, 1904.

"Fellowship with the Father and the Son (1 John 1:3)." In *The Metropolitan Tabernacle Pulpit Sermons*, 50:493–502. London: Passmore & Alabaster, 1904.

"Fellowship with God (1 John 1:3)." In *The Metropolitan Tabernacle Pulpit Sermons*, 7:489–96. London: Passmore & Alabaster, 1861.

"Fulness of Joy Our Privilege (1 John 1:4)." In *The Metropolitan Tabernacle Pulpit Sermons*, 60:229–39. London: Passmore & Alabaster, 1914.

"How to Become Full of Joy (1 John 1:4)." In *The Metropolitan Tabernacle Pulpit Sermons*, 57:493–502. London: Passmore & Alabaster, 1911.

"The Incomparable Bridegroom and His Bride (Song 5:9)." In *The Metropolitan Tabernacle Pulpit Sermons*, 42:277–85. London: Passmore & Alabaster, 1896.

1 John 1:5–10

"The Child of Light Walking in Light (1 John 1:6–7)." In *The Metropolitan Tabernacle Pulpit Sermons*, 33:553–64. London: Passmore & Alabaster, 1887.

"The Evil and Its Remedy (1 John 1:7)." In *The New Park Street Pulpit Sermons*, vol. 4:465–72. London: Passmore & Alabaster, 1858.

"Exposition by C. H. Spurgeon: 1 John 1, and 2:1–6." In *The Metropolitan Tabernacle Pulpit Sermons*, 50: 503–4. London: Passmore & Alabaster, 1904.

"Expositions by C. H. Spurgeon: Psalm 33 and 1 John 1." In *The Metropolitan Tabernacle Pulpit Sermons*, 41:369–72. London: Passmore & Alabaster, 1895.

"Expositions by C. H. Spurgeon: Psalm 130; 1 John 1:4–7." In *The Metropolitan Tabernacle Pulpit Sermons*, 61:251–2. London: Passmore & Alabaster, 1915.

"Expositions by C. H. Spurgeon: Psalm 130:1–8; 1 John 1:1–10; 2:1 and 2." In *The Metropolitan Tabernacle Pulpit Sermons*, 57:465–68. London: Passmore & Alabaster, 1911.

"Honest Dealing with God (1 John 1:8–10)." In *The Metropolitan Tabernacle Pulpit Sermons*, 21:361–72. London: Passmore & Alabaster, 1875.

"Justice Satisfied (1 John 1:9)." In *The New Park Street Pulpit Sermons*, 5:241–48. London: Passmore & Alabaster, 1859.

"Walking in the Light and Washed in the Blood (1 John 1:7)." In *The Metropolitan Tabernacle Pulpit Sermons*, 11:673–84. London: Passmore & Alabaster, 1865.

1 John 2:1–11

"1 John 2:1–11." In The Interpreter: Spurgeon's Devotional Bible, 753. Grand Rapids: Baker Publishing House, 1964.

"The Child of Light Walking in Light (1 John 1:6–7)." In *The Metropolitan Tabernacle Pulpit Sermons*, 33:553–64. London: Passmore & Alabaster, 1887.

"Exposition by C. H. Spurgeon: 1 John 2." In *The Metropolitan Tabernacle Pulpit Sermons*, 57:429–32. London: Passmore & Alabaster, 1911.

"Exposition by C. H. Spurgeon: 1 John 2; and 3:1–2." In *The Metropolitan Tabernacle Pulpit Sermons*, 52:442–44. London: Passmore & Alabaster, 1906.

"Expositions by C. H. Spurgeon: Psalm 130:1–8; 1 John 1:1–10; 2:1 and 2." In *The Metropolitan Tabernacle Pulpit Sermons*, 57:465–68. London: Passmore & Alabaster, 1911.

"'Herein Is Love' (1 John 4:10–11)." In *The Metropolitan Tabernacle Pulpit Sermons*, 29:109–20. London: Passmore & Alabaster, 1883.

"In Him: Like Him (1 John 2:6)." In *The Metropolitan Tabernacle Pulpit Sermons*, 29:409–20. London: Passmore & Alabaster, 1883.

"A Sermon to the Lord's Little Children (1 John 2:12–13)." In *The Metropolitan Tabernacle Pulpit Sermons*, 29:157–68. London: Passmore & Alabaster, 1883.

"Sincerity and Duplicity (1 John 2:3–4)." In *The Metropolitan Tabernacle Pulpit Sermons*, 16:169–80. London: Passmore & Alabaster, 1870.

"The Sinner's Advocate (1 John 2:1)." In *The Metropolitan Tabernacle Pulpit Sermons*, 9:337–48. London: Passmore & Alabaster, 1863.

1 John 2:12–29

"Church Increase (Isaiah 49:20–21)." In *The Metropolitan Tabernacle Pulpit Sermons*, 46:433–44. London: Passmore & Alabaster, 1900.

"A Description of Young Men in Christ (1 John 2:13–14)." In *The Metropolitan Tabernacle Pulpit Sermons*, 29:205–16. London: Passmore & Alabaster, 1883.

"Exposition by C. H. Spurgeon: 1 John 2." In *The Metropolitan Tabernacle Pulpit Sermons*, 51:335–36. London: Passmore & Alabaster, 1905.
"Exposition by C. H. Spurgeon: 1 John 2." In *The Metropolitan Tabernacle Pulpit Sermons*, 57:429–32. London: Passmore & Alabaster, 1911.
"Exposition by C. H. Spurgeon: 1 John 2; and 3:1–2." In *The Metropolitan Tabernacle Pulpit Sermons*, 52:442–44. London: Passmore & Alabaster, 1906.
"Fathers in Christ (1 John 2:13–14)." In *The Metropolitan Tabernacle Pulpit Sermons*, 29:637–48. London: Passmore & Alabaster, 1883.
"The Light of the World (Matthew 5:14)." In *The Metropolitan Tabernacle Pulpit Sermons*, 19:241–52. London: Passmore & Alabaster, 1873.
"Positivism (1 John 5:18–20)." In *The Metropolitan Tabernacle Pulpit Sermons*, 55:433–44. London: Passmore & Alabaster, 1909.
"Preparation for the Coming of the Lord (1 John 2:28)." In *The Metropolitan Tabernacle Pulpit Sermons*, 35:505–16. London: Passmore & Alabaster, 1889.
"A Sermon to the Lord's Little Children (1 John 2:12–13)." In *The Metropolitan Tabernacle Pulpit Sermons*, 29:157–68. London: Passmore & Alabaster, 1883.
"Unto You, Young Men (1 John 2:14)." In *The Metropolitan Tabernacle Pulpit Sermons*, 14:277–88. London: Passmore & Alabaster, 1868.

1 John 3:1–10

"'And We Are': A Jewel from the Revised Version (1 John 3:1)." In *The Metropolitan Tabernacle Pulpit Sermons*, 32:673–84. London: Passmore & Alabaster, 1886.
"The Beatific Vision (1 John 3:2)." In *The New Park Street Pulpit Sermons*, 2:57–69. London: Passmore & Alabaster, 1856.
"The Christian's Manifestation (1 John 3:2)." In *The Metropolitan Tabernacle Pulpit Sermons*, 52:433–44. London: Passmore & Alabaster, 1906.
"Exposition by C. H. Spurgeon: 1 John 3." In *The Metropolitan Tabernacle Pulpit Sermons*, 42:514–16. London: Passmore & Alabaster, 1896.
"Exposition by C. H. Spurgeon: 1 John 3." In *The Metropolitan Tabernacle Pulpit Sermons*, 43:141–44. London: Passmore & Alabaster, 1897.
"Exposition by C. H. Spurgeon: 1 John 3." In *The Metropolitan Tabernacle Pulpit Sermons*, 51:526–28. London: Passmore & Alabaster, 1905.
"The Hope That Purifies (1 John 3:3)." In *The Metropolitan Tabernacle Pulpit Sermons*, 57:49–60. London: Passmore & Alabaster, 1911.
"Light, Natural and Spiritual (Gen 1:1–5)." In *The Metropolitan Tabernacle Pulpit Sermons*, 11:637–48. London: Passmore & Alabaster, 1865.
"A Present Religion (1 John 3:2)." In *The New Park Street Pulpit Sermons*, 4:249–56. London: Passmore & Alabaster, 1858.

"A Sermon to the Lord's Little Children (1 John 2:12–13)." In *The Metropolitan Tabernacle Pulpit Sermons*, 29:157–68. London: Passmore & Alabaster, 1883.

"The Sinful Made Sinless (1 John 3:4–5)." In *The Metropolitan Tabernacle Pulpit Sermons*, 43:133–41. London: Passmore & Alabaster, 1897.

"The Works of the Devil Destroyed (1 John 3:8)." In *The Metropolitan Tabernacle Pulpit Sermons*, 29:361–72. London: Passmore & Alabaster, 1883.

1 John 3:11–18

"Am I Clear of His Blood? (Genesis 4:10)." In *The Metropolitan Tabernacle Pulpit Sermons*, 8:409–20. London: Passmore & Alabaster, 1862.

"Christian Sympathy—A Sermon for the Lancashire Distress (Job 30:25)." In *The Metropolitan Tabernacle Pulpit Sermons*, 8:625–36. London: Passmore & Alabaster, 1862.

"The Church's Love to Her Loving Lord (Song 1:7)." In *The Metropolitan Tabernacle Pulpit Sermons*, 11:349–60. London: Passmore & Alabaster, 1865.

"The Death of Christ for His People (1 John 3:16)." In *The Metropolitan Tabernacle Pulpit Sermons*, 46:1–8. London: Passmore & Alabaster, 1900.

"Exposition by C. H. Spurgeon: 1 John 3." In *The Metropolitan Tabernacle Pulpit Sermons*, 42:514–16. London: Passmore & Alabaster, 1896.

"Exposition by C. H. Spurgeon: 1 John 3." In *The Metropolitan Tabernacle Pulpit Sermons*, 43:141–44. London: Passmore & Alabaster, 1897.

"Exposition by C. H. Spurgeon: 1 John 3." In *The Metropolitan Tabernacle Pulpit Sermons*, 51:526–28. London: Passmore & Alabaster, 1905.

"Exposition by C. H. Spurgeon: 1 John 3:10–24." In *The Metropolitan Tabernacle Pulpit Sermons*, 55:588. London: Passmore & Alabaster, 1909.

"God's Love to the Saints (1 John 3:16)." In *The Metropolitan Tabernacle Pulpit Sermons*, 51:517–26. London: Passmore & Alabaster, 1905.

"Life Proved by Love (1 John 3:14)." In *The Metropolitan Tabernacle Pulpit Sermons*, 44:73–82. London: Passmore & Alabaster, 1898.

"A Sermon to the Lord's Little Children (1 John 2:12–13)." In *The Metropolitan Tabernacle Pulpit Sermons*, 29:157–68. London: Passmore & Alabaster, 1883.

"What Is the Verdict? (1 John 3:21)." In *The Metropolitan Tabernacle Pulpit Sermons*, 31:445–56. London: Passmore & Alabaster, 1885.

1 John 3:19–24

"The Conditions of Power in Prayer (1 John 3:22–24)." In *The Metropolitan Tabernacle Pulpit Sermons*, 19:169–80. London: Passmore & Alabaster, 1873.

"Exposition by C. H. Spurgeon: 1 John 3." In *The Metropolitan Tabernacle Pulpit Sermons*, 42:514–16. London: Passmore & Alabaster, 1896.

"The Lower Courts (1 John 3:20–21)." In *The Metropolitan Tabernacle Pulpit Sermons*, 55:325–36. London: Passmore & Alabaster, 1909.
"The Warrant of Faith (1 John 3:23)." In *The Metropolitan Tabernacle Pulpit Sermons*, 9:529–40. London: Passmore & Alabaster, 1863.
"What Is the Verdict? (1 John 3:21)." In *The Metropolitan Tabernacle Pulpit Sermons*, 31:445–56. London: Passmore & Alabaster, 1885.

1 John 4:1–11

"Expositions by C. H. Spurgeon: Acts 25 and 26; and 1 John 4." In *The Metropolitan Tabernacle Pulpit Sermons*, 55:341–48. London: Passmore & Alabaster, 1909.
"Exposition by C. H. Spurgeon: 1 John 4." In *The Metropolitan Tabernacle Pulpit Sermons*, 40:503–4. London: Passmore & Alabaster, 1894.
"Exposition by C. H. Spurgeon: 1 John 4." In *The Metropolitan Tabernacle Pulpit Sermons*, 47:274–76. London: Passmore & Alabaster, 1901.
"Expositions by C. H. Spurgeon: 1 John 4 and Philippians 4:1–9." In *The Metropolitan Tabernacle Pulpit Sermons*, 41:10–12. London: Passmore & Alabaster, 1895.
"Hearing with Heed (Mark 4:24)." In *The Metropolitan Tabernacle Pulpit Sermons*, 43:169–78. London: Passmore & Alabaster, 1897.
"Helps to Full Assurance (1 John 5:13)." In *The Metropolitan Tabernacle Pulpit Sermons*, 30:397–408. London: Passmore & Alabaster, 1884.
""Herein Is Love" (1 John 4:10–11)." In *The Metropolitan Tabernacle Pulpit Sermons*, 29:109–20. London: Passmore & Alabaster, 1883.
""Herein Is Love" (1 John 4:10)." In *The Metropolitan Tabernacle Pulpit Sermons*, 42:25–33. London: Passmore & Alabaster, 1896.
"Love's Climax (1 John 4:10)." In *The Metropolitan Tabernacle Pulpit Sermons*, 41:1–9. London: Passmore & Alabaster, 1895.
"Love's Logic (1 John 4:19)." In *The Metropolitan Tabernacle Pulpit Sermons*, 17:481–92. London: Passmore & Alabaster, 1871.
"A Sermon to the Lord's Little Children (1 John 2:12–13)." In *The Metropolitan Tabernacle Pulpit Sermons*, 29:157–68. London: Passmore & Alabaster, 1883.
"Sham Conversion (2 Kgs 17:25, 33, 34)." In *The Metropolitan Tabernacle Pulpit Sermons*, 51:145–54. London: Passmore & Alabaster, 1905.
"The Works of the Devil Destroyed (1 John 3:8)." In *The Metropolitan Tabernacle Pulpit Sermons*, 29:361–72. London: Passmore & Alabaster, 1883.

1 John 4:12–16

"Exposition by C. H. Spurgeon: 1 John 4." In *The Metropolitan Tabernacle Pulpit Sermons*, 47:274–76. London: Passmore & Alabaster, 1901.
"Exposition by C. H. Spurgeon: 1 John 4:9–21." In *The Metropolitan Tabernacle Pulpit Sermons*, 38:238–40. London: Passmore & Alabaster, 1892.

"Expositions by C. H. Spurgeon: 1 John 4 and Philippians 4:1–9." In *The Metropolitan Tabernacle Pulpit Sermons*, 41:10–12. London: Passmore & Alabaster, 1895.
"Love's Logic (1 John 4:19)." In *The Metropolitan Tabernacle Pulpit Sermons*, 17:481–92. London: Passmore & Alabaster, 1871.
"A Psalm of Remembrance (1 John 4:16)." In *The New Park Street Pulpit Sermons*, 5:225–32. London: Passmore & Alabaster, 1859.
"The Sealing of the Spirit (Eph 1:13–14)." In *The Metropolitan Tabernacle Pulpit Sermons*, 22:157–68. London: Passmore & Alabaster, 1876.
"Seeing and Testifying (1 John 4:14)." In *The Metropolitan Tabernacle Pulpit Sermons*, 40:493–502. London: Passmore & Alabaster, 1894.

1 John 4:17–21

"Expositions by C. H. Spurgeon: Acts 25 and 26; and 1 John 4." In *The Metropolitan Tabernacle Pulpit Sermons*, 55:341–48. London: Passmore & Alabaster, 1909.
"Exposition by C. H. Spurgeon: 1 John 4." In *The Metropolitan Tabernacle Pulpit Sermons*, 40:503–4. London: Passmore & Alabaster, 1894.
"Exposition by C. H. Spurgeon: 1 John 4." In *The Metropolitan Tabernacle Pulpit Sermons*, 47:274–76. London: Passmore & Alabaster, 1901.
"Exposition by C. H. Spurgeon: 1 John 4:9–21." In *The Metropolitan Tabernacle Pulpit Sermons*, 38:238–40. London: Passmore & Alabaster, 1892.
"Expositions by C. H. Spurgeon: 1 John 4 and Philippians 4:1–9." In *The Metropolitan Tabernacle Pulpit Sermons*, 41:10–12. London: Passmore & Alabaster, 1895.
"Love (1 John 4:19)." In *The New Park Street Pulpit Sermons*, 5:33–40. London: Passmore & Alabaster, 1859.
"Love's Birth and Parentage (1 John 4:19)." In *The Metropolitan Tabernacle Pulpit Sermons*, 22:337–48. London: Passmore & Alabaster, 1876.
"Love's Great Reason (1 John 4:19)." In *The Metropolitan Tabernacle Pulpit Sermons*, 60:133–42. London: Passmore & Alabaster, 1914.
"Love's Logic (1 John 4:19)." In *The Metropolitan Tabernacle Pulpit Sermons*, 17:481–92. London: Passmore & Alabaster, 1871.
"The Secret of Love to God (1 John 4:19)." In *The Metropolitan Tabernacle Pulpit Sermons*, 47:265–74. London: Passmore & Alabaster, 1901.

1 John 5:1–5

"The Blessing of Full Assurance (1 John 5:13)." In *The Metropolitan Tabernacle Pulpit Sermons*, 34:265–76. London: Passmore & Alabaster, 1888.
"Exposition by C. H. Spurgeon: 1 John 5." In *The Metropolitan Tabernacle Pulpit Sermons*, 47:622–24. London: Passmore & Alabaster, 1901.
"Exposition by C. H. Spurgeon: 1 John 5." In *The Metropolitan Tabernacle Pulpit Sermons*, 57:262–64. London: Passmore & Alabaster, 1911.

"Faith and Regeneration (1 John 5:1)." In *The Metropolitan Tabernacle Pulpit Sermons*, 17:133–44. London: Passmore & Alabaster, 1871.
"Love's Logic (1 John 4:19)." In *The Metropolitan Tabernacle Pulpit Sermons*, 17:481–92. London: Passmore & Alabaster, 1871.
"Victorious Faith (1 John 5:4–5)." In *The Metropolitan Tabernacle Pulpit Sermons*, 47:589–600. London: Passmore & Alabaster, 1901.
"The Victory of Faith (1 John 5:1)." In *The New Park Street Pulpit Sermons*, 1:101–8. London: Passmore & Alabaster, 1855.

1 John 5:6–12

"Alive or Dead—Which? (1 John 5:12)." In *The Metropolitan Tabernacle Pulpit Sermons*, 13:325–36. London: Passmore & Alabaster, 1867.
"'By Water and Blood' (1 John 5:6)." In *The Metropolitan Tabernacle Pulpit Sermons*, 57:253–62. London: Passmore & Alabaster, 1911.
"Exposition by C. H. Spurgeon: 1 John 5." In *The Metropolitan Tabernacle Pulpit Sermons*, 53:622–24. London: Passmore & Alabaster, 1907.
"Exposition by C. H. Spurgeon: 1 John 5." In *The Metropolitan Tabernacle Pulpit Sermons*, 57:262–64. London: Passmore & Alabaster, 1911.
"Faith, and the Witness Upon Which It Is Founded (1 John 5:9–10)." In *The Metropolitan Tabernacle Pulpit Sermons*, 21:37–48. London: Passmore & Alabaster, 1875.
"The Priest Dispensed With (1 John 5:10)." In *The Metropolitan Tabernacle Pulpit Sermons*, 21:469–80. London: Passmore & Alabaster, 1875.
"The Sealing of the Spirit (Eph 1:13–14)." In *The Metropolitan Tabernacle Pulpit Sermons*, 22:157–68. London: Passmore & Alabaster, 1876.
"A Solemn Impeachment of Unbelievers (1 John 5:10)." In *The Metropolitan Tabernacle Pulpit Sermons*, 20:685–96. London: Passmore & Alabaster, 1874.
"The Three Witnesses (1 John 5:8)." In *The Metropolitan Tabernacle Pulpit Sermons*, 20:445–56. London: Passmore & Alabaster, 1874.
"The True Position of the Witness Within (1 John 5:10)." In *The Metropolitan Tabernacle Pulpit Sermons*, 24:445–56. London: Passmore & Alabaster, 1878.

1 John 5:13–21

"The Blessing of Full Assurance (1 John 5:13)." In *The Metropolitan Tabernacle Pulpit Sermons*, 34:265–76. London: Passmore & Alabaster, 1888.
"Consulting with Jesus (1 Kgs 10:1, 3)." In *The Metropolitan Tabernacle Pulpit Sermons*, 48:217–28. London: Passmore & Alabaster, 1902.
"Eternal Life! (1 John 5:20–21)." In *The Metropolitan Tabernacle Pulpit Sermons*, 41:25–33. London: Passmore & Alabaster, 1895.
"Exposition by C. H. Spurgeon: 1 John 5." In *The Metropolitan Tabernacle Pulpit Sermons*, 47:622–24. London: Passmore & Alabaster, 1901.

"Exposition by C. H. Spurgeon: 1 John 5." In *The Metropolitan Tabernacle Pulpit Sermons*, 53:622–24. London: Passmore & Alabaster, 1907.
"Exposition by C. H. Spurgeon: 1 John 5." In *The Metropolitan Tabernacle Pulpit Sermons*, 57:262–64. London: Passmore & Alabaster, 1911.
"Praying and Waiting (1 John 5:13–15)." In *The Metropolitan Tabernacle Pulpit Sermons*, 10:597–608. London: Passmore & Alabaster, 1864.
"Helps to Full Assurance (1 John 5:13)." In *The Metropolitan Tabernacle Pulpit Sermons*, 30:397–408. London: Passmore & Alabaster, 1884.
"Idolatry Condemned (1 John 5:21)." In *The Metropolitan Tabernacle Pulpit Sermons*, 53:613–22. London: Passmore & Alabaster, 1907.
"Positivism (1 John 5:18–20)." In *The Metropolitan Tabernacle Pulpit Sermons*, 55:433–44. London: Passmore & Alabaster, 1909.
"Samuel: An Example of Intercession (1 Sam 12:23)." In *The Metropolitan Tabernacle Pulpit Sermons*, 26:277–88. London: Passmore & Alabaster, 1880.

Scripture Index

Old Testament

New Testament

Index of Illustrations by Theme